Kāmarūpa-Kaliṅga-Mithilā

A Politico-Cultural Alignment in Eastern India

History, Art, Traditions

Kāmarūpa-Kaliṅga-Mithilā

A Politico-Cultural Alignment in Eastern India

History, Art, Traditions

CHANDRA DHAR TRIPATHI

INDIAN INSTITUTE OF ADVANCED STUDY
Shimla

ARYAN BOOKS INTERNATIONAL
New Delhi

KĀMARŪPA-KALIṄGA-MITHILĀ
A Politico-Cultural Alignment in Eastern India

ISBN-10: 81-7305-327-8
ISBN-13: 978-81-7305-327-6

First published in **2008** by

INDIAN INSTITUTE OF ADVANCED STUDY
Rashtrapati Nivas, Shimla - 171 005

and

ARYAN BOOKS INTERNATIONAL
Pooja Apartments, 4B, Ansari Road, New Delhi-110 002 (India)
Tel.: 23287589, 23255799; Fax: 91-11-23270385
E-mail: aryanbooks@vsnl.com

Computer Typeset and Printed in India at
ABI Prints & Publishing Co., New Delhi

खीष्टाब्दे द्विसहस्रसंमित इदं प्रारब्धमन्तं गतं
कार्यं शोधमयं त्रिवर्षगमनं यस्या क्षुभाशंसया।
तद्गृह्णात्वरुणाभिधान रमणी मोदाय मे शोभनं
येन स्यां कृतकृत्य उन्नतशिराः श्लोकश्च मे वर्धताम्।।

To

My wife,
Aruna Tripathi

Forty years of love, companionship, support

Preface

The present volume embodies the results of the research work carried out by the author as a Fellow of the IIAS from June 2000 to June 2003. What prompted me to work on this theme has been described at length in its first chapter. By way of preface, therefore, I only propose to narrate the circumstances that enabled me to take it up and to express my gratitude to the various friends and scholars who helped in its successful conclusion. The idea of this theme had lingered in my mind ever since it was sown four decades ago and it became more intense during the last two after I had made some study of the Bhauma-Karas of Orissa and of Sri Sankaradeva of Assam. However, my preoccupation with the official duties and the usual worries of life did not leave me with any spare time to systematically develop it. It was only after my retirement from government service in July 1997 and after becoming reasonably free from the life's worries that I got the time to do so. Then I was fortunate enough to be awarded a Fellowship of the IIAS to work on this topic that I availed of from June 2000. Thus while my retirement from service provided me with all the time needed for serious research work, the IIAS provided me with the necessary financial and academic resources to pursue this long-cherished study. The endless hours spent in the marvellous library of the Institute were some of the most precious moments of my life. The Fellowship award, availed of by me in June 2000, initially for one year, was subsequently extended by two more years and I completed the work in June 2003.

The work naturally involved discussions with a large number of scholars and extensive field visits in the states of Assam, Bihar and Orissa and the list of friends and scholars who helped me in the various ways at different places is fairly long. I would, however, like to mention just a few of them whose assistance was most valuable.

First and foremost, I am grateful to the IIAS, particularly its then chairman Prof. Dr. G.C. Pande for awarding me the Fellowship under which this study became possible. I have been fortunate in receiving the affection, guidance and encouragement from Prof. Pande for over two decades and this time he bound me in a bond of life-long gratitude. It will be impertinent on my part to thank him; I can only offer my respectful *pranam* to this octogenarian embodiment of knowledge and Indian culture.

Before I start thanking the persons who helped me in the various ways in my endeavour I wish to pay homage to the memory of two savants whose blessings and help I had received at the beginning of my study but who departed from the world of the living without seeing its completion. I recall with everlasting gratitude my decades long association with Mm. Dr. Biswa Narayan Shastri of Assam and

Shri Bighna Raj Patel of Orissa. I had known Dr. Shastri, a great Sanskritist, author, renowned Puranic scholar and masterly interpreter of the *Kālikā Purāṇa* and the *Yogini Tantra*, since 1965 and at the commencement of the present study he gave me not only his blessings but also the benefit of learned suggestions and some rare books. The readers will find repeated references to his works in the present volume. Shri Bighna Raj Patel was not only a very senior member of the IAS (Orissa cadre) but also a very sound scholar of history and a sensitive poet and author. It was he who first inducted me into the study of the history and culture of Orissa when I served under him in the Union Public Service Commission during 1982-1984. When I met him at Bhubaneswar in December 2000 he was greatly excited about the scheme of the present study, gave his blessings and also some books that were not easily available elsewhere. Alas, both these savants passed away in 2002 before seeing the conclusion of my project. I can only offer my tearful *śraddhāñjali* to the departed souls.

Coming to the friends and scholars in Assam, I offer my sincere thanks to the eminent art historian Dr. R.D. Choudhury, former Director-General of the National Museum and former Director of Museums, Assam, who has been my companion in the archaeological explorations in Assam for almost four decades. I also thank Dr. N.D. Chowdhury, former Director of Archaeology, Assam and another companion in my archaeological explorations, Shri Hari Prasad Chaliha, a Vaiṣṇava scholar and former administrative colleague, Shri R.C. Das, former Director of Museums, Assam; all of them helped me through discussions and in procuring books and photographs. Dr. N.D. Choudhury and Shri Chaliha were kind enough to escort me to Hajo and sites in the Nagaon district during the visits undertaken specifically for the purpose of the present study. I am thankful to my erstwhile civil service colleague Shri Anil Baruah and his gracious wife, Monica for their generous hospitality at Guwahati. Whenever I went to Assam it was their home that became my Hqs.

Amongst the numerous persons who helped me in Orissa, I gratefully acknowledge the scholarly advices that I received from Prof. K.S. Behera, Dr. (Mrs.) Snigdha Tripathy, and Dr. C.B. Patel. I have known Prof. Behera, the doyen of Orissa historians for a long time and as early as 1983 he had accompanied me and my wife to Ratnagiri and Lalitagiri; he gave me many valuable suggestions regarding my present work. Dr. Tripathy and Dr. Patel, both of the Orissa State Museum, Bhubaneswar extended ungrudging help in studying the museum objects and procuring photographs. Dr. Patel also accompanied me and my wife to Jajpur. I am beholden to the epigraphic works of Dr. (Mrs.) Snigdha Tripathy that proved to be valuable works of reference in the present study; I have extensively quoted from her works in the present volume. I am also extremely thankful to Dr. P.K. Trivedi and Dr. J.K. Patnaik, both of the ASI who escorted me to the various monuments and sites at Bhubaneswar, Ratnagiri, Lalitagiri and Udayagiri and helped me in taking valuable photographs and in library work. They were also kind enough to take me round the excavations in progress (2002) at Udayagiri under the supervision of Dr. Trivedi. Dr. Patnaik is a walking encyclopaedia of the Orissan art and it was a pleasure to visit the various monuments with him as the guide.

At Patna, Dr. Naseem Akhtar, Director of the Patna Museum, Dr. Madhuri Agarwal, Deputy Director (who later succeeded Dr. Akhtar as Director) and Dr. Parashuram Pandey, Asstt. Director were of great help in studying the objects preserved in their museum and in photographing them. Their help is gratefully acknowledged.

During each of my visits to Patna in the course of this study I stayed with my friend Shri K.K. Pandey, a senior IAS officer of the Bihar Government. I can not adequately thank him and his wife Madhu for the excellent hospitality extended by them; not only the lovely couple but their children Tarini and Tushmay went out of their way to make my stay as comfortable and pleasant as possible. In 2002-2003 K.K. Pandey also gave me his car to visit Vaishali, Darbhanga and Madhubani and made the necessary arrangements for my stay at Darbhanga. I am also thankful to Prof. Ramashray Roy, a former colleague (Fellow) at the IIAS and Director of the Centre for Study of Indian Traditions, Madhubani for being my host at Madhubani and particularly for advising me to visit the Rajarajeshwari temple at Dokhar before returning to Patna.

I am thankful to my friend, Shri S.K. Sharma, Chief Artist, ASI for kindly drawing a map of the Eastern and North-Eastern India (showing the regions and places covered in this study) that is being included in this volume. He has also made an accurate representation of the 'Añji' sign as inscribed on a copper-plate inscription of Assam—it is being printed on the cover of this volume. My thanks are also due to Dr. D. Sen, Asstt. Publication Officer of the IIAS for taking great pains to expedite the publication of this volume (that had been delayed for over two years due to administrative reasons) and to ensure its printing to be flawless and its production attractive.

Last but not the least, I offer my gratitude to my scholar wife, Dr. Aruna Tripathi, my companion of forty years, for her ungrudging support to all my literary and academic activities. The high frequency with which I used to be transferred from one place to another during my service career was unusual (ten postings in the first seven years!); even after retirement we have been obliged to change residence six times and live in three towns in less than ten years. The readiness with which she transplanted herself from Delhi to Shimla in the year 2000 only to enable me to pursue my long-cherished study and then kept me free from worries of all kind for three years is praiseworthy. She has also been the first listener of all my literary efforts and I have always benefitted from her critical, though constructive, comments. This volume has, therefore, been rightly dedicated to her. Speaking of the dedication, I am grateful to my senior friend Dr. Madhusudan Mishra, a great linguist and classical scholar for transforming my amateurish Sanskrit words into a beautiful dedicatory verse in Śārdūlavikrīḍita metre, reminiscent of the melodious poetry of the copper plate inscriptions of Kāmarūpa, so heavily relied upon in the present work.

New Delhi
Makara Sankranti/Magh Bihu
14 January 2007

C.D.T.

Contents

List of Plates

Abbreviations

The author has employed the abbreviations commonly used in the works on ancient Indian history and culture such as ASI for Archaeological Survey of India, BI for Bibliotheca Indica, CII for Corpus Inscriptionum Indicarium, IA for Indian Antiquary, IHQ for Indian Historical Quarterly, JASB for Journal of Asiatic Society of Bengal, JRAS for Journal of Royal Asiatic Society, etc. In addition, the following abbreviations have also been used:

ASM	:	Assam State Museum, Guwahati
OSM	:	Orissa State Museum, Bhubaneswar
PM	:	Patna Museum, Patna
JARS	:	Journal of Assam Research Society (Kamarupa Anusandhan Samiti), Guwahati
OHRJ	:	Orissa Historical Research Journal, Bhubaneswar
TCHOA	:	The Comprehensive History of Assam, H.K. Barpujari (ed.), Publication Board, Assam, Guwahati.

EASTERN AND NORTH - EASTERN INDIA

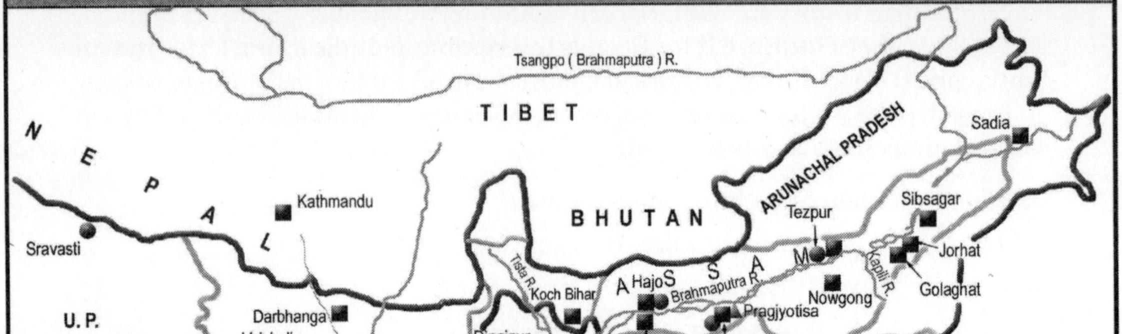

Chapter 1

Prologue

GENESIS OF THE STUDY

One day in July or August of 1963, during my very first official posting at Jorhat, the well-known district town in Upper Assam. I was busy talking to a colleague when he suddenly got up to leave saying he was late for the news. On my expression of concern the colleague said, "Oh, don't worry, I have missed the Assamese news but can still catch the Oriya news." Those days All India Radio used to broadcast the news in Assamese in the morning to be followed by the news in Oriya a short while later. I expressed surprise, "I didn't know that you knew Oriya also." The colleague told me that he did not know Oriya as such but it was so similar to Assamese that he was able to follow at least two-thirds of the news in Oriya. That set me thinking. I had started learning Assamese a few months earlier and had realized that it did not have any great resemblance with Bengali, its immediate neighbour–at least as far as its sound was concerned. But it had great similarly with the language of Orissa, geographically far removed from Assam–it was surely something to think about. A few days later I found an Oriya colleague of mine talking to his young son in Assamese. I asked him whether he was trying to practise his newly-acquired Assamese and he answered, "But I was speaking in Oriya only." This confirmed that the observation of my colleague a few days earlier was not without substance. Then I Myself listened to the Oriya news one day and was wonderstruck with the phonetic similarity between Assamese and Oriya. I started wondering that such close resemblance could not be fortuitious and it really indicated close cultural contacts.

Gradually, as I began to delve deeper in the study of the language and culture of Assam, I found this was indeed the case from the early sixteenth century. Śri Śaṅkaradeva (AD 1449-1568) is regarded as the father of the literature and arts of Assam and he had spent considerable time at Puri, the holy city of Jagannātha in Orissa from where he brought significant elements to be incorporated in the new Vaiṣṇava faith initiated by him and in the literature, music and other arts that he gifted to Assam. A study of the life and works of Śaṅkaradeva and his disciples started unfolding the mystery of the great resemblance between Assamese and Oriya. Twenty years later, when I was posted at Delhi, an Oriya friend requested me to invite him to lunch in the Assam House. It was a surprise, because the food in Assam House was reputed to be anything but tasty. But my friend had his lunch at Assam House and relished it. The reason he gave was that it was like his home cooking. My old ideas about cultural contacts between Assam and Orissa were revived and I realized that these evidently went beyond linguistic contact.

In the intervening years I had made some study of the history of Assam and that of Orissa. I came across a paper by Kanak Lal Barua in the *Journal of Kamarupa Anusandhan Samiti* (Assam Research Society) in which he had surmised that the Bhauma-Kara dynasty of Orissa was established by some prince of Kāmarūpa. On studying more about the Bhauma-Karas I found that this view was—not surprisingly—disputed by some scholars but many others subscribed to it. Then, I came across the works of K.C. Panigrahi who had supported this hypothesis and pointed to the sculptures of Gaṅgā and Yamunā at Dah Parbatia in Assam being the inspiration for the similar images at Ratnagiri and Bhubaneswar in Orissa.

In the course of my study of the Bhauma-Karas I came across the book *Bhauma-Karas–Buddhist Kings of Orissa–and their Times* by Biswarup Das in which the Assamese origin of the Bhauma-Karas had been supported. But more interesting was the fact that in his preface he had mentioned the name of his younger brother as Sri Kamrup Das. Nowhere in India had I ever found any person given the name Kamrup. Did it show that Kāmarūpa had some special place deep in the Oriya psyche? Of Course, I found some Oriyas, particularly among the Kṣatriyas, named after Kāmākhya but I did not attach any significance to it because it is a common occurrence everywhere.

During all these years I had also been keenly aware of the links between Mithilā and Assam. I learnt that the Purāṇic as well as popular legends held that the first Aryan state of Prāgjyotiṣa (ancient Assam) was established by Naraka, son of Janaka, King of Mithilā. Then, while studying the life and works of Śaṅkaradeva, I found that Mithilā and Maithili language had played a significant role in them. It was a scholar from Mithilā, Jagadīśa Miśra, who brought a manuscript of *Śrīmadbhāgawata* to Śaṅkaradeva which became the starting point for his great literary creations. And then to learn that Śaṅkaradeva was one of the earliest and greatest poets of Brajabūlī was almost a discovery. I knew that Brajabūlī was the *lingua franca* of the eastern Vaiṣṇavas and it had its origin in the songs of Vidyāpati, the nightingale of Mithilā, but to realize that the earliest songs of Brajabūlī were composed not in Bengal but in Assam and Orissa was looking at a new landscape.

The more I studied the various aspects of the culture and history of Assam and Orissa–and Mithilā too–the stronger became my conviction that Kāmarūpa, Kaliṅga and Mithilā had such strong links that it would be justified to call it an alignment and that these links deserved to be studied in depth and in detail. I realized that to do justice to the idea, the approach will have to be multi-disciplinary encompassing history, archaeology, literature, arts, anthropology and what not. However, until such an ambitious project is taken up by a team of competent scholars nothing would be lost by undertaking a limited study as the present one.

SCOPE OF THE STUDY

On account of the necessity to complete the present study in less than three years, as stipulated by the Indian Institute of Advanced Study and the resources for the purpose at the author's disposal being extremely limited its scope has been kept severely restricted.

As the title of the subject implies, its comprehensive treatment ought to examine, on the one hand, (i) the political history of the three regions and their inter-connections and, on the other, (ii) the cultural contacts between them.

The first of the two aspects is being dealt with in the present study to the extent of ready availability of material. As regards the cultural aspects, the possible areas of inquiry are (i) Religion and religious traditions, (ii) Affinity in art styles, (iii) Origin and parallel development of the Assamese, Maithili and Oriya languages and their literature with particular reference to the *caryāpadas* of the Siddhas of the eighth to twelfth century AD, (iv) Literature of the three regions from the fourteenth century AD with special references to Brajabūlī, (v) Development of the Dharmaśāstra traditions, (vi) Anthropological aspects including folk traditions of the three regions. Under this last item a special study ought to be made of the folk tales, folk songs and dances, popular religious and other festivals, dress and food of the people of the three regions, etc.

In the above list, the aspect relating to the languages and the earliest literature is undoubtedly one of the most important aspects for our subject and considerable research has already been done in this area by great linguists like George Grierson, Suniti Kumar Chatterjee, Banikanta Kakati, Artavallabha Mahanti, Rahul Sankrityayan, etc. It can, moreover, be easily appreciated that it is a subject of full-fledged independent and rather technical study and adequate justice to it cannot be done in a study like the present one. I have, therefore, refrained from dealing with this aspect in the present study. Similarly, a study of the anthropological aspects is also a subject of full-fledged independent study. In Chapter 2, infra, I have described the three regions under study as 'civilizational regions'. This implies that a study ought to be carried out under the discipline described as "Anthropology of civilizations" as defined by Robert Redfield and his colleagues of the Chicago School of Anthropology. This will indeed require a concentrated effort much beyond the scope of the present study as well as the meagre resources at my disposal. Hence, even though little work has so far been done to compare the folk traditions of the three regions, these aspects have also been excluded from the present study. Finally, while making a preliminary study of the Dharmaśāstra traditions of the three regions, I found that the subject was too vast to be accommodated in the present study. The difficulty is further aggravated by the fact that most of the texts, of which names are available, have not been published and printed as yet. This is particularly true of the texts of the Kāmarūpa school. It is, therefore a stupendous task to locate the manuscripts in different collections and then study them. This task itself is made more difficult by the fact that most of the known collections have yet to prepare and publish their catalogues, even bare lists. This important aspect of the present study has, therefore, been left to be studied by some painstaking young scholars in future.

The examination of the cultural aspects in the present study is therefore, limited to that of some religious traditions, art styles and the literature of the post-fourteenth century period particularly Brajabūlī literature. Some notice of the Dharmaśāstra traditions in the three regions has also been taken under the head Religious Traditions.

The chief sources of this study are (i) epigraphs, (ii) Purāṇic and popular legends, (iii) some medieval Sanskrit and other texts, (iv) Vaiṣṇava literature of Assam, (v) Brajabūlī literature, (vi) sculptures and other art objects preserved in the museums at Guwahati, Bhubaneswar, Darbhanga, Vaishali and Patna, and (vii) the archaeological remains and monuments at the various sites, particularly Dah Parbatia and Hajo in Assam and at Jajpur and Bhubaneswar in Orissa.

Apart from the constraints of time and resources a major limiting factor in the present study has been the non-availability of a number of old Sanskrit texts. Many of them, though reportedly published, are not available in most of the libraries. The author has also been handicapped inasmuch as he does not know Oriya. It has, therefore, not been possible to utilize some valuable sources like the *Mahābhārata* of Sāralādāsa as well as the modern works in Oriya.

Chapter 2

Geographical and Historical Background

THE REGIONS SPECIFIED

Kāmarūpa in modern Assam, Kaliṅga in Orissa and Mithilā in north Bihar are three civilizational regions of eastern India as well as political entities that existed in different periods of Indian history. The Purāṇas, the *Rāmāyaṇa* and the *Mahābhārata* as well as other Sanskrit, Pali and Prakrit texts abound in references to them. Their names also figure in the later Vedic literature. We have also adequate archaeological material including epigraphs to help us reconstruct the political, social and cultural history of the three regions. Before exploring the inter-connections between the three regions it is necessary to define or delineate them for the purpose of the present study.

KĀMARŪPA[1]

The region of Assam is known by different names in the epic, Purāṇic and other early literature. In both the epics it is mentioned as Prāgjyotiṣa which was the territory around the city of that name. Later the same region came to be known as Kāmarūpa; the *Kālikā Purāṇa* is, in fact, very specific in stating that the name of the country was so changed after the arrival of Naraka from Mithilā. In the historical period, the earliest mention of Kāmarūpa is found in the Allahabad pillar inscription of Samudragupta in the fourth century AD. The name Prāgjyotiṣa went out of use in the early medieval period though the rulers continued to employ it till as late as the eighteenth century. Kāmarūpa has been stated to be both a country as well as a state from its earliest available mention. Its boundaries, of course, changed from time to time. Its traditional boundaries were Mount Kāñcana in Nepal, the confluence of Brahmaputra, the Karatoyā and the Dikkavavasinī, apparently in the north, south, west and east respectively. In the sixth century AD, however, the western boundary of the state of Kāmarūpa, was apparently the Kosi river in north Bihar which was flowing considerably east of its present course. During this period, the kingdom of Kāmarūpa apparently included the ancient Aṅga, now a part of Mithilā or Tīrabhukti and Puṇḍravardhana, a bhukti in north Bengal, earlier a part of the Gupta empire. Thus, during the beginning of the period covered by the present study Kāmarūpa had a common border with Mithilā which was under the rule of the Later Guptas or the Maukharīs or the Cedis. On its south and south-west were the regions of Gauḍa and Vaṅga. In the north it included the entire Himalayan foothills from eastern Nepal to the eastern end of Arunachal Pradesh. In the east it perhaps reached the border of what is now Myanmar and China. Trade routes from Kāmarūpa went to Nepal, Magadha and Mithilā in the west, to Vaṅga and Gauḍa in the south and thence to the shores of the Bay of Bengal, to Tāmralipti and Kaliṅga. Routes from Madhyadeśa, Gauḍa and Kaliṅga also passed through Kāmarūpa to Tibet, China and South-east Asia.

KALIṄGA[2]

In the present study the name Kaliṅga has been used to denote the region of Orissa. Parts of Orissa have been known as Oḍra, Utkala, Tośala or Tośalī, Kośala, Koṅgoḍa and Kaliṅga in the various periods of history. Kośala also included parts of Chhattisgarh, Jharkhand and Madhya Pradesh in addition to western Orissa while the major portion of Kaliṅga was generally located in Andhra Pradesh to the south of the river Mahanadi (perhaps not the well-known river but another river of the same name considerably south-west to it) and north of Godavari. The names and boundaries of the various regions in early India considerably varied from time to time and these regions of Orissa were no exception to this. These Orissan territories often overlapped and were variously designated as deśa, viṣaya, maṇḍala, bhukti, etc. Of the various names noted above it is Oḍra that transformed itself into Oḍeṣā or Oreśā around the thirteenth-fourteenth century and was later Anglicized into Orissa. The name Utkala, probably a contraction of Utkaliṅga, i.e, Upper Kaliṅga, was a favourite of the Sanskrit composers of Purāṇas and, in later times, the nibandhakāras and continues to be used for all Hindu ritualistic purposes. However, it is the name Kaliṅga that is met with in the earliest epigraphic record, viz., the Rock Edict XIII of Aśoka. From the Aśokan inscription it does not become clear whether Kaliṅga was just a territory in the third century BC or it was also a state. But in the following centuries it was definitely a state as we find Khāravela being described as *Kaliṅgādhipati.* It is this name that has been most popular and most widely used right from the time of the writing of the epics through the medieval age of *Kaliṅgādhipatis* to the modern days of the Kaliṅga Prize and Kaliṅga Industries.

MITHILĀ[3]

A modern historian says, "There are few regions of India possessing an ancient civilization about which we have less historical information than the region north of Ganga, variously known as Videha, Tīrabhukti or (after the name of its capital) Mithilā."[4] The reason for this is perhaps, in the words of the same author, "Its history does not centre round feats of arms but round courts given to higher pursuits of learning."[5] Of the three regions under study, Videha is surely the most ancient as its name, both as a country and as a state, prominently figures in the later Vedic literature. The name Videha is said to be derived from Videgha Māthava whose legend is mentioned in the *Śatapatha Brāhmaṇa.* Scholars have viewed this legend as an allegorical reference to the eastward spread of the Aryan or Vedic culture beyond Kāśī and Kośala in the later Vedic times.

Sadānīrā or Gaṇḍaka, the river crossed by Videgha Māthava has always been regarded as the western boundary of Videha, the other boundaries being the river Kosi in the east, Gaṅga in the south and the Himalayan foothills in the north. Videha was the seat of an ancient kingdom whose rulers were styled as Janaka. Then, at least from the time of the Buddha the republic of Vaiśālī also flourished in this region. The republic perhaps lasted till the rise of the Mauryas when Vaiśālī became a part of their empire. The Licchavis of Vaiśālī perhaps re-established a republic or a kingdom in the post-Kuṣāṇa era to be incorporated in the Gupta empire through a matrimonial alliance of Candragupta I. Thus, from the early fourth century till the end of the eleventh century Videha or what was now known as Tīrabhukti ceased to be a state, neither independent nor subordinate, and the territory came to be annexed by the various contending powers of north India like the Later Guptas, Harṣa, the Maukharis and the Cedis. Finally, in the year 1097 a Karṇāta prince, Nānyadeva, established an independent state of Mithilā that lasted till AD 1324 when it was lost to the Delhi Sultanate. Politically independent or not, important or not, the ancient tradition of learning never lost its strength and throughout the early medieval period we find the Maithila scholars making significant contributions to all branches of knowledge. The tradition continued even after the fall of the Karṇāta dynasty.

In the eastward extension of the Aryan or Vedic culture as shown by the legend of Videgha Māthava, Mithilā was an important stage from where it moved forward to Gauḍa, Vaṅga and Kāmarūpa in the east and Magadha and Kaliṅga in the south. The role of Maithila Brāhmaṇas in this extension is a fascinating subject; in the present study it has been possible only to touch its fringes.

COMMON POLITICAL DESTINY

The three regions covered by the present study appear to have shared a common political destiny at the various periods of history.

In the legendary times the first noticeable episode in this context is the epic battle of Mahābhārata.[6] Prāgjyotiṣa (the earlier name of Kāmarūpa), Kaliṅga and Mithilā (or Videha) are mentioned as powerful kingdoms in eastern India and their kings fought on the side of the Kauravas in the great war. The king of Prāgjyotiṣa, Bhagadatta, has been praised for his bravery; he was killed by Arjuna in the war. The rulers of Kaliṅga and Mithilā were also killed in the war but their names are confusing. *Sāṁkhyāyana Śrauta Sūtra*, however, mentions the name Kṣemadhūrti as the Videhan king who fought against the Pāṇḍavas.[7] As regards the Kaliṅga army, the *Mahābhārata* itself mentions the names of some of its warriors, e.g., Śrutāyusa, Śakradeva and Bhānumata, the last two being the sons of the king of Kaliṅga. The Kaliṅga army also included a contingent of the Niṣādas, headed by Ketumata, son of their king. The name of the king, however, is not given during the war episode.[8] In another context, though, the king of Kaliṅga is named as Citrāṅgada whose daughter's *svayaṁvara* was attended among others by Duryodhana without success.[9] A look at the list of warriors who came to Kurukṣetra to fight from the two sides reveals an interesting fact, viz., the kings from eastern India were generally on the side of the Kauravas. To illustrate the point, we may note that Daṇḍadhāra of Girivraja and king of Aśmaka are said to have laid down their lives fighting for Duryodhana. The credit for obtaining the support of the eastern rulers should perhaps go to the great warrior, Karṇa, who was crowned king of Aṅga by Duryodhana. In fact, there is a specific reference in the *Droṇa parva* of *Mahābhārata* that the Utkalas were vanquished by Karṇa for Duryodhana and these Utkalas are combined with the Mekalas and Kaliṅgas.[10] Jarāsandha, the dreaded king of Magadha, who was killed by Bhīma, the Pāṇḍava, shortly before the war, may also have terrorized his neighbouring kings in supporting Duryodhana, his great friend. It will, however, be too conjectural to view the Bhārata war as a confrontation between the eastern and western India, particularly because we find notable exceptions to these alignments. Thus, Jayadratha, the king of Sindhudeśa, the Madras, the Kekayas, the Gāndhāras, the Trigartas, Vinda of Avanti, Prātipeya and Somadatta, kings of Vāhlīka, all from the west, are seen fighting on the side of Duryodhana. On the other hand, the Pāṇḍavas are found to be supported by some rulers of the east like the king of Kāśī and Sahadeva, the son and successor of Jarāsandha himself. However, one relevant point does emerge from the above observation and it is that the rulers of

Prāgjyotiṣa, Kaliṅga and Mithilā being on the same side points to a probability of the existence of friendly relations among them at the time of the composition of the great epic. Interestingly, we get a corroboration of this supposition from the fact that during the war the army of Kaliṅga is said to have followed the lead of Bhagadatta, the king of Kāmarūpa.[11]

Another significant fact relating to the *Mahābhārata* is that among the noteworthy kingdoms that continued to exist after the Kurukṣetra war there is specific mention of the Maithilas (of Videha), Bārhdrathas (of Magadha which probably included Aṅga) and Kaliṅga.[12] The list does not include Prāgjyotiṣa of Bhagadatta but history more than compensated for it for the kingdom continued to exist right down to the medieval period.

Coming to the historical times we find that the common factors in the history of the three regions under study are dictated primarily by their geographical location. Magadha and Vaṅga or Gauḍa were the immediate neighbours of all the three states of Kāmarūpa, Kaliṅga and Mithilā; it was, therefore, natural that whenever the rulers of one or the other of these kingdoms entertained any imperial designs these three states became their immediate targets.

During the Early Medieval period Kāmarūpa and Kaliṅga were definitely independent kingdoms while Mithilā (now more commonly referred to as Tīrabhukti) had ceased to be so since long. The region of Mithilā was certainly a part of the Gupta empire and in the post-Gupta age it had become a part of the kingdom of the Maukharis, Harṣa or the Cedis. The attempts of the rulers of Magadha were, therefore, to subjugate the kingdoms of Kāmarūpa and Kaliṅga while in case of Tīrabhukti these were aimed at just annexation of territory. Whether the Later Guptas originated from Malwa or not, it is certain that they became the masters of Magadha and it is from Magadha that they mounted their campaigns against their neighbouring states. From the Aphsad inscription of Ādityasena[13] we learn that his grandfather Mahāsenagupta had defeated Susthitavarman, the king of Kāmarūpa in the later part of the sixth century. We have no record of any Later Gupta ruler trying to subjugate Kaliṅga, possibly because during this period the powerful Śaśāṅka was entrenched there. As regards Tīrabhukti, however, they certainly succeeded in including it in their kingdom. It is likely that they wrested it from the Maukharis. The Aphsad inscription says that Kumāragupta, the fourth ruler of the Later Gupta dynasty had defeated the Maukhari king Iśānavarman. Then, we find that Jīvagupta, five or six generations after Ādityasena, issued the Katra copper plate from the victory camp of Tārā by which he donated three villages in the Cāmuṇḍā *viṣaya* of Tīrabhukti. This was in the early eighth century AD.[14]

The Pālas of Bengal are the known empire builders in Indian history. Dharmapāla, the second ruler of the dynasty, embarked upon a course of expansion in the later part of the eighth century AD. and conquered territories right up to Kānyakubja in the west.[15] From the Bhagalpur charter of Nārāyaṇapāla,[16] who was the third in succession from Dharmapāla, we learn that his nephew, Jayapāla, who was the commander-in-chief of Devapāla, the son and successor of Dharmapāla, defeated the king of Utkala and entered into a treaty with the king of Prāgjyotiṣa.[17] The Nalanda plate of Devapāla[18] as well as the Badal pillar inscription[19] confirm that he fought against the Utkalas and Kāmarūpas. In Utkala he must have defeated a Bhauma-Kara king of which scholars have found a hint in the Hindol plate of Subhakara (IV) of the year 103 (AD 839)[20]. The Kāmarūpa king with whom Jayapāla entered into a treaty is likely to have been Vanamālavarmadeva whose charters reveal him as a great king.[21] Thus, from the end of the eighth century AD. Kāmarūpa and Utkala had become prime targets of the Pālas. Further, the Muṅger plate of Devapāla[22] indicates his possession of Tīrabhukti as it was issued from the victory camp of Mudgagiri which was undoubtedly located in the Tīrabhukti region that included the territory of ancient Aṅga during this period. His grandson, Nārāyaṇapāla, continued to possess this region as is attested to by his Bhagalpur charter. Significantly, the lands donated by this charter are specified as located in the Kakṣa *viṣaya* of Tīrabhukti. The Pālas continued to enjoy the same position in Utkala, Kāmarūpa and Tīrabhukti for quite some time.

In fact, Mahīpāla (I), the fourth in succession from Nārāyaṇapāla, seems to have gained more territories. His Banagada charter[23] indicates that he was in control of Puṇḍravardhana, which was undoubtedly under the Kāmarūpa rule earlier. Mahīpāla had a hold over Mithilā also.[24] That the Pālas continued to maintain their sway over Mithilā right down to the time of Rāmapāla is attested to by the Bongaon copper plate of Vigrahapāla III. The expansionist designs of the Pālas reached their culmination in Kāmarūpa when Rāmapāla, the great-grandson of Mahīpāla (I) finally defeated its ruler (either Dharmapāla, or more probably, his successor, Jayapāla) and appointed one Tiṅgyadeva as its Governor. This Tiṅgyadeva, however, revolted against the next sovereign, Kumārapāla, the son and successor of Rāmapāla. Kumārapāla removed the recalcitrant subordinate and crowned his minister, Vaidyadeva, as king of Kāmarūpa. Vaidyadeva also became independent very soon as we find from his Kamauli grant[25] issued in AD 1142. Rāmapāla had also invaded Orissa and his general Jayasiṁha ousted the last Somavaṁśī ruler, Karṇadeva from the throne.[26] The Orissan kingdom was, however, soon reclaimed by

Coḍagaṅga very early in the twelfth century.[27] Later, Madanapāla, the grandson of Rāmapāla, defeated Codagaṅga but was himself finally defeated by Vijayasena, the founder of the new Sena dynasty.[28]

Bengal's hostility towards Kāmarūpa, Kaliṅga and Mithilā continued undiminished during the Sena period as well. In his Deopada inscription, Vijayasena claims to have vanquished the kings of Gauḍa, Kaliṅga and Kāmarūpa and Nānya.[29] This Nānya is undoubtedly Nānyadeva, founder of an independent state of Mithilā in AD 1097 and the originator of the Karṇāta dynasty. As regards Utkala, Vijayasena perhaps had a friendly alliance with Coḍagaṅga because the latter had helped him in ousting the Pālas from the Vaṅga throne.[30] Vallālasena, the son and successor of Vijayasena is credited with conquerring Mithilā during the life time of his father.[31]

His son and successor, Lakṣmaṇasena, in his Madhainagar[32] and Sunderban[33] plates, claims to have vanquished the kings of Kaliṅga and Kāmarūpa. This Kāmarūpa king is identified with Rāyārideva,[34] grandfather of Vallabhadeva who issued his Tezpur grant in the Śaka era 1107 (AD 1185)[35] and who appears to have belonged to the line of Vaidyadeva. The Kaliṅga king vanquished by Lakṣmaṇasena has not been identified but it is interesting that the friendly relations between Vaṅga and Kaliṅga established during Vijayasena's time were replaced by the traditional hostility within two generations.

The discussion so far clearly shows that Magadha, Gauḍa and Vaṅga remained the common enemies of Kāmarūpa, Kaliṅga and Mithilā throughout the early medieval period from the sixth to the twelfth century AD. None of the three kingdoms could, however, be permanently annexed by any of them. Consequently, we find the successive rulers of the various dynasties claiming victories over the same lands. In the struggle between Kāmarūpa and Gauḍa and Magadha the regions of north Bengal and eastern Mithilā appear to have been the perpetual bones of contention. These areas were apparently annexed by Bhūtivarman of Kāmarūpa in the early sixth century but were lost to Śaśāṅka or Mahāsenagupta within fifty years. The loss was, however, temporary because in the first decades of the seventh century Puṇḍravandhana was re-occupied by Bhāskaravarma as evidenced by the Dubi and Nidhanpur plates. Later, in the Pāla times, we have noted that Devapāla had entered into a treaty with the king of Prāgjyotiṣa (i.e., Kāmarūpa) but Mahīpāla (I) appears to have occupied Puṇḍravandhana, the westernmost part of the Kāmarūpa kingdom five generations later. Evidently, the treaty had no permanent value. And finally, Rāmapāla is found to be completely subjugating the Kāmarūpa kingdom. It is clear that none of the Pāla victories in Kāmarūpa had a lasting effect. Similar was the case in Utkala where most of the Pāla rulers from Devapāla to Madanapāla had to mount military campaigns. In case of Mithilā the situation was somewhat different because during the Pāla period there was no independent state in Mithilā. Yet, it seems that right from the time of Dharmapāla up to Vigrahapāla III they had to continually take recourse to show of strength for retaining their possessions as is evidenced by establishment of victory camps in the region from time to time.

From the end of the twelfth century the history of eastern India enters a new phase with the occurrence of the Turko-Afghan invasions, but here again there are some common features in the histories of Kāmarūpa, Kaliṅga and Mithilā. In the eastern India, Bengal was the first to succumb to the Muslim onslaught. The octogenarian Lakṣmaṇasena was driven out from his capital in AD 1199 by Bakhtiyār Khiljī, the general deputed by Mohammad Ghorī to conquer eastern India. The conquest of Kāmarūpa, Kaliṅga and Mithilā, however, could not be effected so easily by these early invaders; all these kingdoms valiantly resisted them for a long time and this is a most remarkable common feature of their character and history. Such resistance was perhaps ingrained in them due to five centuries of continuous resistance to the Gauḍas, Vaṅgas and Māgadhas. Of the three, the performance of Kāmarūpa was the most remarkable inasmuch as in the year 1205, the entire army of Bakhtiyār, the destroyer of Nalanda and victor of Bengal, was annihilated by the king of Kamatā, the successor state of Kāmarūpa, as we learn from the Kanāī Barsī Bowā rock inscription in North Guwahati.[36] This king is named as Barthu in the Muslim chronicles and has been identified with Pṛthu of the lineage of Vaidyadeva and Vallabhadeva.[37]

The subsequent history of Assam shows that the Muslim governors of Bengal made repeated attempts to conquer this land but never succeeded. Subsequently, in the sixteenth and seventeenth centuries only the Mughals succeeded in subordinating the Koch Kings (the successors of the Kamatā kingdom) and establishing some outposts in western Assam and Koch Bihar. Even they failed to annex the country. In the seventeenth century the Ahom kingdom was invaded under the orders of the emperor Aurangzeb by a strong army led by Raja Ram Singh of Āmer but it suffered a crushing defeat at the battle of Sarāīghāṭ in the year 1671, which has become a great national memory for the people of Assam.[38]

The kingdom of Mithilā under the valiant Karṇāta dynasty successfully resisted the Muslim invasions from Bengal, Jaunpur and even Delhi until in the year 1324, the king Harisimhadeva was defeated by Sultan Ghiyāsuddīn Tughlak and compelled to flee to Nepal.[39] Thereafter, the kingdom of Mithilā passed into the hands of dynasties set up by the Sultans of Delhi. In Orissa the same story of resistance to the Muslim invasions is repeated for three and a half centuries after the fall of Bengal. The Gaṅga and Gajapati kings of Orissa had to face invasions not only from Bengal but also from the Muslim Sultans of the southern states but maintained their independence. It was only in 1568, that the last Hindu king of Orissa, Mukundadeva, finally submitted to the Muslim army of Bengal.[40]

In the light of the above observations, it is pertinent to suggest that tough resistance to the Muslim onslaught by Kāmarūpa, Kaliṅga and Mithilā for centuries after the year 1199 when Bengal fell to the Muslim sword ought to be considered as a characteristic of the history of eastern India. These three regions succeeded in performing a feat in which Bengal had failed.

NOTES AND REFERENCES

1. For a detailed treatment of the topic, see D.C. Sircar, 'Pragjyotisha-Kamarupa' in *TCHOA*, vol. 1, chapter 4, pp. 59-78. His identification of the river Kauśikā of the Nidhanpur plates of Bhāskaravarma with the modern Kusiyara, a branch of the Surma or Barak in Sylhet (and Cachar) is, however, hardly acceptable in view of the arguments of K.L. Barua in his article, 'Kauśika and Kusiara' in *Indian Culture*, vol. 1, No. 3, January 1935, pp. 421-32.
2. Amarchand Mittal, *An Early History of Orissa* discusses the divisions of Orissa in early times in detail in Chapter 1, pp. 18-43 and the traditional history of Kaliṅga in Chapter 2, pp. 81-121.
3. For a detailed treatment of the topic, see Upendra Thakur, *History of Mithila (Circa 3000 B.C. - 1556 A.D.)*, Chapter 1, pp. 1-19.
4. Ibid., p. 1.
5. Ibid., p.1.
6. The information in this and the next paragraph is taken mostly from *Dharmarāja Yudhiṣthhira* by Pt. Chandra Bali Tripathi (in Hindi), Chapters 12 and 13.
7. Upendra Thakur, op. cit., p. 59.
8. Mittal, op. cit., pp. 96-98.
9. Ibid., p. 95.
10. Ibid., p. 102.
11. R.D. Banerji, *History of Orissa*, vol. 1, p. 47.
12. Ibid., p. 45.
13. K.K. Thaplyal, *Inscriptions of the Maukharis, Later Guptas, Pushpabhutis and Yasovarman of Kanauj*, pp. 160-66.
14. Ibid., pp. 174-76.
15. Ramaranjan Mukherji & S.K. Maity, *Corpus of Bengal Inscriptions bearing on History and Civilisaton of Bengal*, p. 12.
16. Ibid., pp. 163-184.
17. Ibid., p. 179.
18. D.C. Sircar, *Select Inscriptions*, vol. 2, p. 71.

19. Ibid., p. 87.
20. Snigdha Tripathy, *Inscriptions of Orissa,* vol. II, p. 125. Panigrahi designates the donor as Subhakara II, but according to Tripathy's revised geneology it should be Subhakara IV (see relevant reference in chapter 3, infra).
21. P.C. Choudhury, *The History of Civilisation of the People of Assam to the Twelfth Century A.D.*, pp. 217-220 for an estimate of Vanamāla and p. 215 for alternative identifications of the Kāmarūpa king in the Bhagalpur grant.
22. Mukherji & Maity, op. cit., pp. 114-32.
23. Ibid., pp. 197-207.
24. Ibid., p. 18.
25. Ibid., p. 370-86; Also, P.C. Choudhury, op. cit., p. 254 for the date of this plate.
26. K.C. Panigrahi, *History of Orissa,* p. 155.
27. Ibid.
28. Mukherji & Maity, op. cit., p. 21.
29. Ibid., pp. 244-58.
30. K.C. Panigrahi, op. cit., p. 155.
31. Mukherji & Maity, op. cit., p. 35.
32. Ibid., pp. 277-89.
33. Ibid., pp. 290-94.
34. P.C. Choudhury, op. cit., p. 255 discusses the question and holds that it was Vallabhadeva who was defeated by Lakṣmaṇasena.
35. Ibid.
36. D. Sarma, *Kamarupaśāsanāvalī,* Part II - Texts. pp. 140-41.
37. P.C. Choudhury, op. cit., pp. 255-56 discusses the identification of Barthu and asserts that he was not a scion of the family of Vaidyadeva but a king of an entirely different line.
38. J.N. Sarkar, 'Failure of Ram Singh in Assam, 1668-71,' in *TCHOA,* vol. II, chapter 8, section IV gives full details of this momentous event.
39. Upendra Thakur, op. cit., pp. 281-85.
40. K. C. Panigrahi, op. cit., pp. 241-49.

Chapter 3

Kāmarūpa and Kaliṅga

POLITICAL ROLE OF KĀMARŪPA IN KALIṄGA-UTKALA: THE BHAUMA-KARA DYNASTY (C. 736-940 AD)

Harṣavardhana of Kānyakubja, Śaśāṅka of Gauḍa, Pulakeśin II of Vātāpi and Bhāskaravarmā of Kāmarūpa were the four greatest rulers of India in the early seventh century AD. The friendship and alliance between Harṣavardhana and Bhāskaravarmā is well-known to all students of Indian history. Harṣavardhana is said to have waged war against Śaśāṅka who was alleged to have treacherously murdered Rājyavardhana, the elder brother and predecessor of Harṣa on throne. It is generally accepted that in this punitive expedition he was helped by Bhāskaravarmā. This must have happened around AD 610-12. It is logical to presume that Śaśāṅka was simultaneously attacked by Harṣa from the west and Bhāskara from the north-east. Śaśāṅka was defeated and fled southwards to Orissa where he established his rule. His capital city, Karṇasuvarṇa was occupied by Bhāskaravarmā as we find the latter issuing land grants from this place (Dubi and Nidhanpur charters). Śaśāṅka was in possession of Daṇḍakabhukti and Koṅgoḍa at least till AD 619, the date on which we find the rulers of these regions declaring themselves to be vassals of Mahārājādhirāja Śaśāṅka.[1] Towards the later part of his life around AD 640, Harṣavardhana is seen to mount a campaign against these Orissan kingdoms and ousting Śaśāṅka for good.[2] The ruler of Koṅgoḍamaṇḍala, Mādhavarāja, who was a vassal of Śaśāṅka in AD 619, is found to have assumed sovereignty within a few years thereafter and become the *de facto* founder of the Śailodbhava dynasty.[3]

There is a hypothesis that in his Orissan campaign Harṣavardhana was also joined by his old friend and ally, Bhāskaravarmā and the latter established his rule in this region for some time. We have really no epigraphic or other archaeological evidence to support this hypothesis but K.C. Panigrahi has found an allegorical passage in the *Ekāmra Purāṇa* to support it.[4] The said Purāṇa was evidently composed in Utkala and is essentially a *Sthala Purāṇa* of the Ekāmrakṣetra (Bhubaneswar) and does not appear to be a work composed earlier than the fourteenth century;[5] it is, therefore, not prudent to rely just on an allegorical passage of the said Purāṇa and for establishing the occupation of a part of Orissa by Bhāskaravarmā as a historical fact we must wait for new and definite evidence that does not seem to be forthcoming at present.

However, we are on much firmer ground about Kāmarūpa's political role in Utkala-Kaliṅga a century later when the Bhauma-Kara dynasty was established in AD 736-37.

Up to the early twentieth century the Bhuma-Karas as a ruling dynasty of Orissa were unknown to scholars but in course of time a very large number of inscriptions belonging to this dynasty were discovered, deciphered and commented upon by eminent scholars. A collection of fourteen such inscription was first published by Pandit Binayak Misra in his monograph *Orissa Under the Bhauma Kings* in 1934. Since the publication of this work several more important inscriptions of this dynasty have been discovered and they throw considerable light on the history of this dynasty. As the male members of this dynasty bear the names mostly ending with *Kara*, it has been described as the *Kara* dynasty. But their epigraphs also mention them as *Bhauma* monarchs, so the dynasty is now generally known as Bhauma-Kara dynasty.[6]

Origin of the Bhuma-Kara dynasty has been a matter of considerable controversy. The question has also been linked, not unnaturally, with their chronology. This too was equally controversial for a long time since the copper-plate charters of the dynasty are dated in an unspecified era. It was, however, clear that the Bhaumas established an era, at least for their official purposes, counting it most probably from the accession of the first ruler of the dynasty, viz., Kṣemaṅkaradeva. The date of the commencement of this era also remained controversial for a long time. Pandit S.N. Rajaguru and K.C. Panigrahi have, however, convincingly established that the era commenced in the year AD 736.[7]

One of the most important epigraphs in consideration of the chronology and origin of the Bhauma-Karas is the Paśupati inscription of Jayadeva (II) of Nepal.[8] In this inscription, Rājyamatī, the queen of Jayadeva, has been described as a daughter of Harṣadeva, as well as born in the family of Bhagadatta. Futher, this Harṣadeva has been described as the ruler of Gauḍa, Oḍra, Kaliṅga, Kośala, etc. The relevant expressions are '*Bhagadattarājakulajā*' and '*Gauḍoḍrādikaliṅga-Kośalapati Śriharṣadevātmajā.*' The date of this inscription was earlier read as 153 of an unspecified era by Pt. Bhagwanlal

Indraji and 159 by R. Gnoli. The correct date, however, appears to be 157 as given by Shankar Mana Rajbansi.[9] Early scholars belived it to be the Harṣa era, thus fixing the date of the inscription as 606+153= AD 759. It has now been established that neither the empire of Harṣa (of Kanauj) included Nepal nor his era was ever used in that country. The era used in the Nepal inscriptions of this age commenced in AD 595, and has been designated as Aṁśuvarman era.[10] The date of the Paśupati inscription is therefore, 595 + 153 = AD 748 or 595 + 157 = AD 752.

Fortunately, we know the following facts as certain:

1. All the three ruling dynasties of early Kāmarūpa, viz., Varman, Śālastaṁbha and Brahmapāla claimed their descent from Naraka and Bhagadatta and are described as Bhauma.[11]
2. The Śālastaṁbha dynasty that succeeded the last and the most illustrious Varman King, viz., Bhāskaravarmā, between AD 650 and 660 actually had a king named Harṣavarmadeva or simply Harṣadeva, who was the sixth in descent from Śālastaṁbha, the founder of this dynasty.[12] Allowing seventy to eighty years for the first five rulers, Harṣadeva must have ascended the throne between AD 720 and 730. We shall presently comment on the importance of this date for the Bhauma-Kara dynasty of Orissa.

The Neulpur inscription of Śubhakaradeva is one of the earliest charters of the Bhauma-Karas. Its date was earlier read as the year 54 when it was edited by R.D. Banerji in E.I. vol. XV. but the latest reading given by Snigdha Tripathy is the year 30. The donor of the plate has used the term *Bhaumānvaya* for his lineage.[13] Banerji suggested that this family of Orissa was connected with the Naraka or Bhauma dynasty of Kāmarūpa-Prāgjyotiṣa.[14] Pandit Binayak Misra and certain other scholars disputed it and sought to link them with the present Bhuiyāṅ tribe of Orissa. K.C. Panigrahi, however, has given a number of cogent arguments to establish that the Bhaumas of Kāmarūpa and Orissa were definitely two branches of the same family.[15] Notwithstanding the arguments put forward by Panigrahi, it would be worthwhile to examine the arguments of Pandit Binayak Misra, particularly those against this hypothesis because the same have not been pointedly dealt with by Panigrahi. Misra says, "It can not be assumed that the former (i.e., Bhauma) family hailed to Orissa from Assam; for it is expressly stated in plate B (i.e., the Chaurasi plate of Śivakaradeva) that the Bhauma family emanated from amongst the people of Utkala:

'*Bhaumyasya mahatīkhyāte guṇa mālotkale kule nṛpobhūd....*'[16]

In the light of this observation, the main arguments of Misra against the Kāmarūpa origin of the Orissa Bhaumas may be summarized as follows:

(i) The donor of the Talcher plate (Śubhakaradeva IV) is said to be the 'final incarnation of Bharata, Bhagadatta and Bhagīratha'. Had the donor belonged to the family of Bhauma Bhagadatta of Assam, he would have mentioned Bhagadatta in a different way.
(ii) The Orissa Bhauma kings have addressed orders in one way and the Bhauma kings of Assam in the other.
(iii) The imprecatory verses of the Orissan Bhauma plates are not found in the Bhauma plates of Assam.
(iv) The Bhauma family of Assam professed Śaivism and that of Orissa Buddhism.

On these considerations, the learned Pandit concluded, "Apparently, there is no clue, which can lead us to assume that the Bhauma family being ousted from Assam ruled in Orissa" and further, "It is recorded in the Kathmandu inscription that queen Rajyamati in AD 757 was the daughter of Harṣadeva and this Harṣadeva was the king of Gauḍa, Udra, Kaliṅga and Kośala. It does not appear from this statement that the Bhauma family of Orissa hailed from Assam."[17]

We may examine these points one by one.

1. Bhagadatta is not such a great hero in the Indian Purāṇic tradition as to be mentioned along with the names of the greats like Bharata and Bhagīratha. The donor of the Talcher plate apparently did so only because he had some special reason for doing so, viz., that Bhagadatta was his remote ancestor. Bharata and Bhagīratha represent respectively the lunar (Candra) and solar (Sūrya) dynasties of India. It is easy to see that the donor was equating himself with the greatest of the two great traditions. Simultaneously, he could not forget his own illustrious lineage and hence mentioned Bhagadatta. In short, if he had not belonged to the family of Bhauma Bhagadatta of Kāmarūpa, he would not have mentioned him at all!
2. As regards (ii) and (iii) the learned Pandit has so averred, I am constrained to note, because his knowledge of the Assam plates does not seem to go beyond a nodding acquaintance. By the time he published his book in 1934, as many as ten Assam plates had been compiled in a book *Kāmarūpas;āsanāvalī* by Pandit Padmanath Bhattacharya Vidyavinod published in 1931. If Pandit Misra had taken sufficient pains to go through this volume he would not have committed the blunder of making these

assertions. The factual position is that from the earliest available copper plates, viz., the Dubi and Nidhanpur plates of Bhāskaravarmā of the early seventh century to the latest plates of the Śālastambha dynasty, viz., the Nowgong plate of Balavarmā III of the late ninth century, all address their orders exactly in the same manner as done in the Orissa plates.[18] The only difference between the Assam and Orissa charters is that while the former begin with an invocation to the favourite deity of the donor (Śiva, in practically all of them) the latter omit it. Except this difference, all the inscriptions in both cases begin with the name of place of issue followed by the genealogy of the donor declaring him or her as in sound condition (Kuśalī). It is interesting to note that the charters seem invariably to have been issued from the capital city but in both cases it is described as the victorious camp (*Jayaskandhāvāra*). Then follows the list of officers to whom the charter is addressed followed by the list of the donee Brāhmaṇas and description of the donated land with its boundaries. The privileges conferred by the charter are also indicated. The date, i.e., the regnal year, and occasionally the month and the day too, of the issue is mentioned either in the beginning or at the end.

The factual position regarding the imprecatory verses is also the same; not only do the Assam plates contain these verses but these are the same as those used in the Orissa plates, viz.,

"*Svadattaṁvāparadattāṁvā yo haret vasundharāṁ sa viṣṭhāyāṁ kṛmirbhūtvā pitṛbhiḥ saha pacyate.*"

Similarly, regarding the merits of donation of land also the same verses are found in both Assam and Orissa plates, viz.,

"*Bahubhirvasudhādattā rājabhiḥ sagarādibhiḥ*
Yasya yasya yadā bhumistasyatasyatadā phalaṁ."
and "*Svadānātphalamāntyaṁ paradattānupālane....*"

Finally, the officials participating in the ceremony of the donation and prepation of copper plates are specified by name in both Assam and Orissa plates.

3. The contention that the Assam Bhaumas were Śaivas while those of Orissa were Buddhists does not prove or disprove any point. Suffice it to say, that the sectarian affiliation of a ruler in ancient India was never a hereditary matter. There is nothing to prevent us from holding that the ancestors of Kṣemaṅkaradeva in Kāmarūpa were Śaivas; when he came to Utkala he found Buddhism–in all probability, of the Vjrayāna variety–in a flourishing

state and he himself became its follower and patron. In this connection, it is relevant to note that in the Bhauma-Kara dynasty itself two immediate successors of Kṣemaṅkara were Buddhists but further down the line they followed other sects. For example, the tenth ruler. Śivakara (IV) in the Talcher plate is described as *Parama Māheśvara* and the eighth ruler, Tribhuvanamahādevī was a *Parama Vaiṣṇavī* (Dhenkenal plate). Further down the line, Daṇḍī Mahādevī was again *Parama Māheśvarī* (Kumrung plate).[19]

Finally, we examine the argument regarding the statement that the Bhaumas emanated from amongst the people of Utkala. This statement occurs in the Chaurasi plate issued by Śivakaradeva, son of Śubhakaradeva. Its date was earlier read as the year 73 by Pandit Binayak Misra and the year 13 by Narayan Tripathy. In the latest reading in 1996, Snigdha Tripathy has corrected it as the year 12 making it the earliest dated inscription of the Bhauma-Karas discovered so far. After a reconsideration of all the Bhauma-Kara inscriptions, particularly their dates, she has proposed a revised chronology and genealogy of this dynasty.[20] She holds that Kṣemaṅkara, who is mentioned only in the Neulpur plate, is identical with Śubhakara I. He was the son of Śivakaradeva I. The Chaurasi plate of the year 12 was issued by his son, Śivakara II, who is also given the names Unmattasiṁha and Bhārasaha in the later charters. As noted above, the name of Kṣemaṅkara as the earliest member of the dynasty is found only in one epigraph, viz., the Neulpur plate of the year 30; the later plates of the family speak of Lakṣmīkara as the earliest ruler. In fact, the plates after the year 141 ignore both Kṣemaṅkara and Lakṣmīkara and commence the dynastic reckoning from Unmaṭṭasiṁha alias Bhārasaha. Tripathy has opined that while Śivakara I was the first member of the dynasty he was only a subordinate ruler and the real maker of the family's fortunes was his son Śubhakara I alias Kṣemaṅkara. In the Chaurasi plate Śivakara I is not given any royal title but Śubhakara (I) is described as *Paramabhaṭṭāraka Mahārājādhirāja Parameśvara* implying that he had acquired sovereign status. The donor, Śivakara, is also given the same titles. In the next plate, viz., the Neulpur plate of Śubhakara II of the year 30, Kṣemaṅkara is not given any royal title and his son Sivakara is called simply as *Narapati.* For that matter, the donor of the plate, Śubhakara II is also mentioned only as 'Mahārājā.' Being the son and grandson of '*Mahārājadhirājas*' he was also one. Significantly, in the later plates, e.g., the Hindol plate of Śubhakaradeva (IV) of the year 103 and the Dharakote plate of the same ruler of the same year, only the donor is described with the full regal titles while the earliest members of the dynasty are enumerated as just *Lakṣmīkarādi, Nṛpati Śubhakara,* etc.

The irresistible conclusion is that these rulers did not consider it necessary to use full regal titles for all their predecessors and used just one or two honorifics as may have met the metrical demands. At the same time, it is noteworthy that the donor of the Chaurasi plate, Śivakara II, has taken special care to mention his father Śubhakara (I) with full regal titles, no doubt because he was the first member of the dynasty to assume them and establish the family's sovereignty and that too only a few years earlier. In the subsequent plates the donors are usually named with full regal titles as was customary and necessary to impress upon all concerned that they had full legal authority to make the impugned donation.

After examining the epigraphic evidence Panigrahi concluded that the conquest of Orissa by Harṣavarman should be taken as a historical fact and states, "After his conquest the Assamese king would have made arrangements for its administration as a result of which the kingdom of the Bhaumas in Orissa owed its origin. Kṣemankaradeva, the first member of the ruling family of the Bhaumas, seems to have been the first administrator or governor of this newly conquered kingdom."[21] Snigdha Tripathy supports the same hypothesis but, in view of the revised genealogy as worked out by her, she also says, "Śivakara I was probably a contemporary and a subordinate ruler under Harṣa or Bhaskaravarman."[22] She has evidently made a chronological slip here because contemporaniety with Harṣa or Bhāskaravarman will take Śivakara I to the first half of the seventh century whereas his date should be around AD 736. The correct position, therefore, seems to be that Śivakara I, a relation of Harṣavarmādeva, was appointed as the subordinate ruler at Tośalī by him after he conquered Oḍra, Kaliṅga and Kośala but within a few years his son Śubhakara I alias Kṣemaṅkara declared independence and assumed full sovereignty. We may note here that in the first two charters of the dynasty there is little to enlighten us about the deeds of the first three rulers of the dynasty, including the two sovereign rulers, Śubhakara I and Śivakara II. The Talcher plate of Śivakaradeva IV of the year 149 (AD 885), however, informs us that Unmaṭṭasiṁha or Śivakara II had defeated the king of Rāḍha and taken away his daughter and that his son, Śubhakara II conquered Kaliṅga. Panigrahi has, however, held that Kaliṅga was conquered actually by Unmaṭṭasiṁha himself as evidenced by the Ganjam plate of Jayavarmadeva.[23] Thus it becomes clear that it was Śubhakara I alias Kṣemaṅkaradeva who severed the links of subordination to the Kāmarūpa house but the Utkala Bhaumas embarked on their march to greatness from the time of his son, Śivakara II alias Unmaṭṭasiṁha. When Śivakara II was going to issue the Chaurasi plate he was faced with the question of the date to be recorded therein. Clearly, in the absence of any well-established common era in use, he had three alternatives before him, viz., (i) use his own regnal year, (ii) use the years elapsed since his father's assumption of sovereignty and (iii) use the years elapsed since the appointment of his grandfather to the Utkala throne. It was logical to rule out the third choice for a sovereign ruler because ir really was the date of conquest of his country by a 'foreign' power. Then, this plate was perhaps issued at the time of his own succession or coronation and thus the first alternative was not relevant. He adopted the second alternative which was also the most glorious. The relevant year was AD 736 making the date of the Chaurasi plate as AD 748. This would imply that Harṣadeva must have effected his conquest and appointment of Śivakara I as viceroy at Tośalī a few years before AD 736, say around AD 725. We have noted earlier that Harṣavarmādeva succeeded to the Kāmarūpa throne between AD 720 and AD 730. He seems to have immediately pressed the military resources of his already extensive domains into campaigns in the direction of Gauḍa and Utkala and soon thereafter also came into conflict with Yaśovarman of Kanauj. K.L. Barua has shown that the Gauḍa king killed by Yaśovarman as described in the poem *Gauḍa-vaho* was Harṣavarman.[24] The date of this event is not known. However, the reign period of Yaśovarman is assumed to be *c.* 690 to 740 AD by R.C. Majumdar[25] and his Gauḍa campaign is presumed to have taken place in the later part of his reign. Barua had taken it to be after AD 748, the date of the Paśupati inscription, on the presumption that Harṣadeva was alive at the time of this inscription. There is, however, nothing in this inscription to warrant such a presumption and the chronological logic of the contemporary events suggests that Harṣadeva was perhaps defeated and killed by Yaśovarman soon after AD 730, say, around AD 733, throwing his extensive dominions into a state of confusion and chaos. R.C. Majumdar, though identifying the Gauḍa king of *Gauḍa vaho* differently, also holds that Yaśovarman set out on his victorious campaign in the east sometime in the second quarter of the eighth century AD.[26] Taking advantage of this chaos and the fact that the successor of Harṣadeva on the distant Kāmarūpa throne was perhaps a weakling, Śubhakara alias Kṣemaṅkara, son and successor of the viceroy, Śivakara I, declared independence and assumed full sovereignty in AD 736. He appears to have ruled for not more than twelve years as his son and successor, Paramabhāṭṭāraka Mahārājādhirāja Parameśvara Śrī Śivakaradeva (II) is found to be issuing the Chaurasi plate in the year 12. It was probably issued on the occasion of his coronation. The assumption of sovereignty by Kṣemaṅkara must have been accompanied by the usual difficulties in such matters and the matters may have been further worsened because of his 'foreign' origin. The assertion of Śivakara II that he belonged to the Bhauma family of Utkala should be viewed in this light. He was the third generation of the Bhaumas who came from Kāmarūpa and was brought up and perhaps also born in Utkala where the family had become 'naturalized' by now. At the same time the original Bhaumas were still ruling in Kāmarūpa and were undoubtedly very famous in the eastern, if not the whole of India. The donor of the Chaurasi plate thought it prudent to distinguish himself from these Bhaumas and to emphasise his status as a 'son of the soil' to gather local support. By doing so, he was clearly washing away the stigma of 'foreign' origin that might still have been sticking, though diluted, over three generations. Significantly, the donor of the Neulpur plate in the year 30 does not speak of his Utkala origin clearly because after four generations the 'naturalization' of the family had become total and no resentment against the family was now left. Similarly, the later plates of the year 100, 103, 141, 149, 158, 180, 183, 187 and 204 also do not care to mention that the Bhaumas belonged to Utkala because it would have been not only unnecessary but rather incongruous and totally redundant and superfluous to do so.

At this stage we may take note of the reading of the Chaurasi plate, as emended by Snigdha Tripathy. According to her, the relevant portion of the inscription given by Binayak Misra as *guṇamālotkale Kule nṛpobhūd* should be read as *guṇamālākule (?) kule abhūdbhūt.*[27] There is reason to accept this reading because Pandit Misra himself was not satisfied with the decipherment of the Chaurasi plate; so much so that he did not include it in his compilation stating, "The published text of this plate is full of mistakes. I have found no opportunity to examine the original plate nor is its facsimile-print clear. Therefore, I could not reproduce here the revised text." Exclusion of this plate from his compilation resulted in his, and following him, other scholars, ignoring the data of this plate and arriving at a defective genealogy and chronology of the Bhauma-Karas. Of our immediate interest, however, is the fact that in view of the new reading there remains no particular reason to consider the point regarding the Utkala origin of the family. It is, however significant to note that the donor of the Chaurasi plate describes his father, Śubhakara, with the peculiar epithet *Mahān Utkalendra.*[28] The implication perhaps is to recall that his grandfather, Śivakara (I) had founded the new dynasty of Utkalendras to which his father and he himself belonged.

Having disposed of the specific points of Pandit Binayak Misra against the Kāmarūpa origin of the Orissa Bhaumas we may, in passing, take up some points by which he supports the hypothesis of their local origin. He has stated that "the Bhuyans, now inhabiting the northern hilly tracts of Orissa, seem to be the representatives of the Bhaumas of Purāṇas. The word 'Bhuyan' can be taken as the variant of Bhauma... the Bhuyans have been living in the north-west hilly tracts of Orissa since remote past and they had come into the pale of civilization even before Buddha's time."[29] Needless to say, this is nothing but pure conjecture based on the dangerous principle of phonetic similarity of words. It is also noteworthy that the surname Bhuyan is also fairly common in Assam and Bengal and the communities using it have no connection with the Orissa Bhuyans. The word Bhuyan perhaps became a common title for landholders from the fourteenth century onward. The only specific point in support of this hypothesis cited by him is that "each of the Bhumas Kings took a name after his grandfather as the Bhuyans do to-day."[30] Here the learned Pandit has failed to refer to the chronological table prepared by himself and given at p.71 of section II (Historical Notes) of his monograph under discussion. He seems to ignore the fact that Śubhakaradeva II alias Siṁhaketu alias Kusumahāra is not named after his grandfather, viz., Śantikaradeva who was the son of Śubhakara I. In any case, naming a son after one's own father has been a rather frequent occurrence and does not amount to a family custom. The name of Candragupta II, son of Samudragupta and grandson of Candragupta I immediately comes to mind. Naming one's son after an illustrious ancestor also was a common practice and this is what was done by the Bhaumas of Orissa. For that matter, this practice also obtained in the Bhauma family of Harṣadeva of Kāmarūpa. Harṣadeva's son and successor was named Balavarmā. Historians designate him as Balavarmā II because there was another Balavarman in the previous Varman dynasty four centuries earlier. Then, in the line of Harṣadeva-Balavarmā II we have Balavarmā III, sixth in descent from Balavarmā II.

The above discussion, I believe, satisfactorily takes care of Pandit Binayak Misra's arguments and a *prima facie* case for the Kāmarūpa origin of the Orissa Bhaumas is established. We may now turn to some peculiar similarities between the copper plates of Assam and Orissa. It would be worthwhile to discuss this matter in some detail particularly because it has not been attempted by any scholar so far. Panigrahi also focussed essentially on the similarities between the art styles of the Bhauma Orissa and early Assam and did not care to take note of the epigraphic evidence.

First, the size of the plates. The dynasties immediately preceding the Bhauma-Karas in Orissa are the Śailodbhava, Vasiṣṭha and Māṭhara dynasties. The Māṭhara plates are generally thin rectangular. Thus the Ningondi plate (single) of Prabhañjanavarman measures 6.9" x 2" resembling a palmleaf.[31] Similarly, the Baranga plates (three) of the same ruler[32] measure 6.6" x 2.6".

This, therefore, appears to have been the norm in the pre-Bhauma period. Coming to the Bhauma charters we find that these are much larger and the proportion of the length and breadth also changes. Thus the Chaurasi plate of Śivakara II of the year 12 measures 7.6" x 5.6".[33] The Neulpur grant of Śubhakaradeva II of the year 30 is as large as 45cm x 20.5cm.[34] Similarly the Terundia plate of Śubhakardeva II of the year 100 measures 41cm x 21.8cm, i.e., very similar to the Neulpur plate.[35]

As regards the Assam plates, the Dubi plates of Bhāskaravarmā of the first quarter of the seventh century measure 25.5 x 12 cms.[36] Nidhanpur plates of the same ruler measure 28.5 x 16 cms. Coming to the Śālastambha dynasty, we find that the Hayunthal plate of Harjaravarmā (single) measures 20.2 x 12.6 cms. while the Parvatiya plate of Vanamālavarmā is 25.2 x 15.6 cms.[37] It is also noted that the Māṭhara and Vasiṣṭha plates are made of thin sheets of copper[38] while the Bhauma Kara plates are much thicker like their Kāmarūpa counterparts.

It is easy to see that the Bhauma-Karas deviate from the earlier Māṭhara norm of the plates being thin rectangular in shape resembling palm leaves. The size adopted by them is very similar to the Assam plates. No doubt, the actual size of the plates depended upon the size of the text to be inscribed on them as well as the personal preference of the official preparing the plates but the proportion of length and breadth was now similar to the Assam plates and quite different from that adopted in the Māṭhara plates.

Secondly, coming to the texts of the plates we have already noticed above that the place of issue of a grant is invariably mentioned in the beginning of the plate both in the Assam and the Orissa plates. This was perhaps a universal custom but what is interesting to note is that the place which is undoubtedly the capital city is described as *Jayaskandhāvāra.* Thus the Orissa plates always mention *Jayaskandhāvārat Guhadevapāṭakāt* or *Guheśvarapāṭakāt.*[39] The Hayunthal plate of Hajaravarmadeva mentions *Haruppeśvaravasī Jayaskandhavāra.*[40]

EPIGRAPHIC EVIDENCE CONSIDERED FURTHER

The reason for using the term *jayaskandhāvāra* for the capital city has not been explained by any scholar so far. In his *Indian Epigraphical Glossary,* D.C. Sircar simply writes that the term meaning 'camp of victory' implies the royal camp or capital. He has not offered any explanation as to why the term was used for the capital. One should expect the capital to be described as a *rājadhānī, rājapurī, rājagṛha* or by some other similar term. Instead, the word *jayaskandhavāra* has been used in many charters where we know the reference is not really to a camp but to the capital city itself. A close examination of the copper plates of the Kāmarūpa kings perhaps gives us some clue in this regard.

The only epigraphs of the Varman dynasty that have been discovered are the Dubi and Nidhanpur grants of Bhākaravarmā. While in the first charter the name of the place is obliterated, the Nidhanpur charter records it as *Skandhāvārāt Karṇasuvarṇa vāsakāt.*[41] It is quite appropriate, since Karṇasuvarṇa, the erstwhile capital of Śaśāṅka, was really the victorious camp of the donor. Coming to the next dynasty, the earliest charter is the Hayunthal plate of Harjaravarmā, who was the tenth in descent from Śālastambha, the founder of the dynasty. The donor is stated to be *Śrīmān Haruppeśvaravasī jayaskandhāvāra.*[42] We know that Śālastambha occupied the throne of Kāmarūpa some years after the death of Bhāskaravarmā. Being a tribal chief–*mlecchādhināthā*[43]—with no legitimate claim to succeed Bhāskaravarmā, he must have won the throne after considerable struggle against the rival claimants and it appears he celebrated the occasion at a victory camp at Haruppeśvara which subsequently became his capital city. For his successors it was no more a victorious camp but the capital city; yet they continued to describe it as a victorious camp to perpetuate the victorious deed of the dynasty's founder. Significantly, the rulers of next, i.e., the Brahmapāla dynasty, who issued their charters from the city of Durjayā do not use the term *jayaskandhāvāra* for it. The earliest record of the dynasty, viz., Bargaon plates of Ratnapāla, son of Brahmapāla, simply mentions *Prāgjyotiṣeṣu Durjjayākhyāpuramadhyuvāsa.*[44] We come across the name of this city for the first time in this record; it was evidently founded by either Brahmapāla or Ratnapāla. The reason why the term *jayaskandhavāra* has not been used for this city, I venture to suggest, is that it was not connected with any victory whatsoever. We should remember that Brahmapāla became king not by use of arms but the elders of the realm had elected him to the throne of Kāmarūpa lying vacant after Tyāgasiṁha, the last Śālastambha ruler, who died intestate.[45] Successors of Ratnapāla too do not use the term *jayaskandhāvāra* for their Durjayā nagarī.

In view of the above discussion, I propose a hypothesis that the term *jayaskandhāvāra* for the place of issue of a charter in the first instance was used by a donor if the place was really a victorious camp but even after such place became the capital or the major city of the kingdom the term continued to be used for it by the successors of the original victor because such use became conventional.

Applying this hypothesis to the Bhauma-Kara charters, we conclude that Guheśvarapāṭaka or Guhadevapāṭaka was originally a place of a military camp and hence a *jayaskandhāvāra.* With the passage of time the use of this term for this place became conventional and every ruler of the dynasty described the capital city of Guhadevapāṭaka as a *jayaskandhāvāra*. It would appear that during his Orissa campaign around AD 725 Harṣadeva selected this place as his campaign headquarters on account of its strategic location in Tośalī and in what was perhaps Oḍra at that time. From this place the regions of Kaliṅga and Kośala towards the west could be easily approached and subjugated and the supply line from Kāmarūpa through the already subjugated land of Gauḍa could also be effectively maintained. Its proximity to the shrine of Virajā may also have been a factor as Harṣadeva came from the land of Kāmākhyā and may have had some Śakta leanings. In fact, it was an ideal location for not only the campaign headquarters but also for the seat of the viceroyalty that was established here under Śivakara (I). There is every likelihood that the city of Guhadevapāṭaka grew out of this military camp only. This view would find support in the fact that in and around Jajpur hardly any antiquities anterior to the eighth century AD have been found; in fact, the two-armed idol of Mahiṣāsuramardinī known as Virajādevī is perhaps the only item of this class.[46] It thus appears that the most important city of Orissa in the early medieval period owes its foundation to the Kāmarūpa king Harṣavarmādeva around AD 725 and it is this city that in AD 736 became the capital city of the Bhauma-Karas who ushered in a golden era of the arts in Orissa.

We may test this hypothesis in the case of the pre-Bhauma-Kara inscriptions. In the copper plates of the Māṭharas, Vasiṣṭhas, Pitṛbhaktas, Śailodbhavas and Mudgalas the place of issue is simply named with the prefix *Vijaya* (in some cases) without any mention of *skandhāvāra*. There appear to be only three exceptions to this rule and these are (a) the Khurda plates of Śri Mādhavarāja[47] and (b) two plates of Śambhuyaśas, viz., the Erbang plate of the year 235 and the Soro plate of the year 260.[48]

The Khurda plates of Śri Mādhavarāja alias Śri Sainyabhīta, son of Śri Yaśobhīta and grandson of Śri Sainyabhīta uses the words *jayaskandhāvārāt Koṅgoḍavāsakāt*. We do not know the date of this record but we do know that the same Mādhavarāja was earlier ruling as a vassal–*Mahāsāmanta*–of Mahārājādhirāja Śaśāṅkarāja in which capacity he issued the Ganjam plates in the Gupta Saṁvat 300 (i.e., AD 619).[49] In the Ganjam plates the reigning king is clearly stated to be Śaśāṅka and Mādhavarāja is just a *Mahāraja Mahāsāmanta* but in the Khurda plates he himself is the reigning king and addresses his order to the various subordinates including a *Mahāsāmanta*. Evidently, during the period intervening the Ganjam and Khurda plates he had acquired independence, presumably following the death of Śaśāṅka without leaving a legal heir. Mādhavarāja evidently took advantage of the situation and acquired sovereignty by the prowess of his arms. In fact, he confirms this position by proclaiming that he subdued the enemies and acquired the sovereignty of the whole of Kaliṅga country. He must have accomplished all this from his headquarters at the city of Koṅgoḍa which thus qualified to be called a *jayaskandhāvāra.*

Coming to the plates of Śambhuyaśas of the Mudgala family, we find that the Erbang plate was issued from the *jayaskandhāvāra* of Haṇḍaka and the Soro plate from the *jayaskandhāvāra* of Taṁparavadamā. No other plates of the Mudgalas giving the names of these places have been found and, therefore, it is reasonable to assume that neither of the two was their capital city but both of them were only military camps set up in the course of their military campaigns from where they issued these land grants.

The above discussion would seem to confirm our hypothesis regarding the term *jayaskandhāvāra* and its application to Guhadevapāṭaka.

As to the name Guhadevapāṭaka, I am inclined to think that Harṣadeva, leading a victorious army, paid his homage to the *devasenāpati* Kārtikeya or Skanda (also called Guha) by naming his encampment after the god. Alternatively, he may have been prompted by the Purāṇic legend in which a person named Guha is said to have been the first ruler of the land of Utkala, i.e., the land conquered by Harṣadeva. There is a likelihood that the camp of Harṣadeva was named after this Guha to proclaim the advent of a new dispensation in accordance with the destiny of the land. It was a way of saying that a modern Guha had come to Utkala!

Incidentally, it will also not be out of place to examine some copper plate grants of the period sixth to twelfth century AD from the regions other than Assam and Orissa in the light of the present hypothesis. Among the inscriptions of the Later Guptas we have the Katra plate of Jīvagupta issued from the *jayaskandhāvāra* of Tārā, evidently a place in Tīrabukti.[50] The capital of this ruler was surely somewhere in Magadha and he had come to Tārā evidently in course of a military expedition. Then, we have the Banskhera and Madhuban charters of Harṣa[51] issued from the *jayaskandhāvāra* of Śrivardhamānakoṭi and the *jayaskandhāvāra* of Kapitthikā respectively. We know that Harṣa's capitals were Kānyakubja and Sthāṇvīśvara; both the places named in the two charters are, therefore, literally only the victory camps set-up in the course of Harṣa's eastern campaigns. These examples would show that the term *jayaskandhāvāra* was usually employed in its literal meaning.

We may also have a look at the charters of Bengal kings from the time of the Pālas. Khalimpur charter of Dharmapāla is one of the earliest Pāla inscriptions.[52] It has the words *Pāṭaliputra samāvāsita Śrimajjayaskandhāvārāt.* We know that Dharmapāla was a great warrior and the real founder of the

Pāla glory; it appears that he conquered the city of Pātāliputra and made it his capital too. Then we have the Munger grant of Devapāla issued from the *Śrimajjayaskandhāvāra* of Mudgagiri.[53] Devapāla too was a great warrior and Mudgagiri was evidently a victory camp set up during his campaign against either the Kāṁbojas or Kāmarūpas. This place also never became his capital to the best of our knowledge. It is interesting to find that Devapāla's grandson, Nārāyaṇapāla in his Bhagalpur charter also calls the place of issue as *Śrimajjayaskandhāvāra* of Mudgagiri.[54] We know that Nārāyaṇapāla was no warrior and there is no question of his having really set up a victory camp at Mudgagiri. In all probability, after subjugating this region Devapāla had set up a provincial headquarters at Mudgagiri and it became conventional with his successors to call it the 'victory camp'. We notice the use of the expression *Śrimajjayaskandhāvāra* in the twelfth century Belava charter of Bhojavarman for the city of Vikramapura.[55] The Varmans of East Bengal originally belonged to Siṁhapura (which remains unidentified) and one of their early members, perhaps Bhojavarman's grandfather, Jātavarman had conquered the city of Vikramapura.[56] Thus, this city was not a 'victory camp' for Bhojavarman but the seat of his administration; yet he was describing it as 'victory camp' because his grandfather had originally occupied the city as such. Finally, we may take note of the Naihati copper plate of Vallālasena which is issued from the *Śrīmajjayaskandhāvāra* of Vikramapura. In this case also, the city of Vikramapura had already been conquered by Vijayasena, the father of Vallālasena, and made his capital. So, for Vijayasena it was a 'victory camp' but his son continued to described it as such only to perpetuate the memory of the victory.

On the basis of the specimens from the different regions of eastern India from the sixth to the twelfth century AD examined above, I believe, the hypothesis proposed in the earlier paragraphs stands reasonably established and, therefore, so does its implication for the Bhauma-Kara history.

Next, we shall take note of an unusual expression used in the genealogical section of the plates of the Kāmarūpa rulers.

In the inscriptions of the Guptas as well as the Maukharis and Puṣpabhūtis we find the donor kings describing themselves as 'meditating at the feet of his father'–*tatpādānudhyāta*.[57] In the Dubi and Nidhanpur plates, Bhāskasavarmā is seen to be dispensing with this convention, perhaps because of the peculiar circumstances of his succession to the Kāmarūpa throne–his father was succeeded by Supratiṣṭhitavarmā, the elder brother of Bhaskaravarmā and after some time the latter succeeded his elder brother. In the very first available record of the next, i.e., Śālastambha, dynasty, viz., the Hayunthal plate of Harjaravarmā,[58] we find an entirely new expression: the donor king describes himself as *mātāpitṛpādānudhyāta*, i.e., meditating at the feet of his mother and father'. It is noteworthy that this expression is not found in the Gupta inscriptions, nor in any of the north Indian records of the sixth, seventh and eighth centuries; then in the absence of any such convention, from where does Harjaravarmā suddenly adopt this novel expression and why? Most interesting, this expression is found in almost all the Bhauma-Kara inscriptions, from the Neulpur plates of Śubhakaradeva, of the year 30, to the Kumrung plate of Daṇḍīmahādevī, of the year 187. This was not a Bhauma-Kara innovation, for we find the expression used in Orissa earlier by the Māṭharas, Vasiṣṭhas, etc.[60] It appears that the rulers of these dynasties owed their power and kingdom, at least in some measure, to the help rendered by their material relations and, therefore, they thought it prudent to express their regard for their *mātṛkula* in their public documents. In case of the Bhauma-Karas we have definite evidence of the fathers of the Bhauma queens playing important, often decisive, role in their succession affairs. The case of Tribhuvanamahādevī, daughter of the southern king, Rājamalla, is the most glaring instance.[61] In any case, the use of this expression was conventional in Orissa when Harṣadeva conquered the land. Exchange of scholars between Kaliṅga and Kāmarūpa was a natural consequence of this event as a result of which the court poets of Kāmarūpa became familiar with the conventions of Kaliṅga and started using them in their compositions. Question arises as to why did the donor kings readily accept its use. I think it was because of the history of Śālastambha's acquisition of the Kāmarūpa throne. We know that Bhāskaravarmā had no legal heir at the time of his death. Śālastambha, probably a Bodo chief, with the help of some friendly tribes, usurped the vacant throne after defeating other rival claimants. In this struggle he received great help from the Khasi or Garo tribes in one of which he had married. It is likely that his successors continued the tradition of marrying ladies from these tribes and to have their support. The successors of Śālastambha were thus always grateful to their *mātṛkula*; more so, because the Khasis and Garos of Meghalaya were matriarchal tribes and continue to be so to this day. When their court poets composing their copper plates proposed the expression *mātāpitṛpādānudhyata* they found a ready formula for expression of their gratitude to their *mātṛkula*! These court poets were undoubtedly conversant with the Orissan convention; some of them might actually have belonged to Utkala. The convention of using this expression was followed by the successors of Hajaravarmā right down to Balavarmā III, the last Śālastambha ruler whose record is available.[62] Significantly, the rulers of the next, i.e., Brahmapāla dynasty are found to have given up this expression. Thus, in the first charter of the dynasty, we find Ratnapāla[63] describing himself as only *Śri Brahmapālavarmmā-devapādānudhyāta.* The mother is now totally forgotten; evidently, because the family did not have a tribal origin, nor did they marry in the Khasi or Garo tribe. As a matter of fact, the originator of the dynasty, Brahmapāla, who was elected king by the elders of the kingdom, might have been a descendant of the ancient Varman line because the selectors are stated to have been looking for such a person.[64]

We may now take note of a symbol with which some of these inscriptions begin. In Kāmarūpa, it makes its first appearance in the inscriptions of Vanamālavārmā (mid ninth century)[65] and again in those of Balavarmā III (late ninth century) and Indrapāla (late tenth century).[66] It is possibly also present in the Sualkuchi grant of Ratnapāla (middle of the tenth century) but is not distinct.[67] In the Bhauma-Kara plates we come across this symbol as early as the Chaurasi plate (of AD 748)[68] and continue to find it in the plates of the later rulers. The editors of the Bhauma-Kara plates have interpreted it as a symbol for *siddhaṁ.* Pandit Padmanath Bhattacharya Vidyavinod had, however, pointed out that the symbol really represented the Tāntrik divinity *Kuṇḍalinī.*[69] It is called *Añji.* The adoption of this symbol by Śivakaradeva (II) in his Chaurasi plate is significant in view of the fact that he was a Buddhist as we find from the Neulpur plate of his son in which he is described as *Paramatathāgata.*[69] In fact, the first three rulers of the family, viz., Kṣemaṅkara, Śivakara (II) and Śubhakara (II) were Buddhist and they are given the epithets respectively as *Paramopāsaka, Paramatathāgata* and *Paramasaugata.*[71] This was the period when Vajrayāna had just been established in Orissa and the Bhaumas coming from Kāmarūpa became its followers. Adoption of the *Añji* as the auspicious symbol to begin an inscription clearly points to the adoption of the Tāntrik Buddhist faith by these rulers. The subsequent rulers continued to use it as a convention even though they may have followed different faiths. With the exchange of ideas between Kāmarūpa and Kaliṅga-Utkala, the sign of *Añji* found its way to Kāmarūpa where it was adopted from the middle of the ninth century. It is interesting that the expression *mātāpitṛpādānudhyāta* had already been imported in the early ninth century. It is also significant to note that we find some allusions to the worship of the Mother Goddess from the middle of the ninth century. The charters of Vanamālvarmādeva[72] mention Śrī *Kāmeśvara mahāgaurībhaṭṭārikā* and the *Kāmakūṭagiri.* It is, however, not possible to ascertain whether Vanamālā had become a *Śākta.* This was surely the period when the *devī* was being glorified; the *Kālika Purāṇa* was composed in Kāmarūpa in the later part of the ninth century.[73] The Tārā-centred

Vajrayāna was definitely evolving during this period in Kāmarūpa, possibly an import from Oḍḍiyāna, i.e. Utkala and some of the *siddhas* of this system belonged to Kāmarūpa.[74] Towards the middle of the tenth century, king Ratnapāla was converted to Buddhism by either Sarahapā or his disciple, Nāgārjuna.[75] Dharmapāla, five generations later (end of the eleventh century) appears to have been a confirmed follower of the Tāntrik Śaivism as the invocations in his charters are not addressed simply to Śiva, as was the normal practice of his predecessors, but to the *Ardhayuvatīśvara.*[76] We know that by now a blending of the Buddhist and Śaiva Tantras was taking place.

Before concluding this discussion on the epigraphs of Utkala and Kāmarūpa we may also take note of a certain reference in the Bhauma-Kara inscriptions that has often puzzled the scholars. In the Neulpur charter, the founder of the dynasty, Kṣemaṅkaradeva, is credited with having 'established the four *varṇas* in their proper duties'.[77] This king is given the Buddhist epithet *Paramopasaka*; his patronage to the *Varṇāśrama dharma* is apparently strange. The first explanation that comes to mind is that the Buddhism had never completely rejected *Varṇāśrama dharma*; it had only denounced its abuses like the practice of untouchability. If we accept this explanation, there remains no contradiction in the Neulpur plates. But two other explanations, more plausible to my mind, may be as follows:

(i) The composer of the charter was perhaps a man from Kāmarūpa where the kings were conventionally extolled for upholding the *Varṇāśrama dharma.* In the Nidhanpur charter it is stated that the king is created in order that he might make proper arrangements for the maintenance of the *Varṇāśrama dharma* that is in disarray.[78] It appears that the composer of the Neulpur charter was emphasizing that Kṣemaṅkara fulfilled this divine obligation, regardless of being a Buddhist.

(ii) The most probable explanation, however, is that the phrase under discussion really means that Kṣemaṅkara brought peace and order to the country by enforcing the performance of their duties by every citizen. The country had been in a disturbed and unsettled condition at the time of the invasion of Harṣadeva, which no doubt made its conquest easy for the Kāmarūpa invader;[79] the invasion must have further compounded the chaotic condition. To create order out of this chaos was surely a great achievement worthy of note by the panegyrist of the Neulpur charter.

NOTES AND REFERENCES

1. Snigdha Tripathy, *Inscriptions of Orissa*, vol. I, Midnapore plate of Somadatta, year 19 at p. 201 and Ganjam plates of Mādhavarāja, Gupta Saṁvat 300 at p. 209.
2. There is a distinct possibility that Śaśāṅka was already dead by now and this campaign was against the Śailodbhavas.
3. Snigdha Tripathy, op.cit., section V, pp. 209-277 give all the available inscriptions of the Śailobhava rulers including Mādhavarāja as a Mahāsāmanta of Śaśāṅka and as a sovereign independent king.
4. K.C. Panigrahi, *History of Orissa*, pp. 58-60.
5. Ibid., p. 60.
6. Ibid., p. 66.
7. Ibid., p. 70 and K.C. Panigrahi, *Chronology of the Bhauma–Karas and the Somavamsis of Orissa* (the entire monograph)
8. Reniero Gnoli, *Nepalese Inscriptions in Gupta Characters*, Part I, Texts, pp. 115-119.
9. Lallanji Gopal and T.P. Verma, *History and Culture of Nepal*, p. 10, fn no. 39.
10. K.P. Jayaswal, *Chronology and History of Nepal*, pp. 12-17.
11. See D. Sarma, *Kāmarūpaśāsanāvalī*; reference may be made to Dubi and Nidhanpur plates of Bhāskaravarmā for the Varman dynasty, Parvatiya plate of Vanamālavarmā for the Śālastaṁbha dynasty and Khonamukh plate of Dharmapāla for the Brahmapāla dynasty.
12. Ibid., pp. 96-97 of Part I, General Introduction.
13. Pandit Binayak Misra, *Orissa under the Bhauma kings*, Section I (Inscriptions), p. 1 and also Srigadha Tripathy, *Inscriptions of Orissa*, vol. II, pp. 110-115.
14. R.D. Banerji, in E.I., vol. XV, pp. 1-8.
15. K.C. Panigrahi, op. cit., p. 67-71 and his monograph cited above.
16. Pandit Binayak Misra, op. cit., Section II (Historical Notes), p. 81.
17. Ibid., p. 83.
18. See inscriptions in D. Sarma's *Kāmarūpaśāsanāvalī*, op. cit., for Assam and Binayak Misra, op. cit., as well as S. Tripathy, op. cit., for Orissa.
19. See B. Misra, op.cit., or Tripathy, op. cit., for all these epigraphs.
20. Snigdha Tripathy, 'Chronology of the Bhauma-Karas of Orissa–A Reappraisal' in *OHRJ*, vol. XLI, no. 1 to 4, pp. 39-84.
21. K.C. Panigrahi, *History of Orissa*, p. 76.
22. Snigdha Tripathy, op.cit., p. 45.
23. K.C. Panigrahi, op. cit., p. 76.
24. K.L. Barua, 'Kamarupa in the Eighth Century AD' in *JARS*, vol. II, no. 1, April 1934, pp. 19-23.
25. R.C. Majumdar, *The Classical Age*, p. 131.
26. Ibid., p. 127.
27. Snigdha Tripathy, *Inscriptions of Orissa*, vol. II, p. 105.
28. Ibid., p. 105.
29. B. Misra, op. cit., p. 81.
30. Ibid.
31. S. Tripathy gives these measurements in her *Inscriptions of Orissa* cited above.
32. Ibid.

33. Ibid.
34. Ibid.
35. Ibid.
36. See R.D. Choudhury, *Catalogue of Inscriptions in the Assam State Museum* for these measurements.
37. Ibid.
38. Snigdha Tripathy, *Inscriptions of Orissa*, vol. I, p. 15.
39. B. Misra, op. cit., or S. Tripathy, op. cit.–all epigraphs in these collections.
40. D. Sarma, op. cit., Part II-Texts, pp. 37-39.
41. Ibid.
42. Ibid.
43. Ibid., line 3.
44. Ibid., pp. 79-87.
45. Ibid., verse 10.
46. K.C. Panigrahi, *History of Orissa*, p. 438.
47. Snigdha Tripathy, *Inscriptions of Orissa*, vol. 1, p. 212.
48. Ibid., pp. 180, 182.
49. See note 1 above.
50. K.K. Thaplyal, *Inscriptions of the Maukharis Later Guptas Puṣpabhūtis and Yaśovarman of Kanauj*, pp. 174-176.
51. Ibid., pp. 171-181, 182-185.
52. Ramaranjan Mukherji and S.K. Maity, *Corpus of Bengal Inscriptions bearing on History and Civilization of Bengal*, pp. 95-110.
53. Ibid., pp. 114-131.
54. Ibid., pp. 163-184.
55. Ibid., pp. 234-244.
56. Ibid., Introduction, p. 29.
57. See, for example, the Sohang Seal of Avantivarman, Deo Baranark Inscription of Jīvitagupta II, Banskhera Copper-plate Inscription of Harṣa, Madhuban Copper-plate Inscription of Harṣa, all in Thaplyal, op. cit., respectively at pp. 150-51, 171-73, and 177-81.
58. D. Sarma, op. cit., Part, II-Texts, pp. 37-39.
59. See the inscriptions in Snigdha Tripathy, *Inscription of Orissa*, vol. II.
60. See, for example, Siripuram Plates of Anantavarman and Chicacole Plates of Nandaprabhañjanavarman in Snigdha Tripathy, *Inscriptions of Orissa*, vol. 1, respectively at pp. 100-101 and 114-15.
61. Snigdha Tripathy, *Inscription of Orissa*, vol. II, p. 32.
62. Nowgong Plates of Balavarma III, of year 8, in D. Sarma, op. cit., pp. 71-77.
63. Bargaon Grant of Ratnapala, in D. Sarma, op. cit., pp. 78-87.
64. Ibid., verse 10.
65. See Photograph of the Parvatiya Plate of Vanamālā opp. p. 52 in D. Sarma, op. cit., Part II-Texts.
66. See photograph of the Howraghat Plates of Balavarma III opp. P. 66, that of the Nowgong Plates opp. p. 72, that of the Gauhati Plate of Indrapāla opp. p. 91 and that of the Guakuchi Plate of Indrapāla opp. p. 102. in ibid.
67. See Photograph in ibid., opp. p. 90.

68. See Photograph in Snigdha Tripathy, *Inscriptions of Orissa*, vol. II, Plate I.
69. Pandit Padmanath Bhattacharya Vidyavinod, 'The Sign in Ancient Copper Plate Inscriptions of Kamarupa' in *JARS*, vol. I, no. 1, 1933.
70. S. Tripathy, op. cit., pp. 110-15.
71. Ibid.
72. D. Sarma, op. cit., the Tezpur Plates at pp. 43-50 and the Parvatiya Plates at pp. 50-55.
73. B.N. Shastri (tr. & ed.), *The Kālikā Purāṇa*, Introduction, pp. 51-67 discusses in detail the date and place of origin of this *Upa-Purāṇa.*
74. K.L. Barua, 'Kāmarūpa and Vajrāyana' in *JARS*, vol. II, no. 2, July 1934, pp. 44-49.
75. Ibid.
76. D. Sarma, op. cit., Part II-Texts, the Khonamukh Plates at pp. 118-123 and the Subhankarapataka Plates at pp. 124-131.
77. Snigdha Tripathy, op. cit., p. 114.
78. D. Sarma, op. cit., p. 164.
79. K.C. Panigrahi, *History of Orissa*, p. 67 says, 'The accounts of the Tibetan historian Tārānātha indicate that both in Bengal and Orissa there was a period of confusion and anarchy that preceded the foundation of the Pāla kingdom and the Bhauma Kingdom.' The truth of Tārānātha's statement has been established in case of Bengal and there is no reason to doubt it in case of Orissa.

Chapter 4

Kāmarūpa and Mithilā

PURĀṆIC AND LEGENDARY HISTORY

According to the popular legends, the country of Prāgjyotiṣa was originally populated by the *Kirātas* and its first ruler was Mahiraṅga dānava. The memory of this legendary figure is preserved in the name of the hill Mairaṅka parbata at Beltola on the outskirts of Guwahati. He was succeeded by Hāṭaka, Śaṁbara, Ratna and Ghaṭaka, all of them called *asura*. The last of this line, Ghaṭakāsura was killed by Naraka, born of the earth goddess, Pṛthvī, and brought up by Janaka, the king of Mithilā.[1] The story of the birth of Naraka is found in the various Purāṇas.[2] The story of the birth and career of Naraka has been given in great detail in the *Kālikā Purāṇa*[3] in chapters 36 to 42. We are told that Pṛthvī gave birth to Naraka at the same sacrificial ground where Sītā was born in the past and Janaka started rearing up the child in accordance with a promise that he had made earlier to Pṛthvī. We are told that this event took place after Pṛthvī had been relieved of the demons Rāvaṇa, Kuṁbhakarṇa, etc., i.e., during the Rāma incarnation of Viṣṇu even though she had conceived the child Naraka by Viṣṇu in his *Varāha avatāra* aeons ago; Pṛthvī was made to carry the child in her womb all this time by a divine design. Soon after his birth the child crawled away from the sacrificial ground where he was born and when Janaka came looking for him he found the child with his head resting on the skull of a dead man. It is for this reason that the child was named Naraka by the sage Gautama. Soon after the child was taken to the palace of Janaka, his mother disguised herself as a nursemaid named Kātyāyanī and got employed in the palace to look after the child. The boy was brought up as a Kṣatriya prince and grew up into a fine virtuous warrior. When the lad reached the age of sixteen, Kātyāyanī became suspicious that the king might not make him his successor preferring his own sons. Thinking thus, she ran away with Naraka from the palace, told him that his real father was Viṣṇu and not Janaka and summoned Viṣṇu by her divine powers to vouch for her story. Viṣṇu accepted the young man and took him to Prāgjyotiṣa, 'situated in the centre of Kāmarūpa where Kāmākhyā is the supreme Goddess'.[4] A fierce battle took place between Naraka and Ghaṭaka and his army in which Ghaṭakāsura was killed by Naraka. Thereupon, Naraka was annointed to the throne of Prāgjyotiṣa and also became the chief devotee of Kāmākhyā. Viṣṇu instructed him in the ways of righteousness and to remain devoted to Kāmākhyā for ever. Thus began the rule of Naraka over the kingdom of Prāgjyotiṣa and his fame spread far and wide. Hearing of his fame, his foster-father, Janaka, paid him a visit with his family members and stayed with Naraka for quite some time.

Naraka is stated to have ruled through the whole of the *Tretā* and the *Dvāpara Yugas*. All these synchronisms might prove to be of some value if an attempt is made to cull out any historical chronology from the allegorical and mythical time-measurements of the Purāṇas. At the end of the *Dvāpara Yuga*, Naraka became very friendly with Bāṇāsura, the ruler of the neighbouring kingdom of Śoṇitapura and son of the great demon, Bali. Thanks to this association, Naraka started deviating from the right path and developed demonic tendencies. Meanwhile, he annoyed the sage Vasiṣṭha who had come for a *darśana* of Kāmākhyā but was denied entry to the *yonimaṇḍala* by Naraka, the guard and custodian of the place. The sage cursed him saying that the goddess will disappear and remain hidden from Prāgjyotiṣa as long as Naraka remained alive. The *Yoginī Tantra* gives a somewhat different account of Vasiṣṭha's curse. It says that the sage had cursed the Devī herself to the effect that she will become powerless and no merit will accure from worshipping her. On the intervention of Śiva, however, the curse was modified to the extent that it will be effective only for three hundred years during the *Kali Yuga*.[5] However, continuing the version of the *Kālikā Purāṇa*, we are told that on the advice of his friend Bāṇa, Naraka did penance to propitiate Brahmā from whom he received five boons, including one of invincibility but forgot to ask him for release from the curse of Vasiṣṭha. In course of time he appointed many *asuras* as his ministers and commanders. By virtue of Brahmā's boons and with the assistance of his principal commander, Hayagrīva, he vanquished even the god Indra and snatched away the *Kuṇḍalas* from the ears of Aditi, the mother of *devas*. He committed many atrocities and imprisoned a large number of virtuous kings and sixteen thousand *apsarās*. Ultimately, the *devas* and the mother Pṛthvī herself pleaded before Viṣṇu for deliverence from the evil of Naraka and Viṣṇu promised to do so by taking birth as Kṛṣṇa. Accordingly, Kṛṣṇa went to Prāgjyotiṣa from Dvarikā and first killed Hayagrīva, the keeper of the gates of the city of Naraka and then annihilated Narakāsura along with all his *asura* generals. *Kālikā Purāṇa* informs us that in the Kṛṣṇa's fight with Naraka, the goddess Kālikā remained by the side of the former throughout. At the pleadings of Pṛthvī, ŚrīKṛiṣṇa took the son of Naraka, Bhagadatta, under his protection and crowned him king of Prāgjyotiṣa; he also recovered the earrings of Aditi and restored them to her. The other consequence of the killing of Naraka was that the curse of Vasiṣṭha expired and Kāmākhyā returned to Prāgjyotiṣa.

I have summarized the narration of *Kālikā Pūraṇa* at some length only to see if we could make some historical sense out of it and my hypotheses are as follows.

First, there is no doubt that in the proto-historical times a person named Naraka came from Videha or Mithilā to Prāgjyotiṣa, vanquished the tribal chief ruling there and established his own rule. Secondly, the arrival of Naraka heralded not only a political but also a socio-cultural upheaval in Prāgjyotiṣa because it is from this time that the worship of the Mother Goddess seems to have been adopted by the people of this land. This is corroborated by the mention in *Kālikā Purāṇa* (38.130) that the name of the country henceforth became famous as Kāmārūpa. It is to be noted that Prāgjyotiṣa is a secular name; it is perhaps the Sanskritized form of an Austric formation *Par+ger+ju+tic* meaning the land of long and high hills which indeed Assam is.[6] Kāmārūpa, on the other hand, is clearly related to Kāmā or Kāmākhyā as well as to the legend of the burning of Kāmādeva by Śiva to ashes and his regaining his body or *rūpa* which perhaps refers to some Tāntrik ritual.[7] Thirdly, Naraka was probably the son of a tribal chief who had deserted his mother who somehow managed to obtain shelter for the boy in the palace of Janaka, the king of Videha. Here I should mention that Kokāmukha, also known as the Śūkara or Varāha Tīrtha is considered in *Brahma Purāṇa* as the site of the *Varāha avatāra* as well as the birth place of Naraka.[8] This place was located in the hilly region bordering on the northern fringes of Bengal and thus touching the eastern extremity of Mithilā as also the western-most region of Kāmārūpa. This region was perhaps inhabited by some Bodo tribe to which Naraka's real father belonged. That Naraka was born outside the 'Aryan' system is also perhaps alluded to by the fact that he had crawled away from the sacrificial ground–the *yajña bhūmi*. Fourthly, it would appear that Naraka was introduced to the cult of the Mother Goddess in his childhood even while he was growing up under the tutelage of Janaka. Such an inference is strongly suggested by Kātyāyanī being his nursemaid. Devī worship, was perhaps prevalent in the tribe to which Kātyāyanī and Naraka's father belonged. It thus follows that the Devī worship in Kāmārūpa was introduced from Mithilā by Naraka; Kāmākhyā, a minor local tribal deity of the matriarchal people like the Khasis or the Garos was raised to the status of the Supreme Goddess by Naraka. We should remember that the Khasis and Garos inhabit the hills lying to the south of and not far from the Kāmākhyā shrine on the Nīlāchal hill in Guwahati. The word Kāmākhyā itself has been thought of as the Sanskritized version of an Austric formation *Kā-mei-khā* meaning supreme goddess on the hill.[9] Fifthly, in his campaign to Prāgyotiṣa, Naraka was perhaps helped and guided by the chief of the tribe to which he belonged. Viṣṇu, the dark god of the Hindu pantheon being his father and leading him to Prāgyotiṣa seems to refer to such a fact. It was his mother who was instrumental in getting this support; she must have taken the young Naraka to the tribal chief and pleaded that the boy was one of them and they must help him. Sixthly, the Vasiṣṭha episode clearly points to a conflict between the followers of the *Vāmacāra* and *Dakṣiṇācāra*, the two *Śakta* sects, the latter of which was perhaps already prevalent in Kāmārūpa. In this conflict for supremacy not only did the former lose but Naraka also lost his life. It is possible to detect one more point in the narration: as a born tribal and by virtue of training under Kātyāyanī, Naraka had an instinctive inclination towards the tribal ways of life; his "Aryan" upbringing in the palace of Janaka did bring about some changes in him but on his contact with Bāṇāsura, his tribal or *mleccha* mores reasserted. Finally, in the *Yoginī Tantra* version of the Vasiṣṭha's curse one can possibly detect a reference to the suppression of the *Śaktas* and supremacy of the Vaiṣṇava cult in the historical times.

CONNECTIONS IN HISTORICAL TIMES

Some aspects of the connections between Kāmārūpa and Mithilā have already been dealt with in Chapter 2 while discussing the common political destiny of Kāmārūpa, Kaliṅga and Mithilā. Here we may take note of some facts especially about Kāmārūpa and Mithilā.

It is a well-established fact that the boundaries of the *dharma-kṣetra* of the Vedic culture kept on shifting eastwards in the proto-historical times. Until Videgha Māthava crossed the Sadānīrā it was that river which formed the eastern boundary. This river is believed to be the modern Gandak beyond which Mithilā is situated which was purified by Videgha Māthava. It is, however, noteworthy that the *Mahābhārata* treats Gandakī and Sadānīrā as two different rivers. By the time of the *Manusmṛti* the boundary had reached beyond Mithilā up to the river Karatoyā. In deference to the memory of the ancient boundary being Sadānīrā, the Karatoyā now became synonymous with Sadānīrā as is recorded in the *Amara Koṣa*,[10] which is probably a work of the third century AD.[11]

The Karatoyā during this period was the boundary between Tīrabhukti and Puṇḍravardhana. From the late fifth century Puṇḍravardhana had come under the rule of Kāmārūpa or Prāgjyotiṣa (see below) and, therefore, now Karatoyā seems to have been treated as the boundary between Tīrabhuki and Prāgjyotiṣa, a convention that remained current till the twelfth century when Puruṣottamadeva composed the *Trikāṇḍa Śeṣa.*[12] That Tīrabhukti and Kāmārūpa were contiguous may be inferred by their being mentioned together as follows *Prāgjyotiṣāḥ Kāmārūpe Tīrabhuktistu Nicchaviḥ.*[13]

About the ancient history of Mithila from the earliest times till the Gupta age we have considerable knowledge both from the archaeological and literary sources right from the Later Vedic, Buddhist and Jain literature. About Kāmārūpa, however, we have no definite archaeological or literary evidence to enlighten us till the establishment of the dynasty of Puṣyavarman, the Bhauma, whose lineage is traced from Naraka and Bhagadatta. Bhagadatta is really the link between the legendary and historical periods in Assam. It has not been possible to determine the date of Puṣyavarman with any definiteness because no contemporary epigraphs of his have been found. In fact, the only epigraphs of real historical value belong to the last ruler of the line, the great Bhāskaravarmā. P.C. Choudhury has suggested AD 355 as the date of accession of Puṣyavarman and assuming that about twelve rulers of the line had preceded him he fixes first century AD or a little earlier as the date of the beginning of the Varman line.[14]

This date of Puṣyavarman appears to be reasonable because Bhāskaravarmā ascended the throne in AD 594 and he belonged to the eleventh generation from Puṣyavarman and was the twelfth ruler of the line according to the established genealogy;[15] an average of 21 or 22 years for each generation can be regarded to be in order.

At the time of Puṣyavarman in Kāmārūpa, Videha or Mithilā was surely under the Gupta rule. Samudragupta has named Kāmārūpa as a frontier state–*Pratyanta rājya*–whose ruler was subordinated by him but the kingdom was otherwise left undisturbed.[16] Videha or Tīrabhukti was a *bhukti* or province of the Guptas.[17] Eighth ruler of the Varman dynasty, Bhūtivarman or Mahābhūtivarman is found to be donating lands in the Candrapurī *viṣaya* on the banks of the river Kauśikā.[18] This river has been identified as the Kosi and the donated land situated between two dried up abandoned beds of this river.[19] The Candrapurī *viṣaya* was thus a part of the Tīrabhukti and at the time of Bhūtivarnam, i.e., in the early sixth century it was no more a part of the Gupta empire. It appears that from the time of Mahendravarman, the sixth ruler of the Varman dynasty towards the end of the fifth century, the Kāmārūpa rulers were becoming ambitious and started making attempts to throw off the subordinate status imposed on them by Samudragupta He is credited to have performed two *Aśvamedha* sacrifices and his attempts to wrest Puṇḍravardhana and eastern Tīrabhukti from the Guptas may have met with some success as it was the period of decline of the Gupta power. But the final success perhaps came at the time of his grandson, Bhūtivarnam, fifty years later. On the occassion of his victory over the weak Gupta governor of Tīrabhukti he settled a large number of *Madhyadeśa* Brahmāṇas in the Candrapurī *viṣaya*. Between Tīrabhukti and Kāmārūpa lies the Puṇḍravardhana *bhukti* and this was also annexed by Bhūtivarman. Soon after these events, the rule of the Imperial Guptas came to an end and by the beginning of the sixth century the Later Guptas appear on the scene. Mahāsenagupta defeated the Kāmārūpa king Susthitavarman in the middle of the sixth century and apparently wrested the territories of Puṇḍravardhana and eastern Tīrabhukti (in which the Candrapurī *viṣaya* was located) from the Varmans. The setback for the Varmans was, however, temporary as within about fifty years, in the early seventh century these territories were reoccupied by Bhāskaravarmā. To celebrate his victories he re-issued the orders of donation of lands to the Brāhmaṇas in the Candrapurī *viṣaya*. These revenue -free lands were originally donated by Bhūtivarman but the relevant copper plates got destroyed by fire and the lands were assessed to revenue during the period of Mahāsenagupta's rule and, therefore, it became necessary to re-issue the copper plates. Bhāskaravarmā not only wanted to celebrate his victory in Tīrabhukti but also to hanour the commitments and donations made by his ancestor, Bhūtivarman.

We do not know how much of Tīrabhukti came under the Kāmārūpa rule during Bhutivarman's time but we do know that during Bhāskaravarmā's time the Kāmārūpa rule did not extend beyond the Candrapurī *viṣaya* in the west. For, in the early seventh century Tīrabhukti as such was alternately being ruled by the Maukharis, the Later Guptas and Harṣa.[20] In any case, it is reasonable to assume that a century or so of the Kāmārūpa rule in a part of Tīrabhukti must have heralded an era of cultural exchanges between the two regions. Inter-regional movement of Brāhmaṇas dealt with in Chapter 6, infra, must have been an important part of this phenomenon. In the eighth and subsequent centuries the interaction between the two regions was essentially of the cultural nature. No political relations were possible during this period as until the year 1097 there was no independent state in Mithilā. It is precisely because of this reason that in the Paśupati inscription of Jayadeva (II) of Nepal, in the list of countries ruled by the queen Rājyamati's father, king

Harṣadeva, there is no mention of Tīrabhukti or Mithilā, the country lying immediately to the south of Nepal. Clearly, Tīrabhukti was a part of the kingdom of some powerful ruler whom Harṣadeva did not like to challenge. He evidently did not proceed in the westerly direction after subjugating Gauḍa; instead, he turned southwards to conquer Oḍra, Kaliṅga and Kośala. Since we have accepted the identification of the ruler of Gauḍa, killed by Yaśovarman as narrated in the kavya *Gauḍa vāho*, with Harṣadeva (see Chapter 3, supra) it will not be unreasonable to presume that the two powerful kings came into conflict when both tried to establish supremacy over Magadha and Tīrabhukti, the regions left alone so far by Harṣadeva. There is no evidence to suggest that the rulers of Kāmārūpa made any effort to extend their territory westwards beyond the traditional boundary of the river Karatoyā. It is perhaps not without significance that the *Kālikā Purāṇa* compiled in the middle of the ninth century AD[21] unequivocally fixes the perennial river Karatoyā as the western boundary of Prāgjyotiṣa and that too by putting these words as coming from the mouth of Viṣṇu himself.[22] The full import of this speech may be appreciated from the fact that this is the earliest reference to Karatoyā being the western boundary of Prāgjyotiṣa-Kāmārūpa; we find no such mention in the earlier works in which Prāgjyotiṣa or Kāmārūpa finds a mention, e.g. in the *Rāmāyaṇa*, the *Mahābhārata*, the *Bhāgawata Purāṇa*, *Raghuvaṁśa* of Kālidasa, etc. In all these works the river Lauhitya does find a mention but not the Karatoyā. The *Kālikā Purāṇa* was compiled in Kāmārūpa[23] and there is every reason to believe that it was duly honoured by the people and rulers of the land. The rulers, therefore, would not try to violate the boundary specified by the Lord Viṣṇu himself in their favourite scripture! Had such not been the case, some ambitious ruler between the ninth and twelfth centuries would surely have tried to play a second Harṣadeva and, taking advantage of the unsettled political conditions of the times, would have tried to extend his territories in the west. Of course, the presence of the powerful Pālas in Gauḍa, Vaṅga, and Magadha was another effective deterrent and the Pālas were continually making their presence felt in Tīrabhukti by mounting military campaigns as we know from the establishment of victory camp at Mudgagiri (i.e., modern Munger) in eastern Tīrabhukti by Devapāla[24] and Nārāyaṇapāla.[25] Not only that, they even occupied portions of Tīrabhukti, at least for limited periods of time as we find them donating lands in this *bhukti*.[26] Eventually, it is the conflict with the Pālas that proved to be disastrous for Kāmārūpa; towards the end of the eleventh century Kāmārūpa lost its independence to Rāmapāla who appointed Tiṅgyadeva as his viceroy or governor in Kāmārūpa.[27]

Tingyadeva declared independence when Rāmapāla died. The new sovereign, Kumārapāla removed the recalcitrant governor and appointed Vaidyadeva as king on the throne of Kāmārūpa. The history of Kāmārūpa in the twelfth and thirteenth centuries is quite confusing. From the Kamauli Grant of Vaidyadeva,[28] however, we do know that by AD 1142 he had become independent. We have no information about his successors but we find one Vallabhadeva issuing the Tezpur grant in the year 1185 and we also hear of one Rāyārideva who probably set up a kingdom in a part of Kāmārūpa and was an ancestor of Vallabhadeva. It appears that king Pṛthu was born in this family who annihilated the entire army of Bakhtyār Khiljī in the year 1205 when it was proceeding to conquer Bhutan or Tibet.[29] In the Muslim chronicles he is named as Barthu. This was perhaps the last glorious act of Kāmārūpa and now the land got divided into small principalities governed by the rulers of little consequence. In the early fourteenth century we find one Pratāpadhvaja ruling over Kamatā,[30] the new kingdom that had risen over the ashes of the glorious Kāmārūpa. In the next century, Kamatā was ruled by the Khen or Khyān dynasty; we have the names of three Khen rulers between AD 1440 and 1498: Nīladhvaja, Cakradhvaja and Nīlāṁbara.[31] The kingdom of Kāmatā was subjected to continual attacks from the Sultans of Bengal, the representatives of the Delhi Sultanate.[32] Whether the kings of Kāmatā had any political relations with their neighbours, the kings of Mithilā, is not known but there is little doubt about the existence of strong cultural relations. This was the period when the *nibandhakāras* of Mithilā were profoundly influencing those of Kāmārūpa and Bengal and from the early fourteenth century commenced the all-pervasive influence of Vidyāpati over the entire eastern India. This will be discussed in some detail in Chapter 9, infra. One striking feature in the names of the rulers of this period, however, deserves to be noted before we close this chapter. At no time in the previous history of Kāmārūpa do we get any Nārāyaṇa-ending names but in the fourteenth century we have the king Durlabhanārāyaṇa ruling over Kāmatā (c. 1330-50).[33] Such names seem to have been borrowed from Mithilā. After the fall of the Karṇata dynasty in AD 1324, Mithila passed into the hands of the Sultans of Delhi. In 1353, Feroz Tughlak appointed Kāmeśvara Ṭhākura, a Brāhmaṇa, as king of Mithilā who became the founder of the Oinawār dynasty that ruled for two centuries.[34] One ruler of this line, Devasiṁha had adopted a *viruda* Garuḍa-nārāyaṇa.[35] In this family we also come across the names Rūpa-nārāyaṇa[36] and Darpanārāyaṇa.[37] It seems almost certain that the kings of Kamatā like Durlabhanārāyaṇa were imitating these names. In fact, the influence reached for beyond Kamatā in the east. Thus, in the fourteenth century itself we find that the rulers in the far off Sadhayāpurī, in the north-eastern corner of Assam, had the names like Lakṣmīnārāyaṇa, Pratyakṣa-nārāyaṇa and Satyanārāyaṇa.[38]

The practice evidently continued till the sixteenth century. In the year 1515 a Mech or Koch chieftain named Biśu adopted the name Visvasiṁha[39] and founded a new dynasty in Kamatā. His son, Malladeva or Naranārāyaṇa (1540-87)[40] proved to be an exceptional monarch.

Naranārāyaṇa and his brother Śukladhvaja, who was also his commander-in-chief, were great patrons of arts, culture and religion and their courts attracted poets, painters and scholars from far and near.[41] There is enough evidence to show that many scholars from Mithilā adorned the court of Naranārāyaṇa and the monarch encouraged them also to write in the Maithili language. The great Vaiṣṇava saint, Śaṅkaradeva (1449-1568) also took refuge in this court when he had to flee from his home in central Assam due to persecution by the Ahom rulers. Details of Śaṅkaradeva's life have been discussed in Chapter 9, infra. A number of scholars and poets of Assam as well as Bengal were also patronized by this great ruler at whose instance they composed many works in Sanskrit and Assamese. In the royal family of Koch Bihar as well as in the families of its successor states like Darrānga, Beltola, etc., the convention of having Nārāyaṇa - ending names continues to this day. Of course, during the last three centuries 'Siṅgha' has also been added after Nārāyaṇa. The presence of both Maithili and Assamese scholars at the same place must have resulted in extensive exchange of ideas; no wonder, the influences of Maithili on the Assamese of this period is both extensive and intense.

The cultural relations between the two regions continued to flourish in the later periods as well. The Śākta *mahāpīṭha* of Kāmākhyā has remained a place of extraordinary interest for the Śāktas of Mithilā as of the other regions of India and Nepal throughout its history. In the late nineteenth century Mahārājā Rāmeśvara Siṅgh of Darbhanga was a great devotee of the *devī*. It is interesting that he built a rest house on the Kāmākhyā hill where he used to resort for doing *sādhanā*. The building called the Darbhanga Kothi still exists on the hill-top near the temple of Bhuvaneśvarī telling the tale of inseparable links between Kāmārūpa and Mithilā.

NOTES AND REFERENCES

1. P.C. Choudhury, *The History of Civilisation of the People of Assam to the Twelfth century A.D.*, pp. 109-112.
2. Banikanta Kakati, *The Mother Goddess Kamakhya*, p. 23.

3. *Kālikā Purāṇa*, Chapters 36-42.
4. Ibid., 36.100 describes Prāgjyotiṣa as '*Madhyagaṁ Kāmārūpasya Kāmākhyā yatra nāyikā*'.
5. *Yoginī Tantra*, 1.12.41.
6. Banikanta Kakati, op. cit., p. 5-6.
7. Ibid., pp. 6, 34-38.
8. Hemachandra Roychaudhury, 'Kokamukhasvamin' in *Studies in Indian Antiquities*, chapter 18, pp. 205-8.
9. Banikanta Kakati, op. cit., pp. 34-38.
10. Kuberanath Sukul, *Vārāṇasī Vaibhava* (in Hindi), p. 9.
11. Baladeva Upadhyaya, *Sanskrit Śāstroñ Kā Itihās* (in Hindi), pp. 334-36.
12. Ibid., p. 349
13. Upendra Thakur, *History of Mithila*, p. 8.
14. P.C. Choudhury, op.cit., p. 128 and Appendix II.
15. Ibid., Appendix II and D. Sarma, *Kāmarūpaśāsanāvalī*, Part II - Texts pp. 7-18 (Dubi Plates of Bhaskaravama). The seal attached to these plates gives the full genealogy.
16. D.C. Sircar, *Select Inscriptions*, vol. 1, pp. 254-62.
17. Upendra Thakur, op.cit., pp. 185-91.
18. D. Sarma, op.cit., Part II -Texts, pp. 19-32 (Nidhanpur Plates of Bhaskaravarma). These plates record renewal of the grant originally made by Bhūtivarman.
19. K.L. Barua, 'Kausika and Kusiara' in *Indian Culture*, vol. I, no. 3, January 1935, pp. 421-32.
20. K.K. Thapliyal, *Inscriptions of the Maukharīs, Later Guptas, Puṣpabhūtis and Yaśovarman of Kannauj*, Section One, II. Political History, pp. 17 - 86; Also, Upendra Thakur, op. cit., pp. 189-203.
21. Biswanarayan Shastri (tr. & ed.), *Kālikā Purāṇa*, Introduction, pp. 51-67 thoroughly discusses the date of this *Upa-Purāṇa*.
22. *Kālikā Purāṇa*, 36.118.
23. Biswanarayana Shastri, op. cit., Introduction, pp. 51-67 gives many cogent arguments to establish that KP was compiled in Kāmārūpa.
24. Ramaranjan Mukherji and Sachindra Kumar Maity, *Corpus of Bengal Inscriptions bearing on History and Civilization of Bengal*, pp. 114-132(Munger Copper-Plate grant of Devapāla).
25. Ibid., pp. 163-184 (Bhagalpur Copper-Plate Inscription of Nārāyaṇapāla).
26. Ibid. The donated land in Nārāyaṇapāla's grant is situated in the Kakṣa *viṣaya* within Tīrabhukti.
27. P.C. Choudhury in op.cit., p. 250 holds that Rāmapāla did not conquer the whole of Kāmārūpa but only its possessions in Bengal over which Tingyadeva was appointed as vassal. The territory in question, therefore, is that lying to the west of Karatoyā.
28. Mukherji and Maity, op. cit., pp. 370-86 for the text and P.C. Choudhury, op. cit., p. 254 for its date.
29. P.C. Choudhury, op. cit., pp. 255-56.
30. J.N. Sarkar, 'The Turko-Afghan Invasions' in *TCHOA*, Chapter Two, p. 41.
31. Ibid., p. 44.

32. Ibid., the entire chapter.
33. Ibid., pp. 41-42
34. Upendra Thakur, op. cit., Chapter 6, pp. 290-342
35. Ibid., p. 305.
36. Ibid., p. 309.
37. Ibid., p. 333.
38. M. Neog, *Prācdya - Śāsanāvalī*, Introduction, pp. 82-85; Texts, pp. 93-97 give the copper-plates issued by these rulers.
39. J.N. Sarkar, 'Early Rulers of Koch Bihar', in *TCHOA*, Chapter Four, pp. 69-90.
40. Ibid., pp. 74-89.
41. B.K. Barua, *Assamese Literature*, pp. 16-17.

Chapter 5

Affinities in Art Styles

ARCHITECTURE AND SCULPTURE

In his monograph *Chronology of the Bhaumakaras and the Somavamsis of Orissa,* K.C. Panigrahi remarked as follows in 1961:

> A thorough examination of art and architecture is likely to provide evidence of the mutual exchange of styles and art motifs between the two branches of the same family ruling in Orissa and Assam, but here we refer to two images of Gaṅgā, one found at Dah Parbatia in the Tezpur District of Assam and the other from Ratnagiri in the Cuttack District of Orissa, now preserved in the Patna Museum. These are the only two images of Gaṅgā so far discovered in any part of India, which stylistically and iconographically possess such close similarity. The present writer is not aware of a third specimen of the type to be found in any other part of India. The Assamese specimen is earliler to the Orissan one by about three centuries, but yet the continuity of the tradition has been remarkably preserved in the latter. The omission or the occurrence of certain details in both appears to have been occasioned by the exigencies of the available space. The tradition of art exhibited by the Orissan specimen must have come from Assam (pp. 22-24).[1]

Unfortunately, no such 'thorough examination' of the art styles of Assam and Orissa has been undertaken so far. Needless to say, such a task can be taken up only under a large project; yet in the present work an attempt is made towards this objective on the same lines as Panigrahi has adopted in comparing the two Gaṅgā images from Dah Parbatia (Assam)[2] and Ratnagiri (Orissa) (PM no. Arch. 6498)[3]. The present author has noted similar close resemblances in a number of stone and bronze sculptures, including certain features in the decorative motifs that are peculiar to the art of Assam and Orissa.

As regards the architecture, it is unfortunate that in Assam not a single complete structure dateable to a period prior to the sixteenth century AD is found *in situ.* The architectural fragments seen in the ruins of temples dateable from the eighth to the thirteenth century are hardly adequate for any worthwhile study for comparing them with the magnificent architecture of

Orissa still existing. These ruins are scattered in the districts of Kamrup, Nagaon, Sonitpur, Darrang, Goalpara, Dhubri, Sibsagar and Golaghat, i.e., the region of ancient Kāmarūpa (including Davāka mentioned in the Allahabad pillar inscription of Samudragupta). In a number of these ruins the plans of the temples are traceable but that does not help us much. The occurrence of a large number of *āmalakas* (both large and small) in these ruins does, however, indicate Orissan affinity. Only in one temple, viz., the Hayagrīva Mādhava temple at Hajo, situated about 22 km west of Guwahati, the lower portion is still surviving on which the present temple was erected in AD 1583.[4] This lower portion may be dated to the eighth-ninth century and is built on a *Pañcaratha* plan like the Orissan temple (plate 1). We know by the seventh century this type had fully developed in Orissa (for example, the Paraśurāmeśvara temple at Bhubaneswar) and it is quite distinct from the contemporary *Nāgara* types like those at Deogarh. Evidently, the architectural style adopted in the Hajo temple was imported from Orissa in the eighth ninth century AD.

In the extant lower portion of the Hajo temple the decorative motifs in the mouldings are also noteworthy. As in the *Pābhāga* of the Orissan temples, the lowest portion consists of rows of elephants (plate 2). The next two mouldings consist of a mat design, and a floral design respectively. Locally, the three are called *gaja-āsana, Kuśa-āsana and padma-āsana* (plate 3) and are very similar in execution to the designs in the Paraśurāmeśvara and Bharateśvara group of temples at Bhubaneswar (plate 4).

Significantly, in the reconstruction of the temple in the sixteenth century the pattern of the *rekhā deul* of Orissa was adopted (plate 5). The main curvilinear *śikhara* as well as the *aṅga śikharas* have undoubtedly been created by the architects trained in the contemporary Orissan school which was the culmination of its evolution from the sixth-seventh century. There is room to spectulate that these architects may actually have come from Orissa on invitation by the ruler of the eastern Koch kingdom, Raghudeva, who built the temple. It must, however, be noted that the present state of the ruins does not allow us to determine whether the original temple of the eighth-ninth century had a *Jagamohana* or not, nor how the facets of the *śikhara* looked. The sixteenth century temple surely has a porch, as was the style in most temples of the Koch-Ahom type.

The Kāmākhyā temple at Guwahati was also rebuilt in the sixteenth century, in 1563, by the great Koch king Naranārāyaṇa alias Malladeva, uncle of Raghudeva who built the temple at Hajo two decades later. Here too, there was an earlier temple of the eighth-ninth century but of that no trace remains except two massive square pillars in the *calantā* and pieces of sculpture and architectual fragments lying scattered in the vicinity. The present temple of 1563 has a *śikhara* that is quite different from the *rekhā deul* in conception and is more lilke a dome on which pattern some of the Ahom temples were built in the seventeenth century (plate 35). Pradip Sarma has, however, made a detailed study of the plan and the surviving remains of the earlier temple and come to the conclusion that the original temple was of the Orissan *Pañcaratha* type. He, however, places it in the eleventh-twelfth century. Relying on *Darrāṅga Rājavaṁśāvalī*, an eighteenth century chronicle, he has stated that the architects sent by Naranārāyaṇa from Koch Bihar were perhaps not well-versed in the building of a temple *śikhara* and were also influenced by the Islamic architecture which had already reached Koch Bihar and Bengal. In their attempts to build a *vimāna* of stone they failed twice and then chose to construct it of bricks and they built a sixteen-sided dome superimposed on a truncated *rekhā deul* of the *pañcaratha* type.[5] His more interesting finding, however, is that the *calantā* or the first chamber in front of the sanctum, has a peculiar, pyramidal roofing of stone which indicates that the roofing of the original temple was in the from of a *pīḍhā deul*. This surmise would support Sarma's contention that the original temple is not older than the eleventh century because the beginnings of the *pīḍhā deul* in Orissa itself do not go to earlier than the tenth century.[6] As noted by Panigrahi, the *pīḍhā deul* makes its first appearance in the Mukteśvara temple at Bhubaneswar which is dateable to AD 950-975.[7] The repairers failed to reproduce this in their construction and resorted to a type with which they were more conversant. It appears that the architects employed by Raghudeva for building the temple at Hajo learnt a lesson from the failures of the Kāmākhyā architects and succeeded in constructing a proper *vimāna* at Hajo in 1583. It is quite likely that they went to Orissa to learn the technique. It is also possible that Raghudeva invited some architect from Orissa to build this temple. He surely wanted it to be a faultless and magnificent structure as Hajo was his capital city. In the Hayagrīva Mādhava temple inscription it is recorded that it was built on the orders of Raghudeva by his minister, Gadādhara, in the Śaka year 1505 (AD 1583) and its architect was Śridhara. Incidentally, the same Gadādhara is found to be building another temple for Raghudeva two years later, in Śaka 1507 (AD 1585); this time it was the Pāṇḍunātha Hari temple near Kāmākhyā.[8] It will be interesting to extract more information about Gadādhara and Śridhara from the *Darrāṅga Rājavaṁśāvalī* and other Koch records, more particularly to see if they had any connection with Orissa. It will also be worthwhile to explore whether in the Puri-Bhubaneswar region there was a *sthapati* named Śridhara in the sixteenth century.

It is relevant to mention that in the seventeenth and eighteenth centuries the Ahom temples adopted the same *rekhā deul* pattern, except in just one or two examples (like the Jaya dol at Sibsagar and Maghanowa dol in Lakhimpur).

A peculiar characteristic of the temple architecture of Orissa is "Orissan predilection for dark plain interiors, particularly with Śaiva temples where the sanctum is often subterranean."[9] The same characteristic is noticeable in many temples of Assam. The most prominent example is the Kāmākhyā where one has to descend about a dozen steps to reach the deity. In a number of ruins of the temples dateable from the ninth to twelfth century the author has noticed that the sanctum was a few feet below the floor level. And it was not limited to the Śiva temples. For example, in the ruins of the Saubhāgya Mādhava and Gopāla Mādhava devālāyas in the Nagaon district the 'subterranean' nature of the sanctum is clearly noticeable. Interestingly, the sanctum of the Rājarājeśvarī temple at Dokhar near Madhubani (in Mithilā) described below is also subterranean. This seems, therefore, to be a common feature of the temples in all the three regions of our study during the tenth-eleventh century.

Coming to the Mithilā region, we again note that no architectual examples of an early period have survived not only in Mithilā but even in the neighbouring Magadha region, except the antiquities of Bodh Gaya, Nalanda, etc. that are, of course, not relevant for our purpose. Even the plinths or plans of the structures of an early period are not traceable anywhere. The author, however, had an opportunity to visit a very interesting modern temple near Madhubani. The deity of this temple at Dokhar is named Rājarājeśvarī and the present temple is just over a hundred years old. The site of the temple, however, is definitely very old as is evidenced by the image being worshipped in the temple, an inscription on the sanctum's doorway and some broken pieces of sculptures lying in the compound. The image is a typical Pāla-Sena *Umāliṅgana Śiva mūrti* of black basalt. The inscription from its palaeography appears to be of the tenth-eleventh century; I could not ascertain whether it has been deciphered or not. The most interesting aspect of the temple, however, is the *śikhara* of the present temple. It is in the Orissan *Khakhara* style, something that is a rarity in modern temples (plate 6). Its resemblemce to the *śikhara* of the Vetāla temple of Bhubaneswar belonging to the eighth century is unmistakable (plate 36). That this *Śakta* architectural tradition was alive in the Mithilā region till as recently as a hundred years ago is undoubtedly significant. We may recall that Mahārāja Rameśwara Siṅgha of Darbhanga in the late nineteenth century was a devout *Śākta sādhaka* and the Rājarājeśvarī temple at Dokhar was perhaps built by him. He must have known that the *khakhara* style was exclusive to the Devi temples and hence employed it.

We are on a somewhat firmer ground when we consider the styles of sculpture although, here again, the comparisons may be made only between individual pieces as was done by Panigrahi in the case of the two Gaṅgā images. An over-all stylistic comparison will have to await a detailed and systematic study. For the present, we have to be content with noting the striking similarities between some specimens from Assam and Orissa as well as from Bihar and their characteristic common features. Such specimens include stone as well as bronze pieces and some terracotta also. We first take up the stone sculpture.

While discovering the Gaṅgā image from Dah Parbatia it was noted by R.D. Banerji[10] as well as later scholars that it was a very fine example of the Gupta sculpture of Sarnath school of the sixth century AD. The Ratnagiri image of Gaṅgā dateable to the eighth century (PM no. Arch. 6498-plate 37) has been considered by some scholars to be the earliest specimen of the Gupta art found in Orissa. As opined by Panigrahi, the inspiration for this image seems to have come from the Dah Parbatia image (plate 38). In other words, the Gupta art seems to have come to Orissa via Assam during the Bhauma-Kara period. The various characteristics of the Sarnath school discernible in the Dah Parbatia specimen have been faithfully continued in many pieces of the Orissan sculptures of the eighth to tenth century. Before taking note of some such specimens it may incidentally be observed that the Gaṅgā image in the Patna Museum noted by Panigrahi to be from Ratnagiri really came from Udayagiri, where excavations by the Archaeological Survey of India (ASI) are in progress at present (in 2002-03). The error clearly has occurred because Ratnagiri, Udyagiri and Lalitagiri form a complex of three archaeological hill sites, collectively known as Asia hill. When the said image was taken from Udayagiri to Cuttack in the late nineteenth century and finally to Patna, along with many other pieces from this area, no distinction seems to have been made between one site and another. Yet, in the Patna Museum its find-place is correctly shown as Udayagiri. Significantly, a colossal Avalokiteśvara image kept in the court compound at Jajpur is labelled simply as coming from Asia hill, no doubt because the actual site of its provenance nobody now remembers; we do not know which of the three sites it came from. A finely carved gateway now preserved in the Patna Museum (PM no. Arch. 6495-97)[11] is also from Udayagiri. Fortunately, the present excavations have yielded the monastery shrine to which it decidedly belonged. Further, I was fortunate to locate and obtain a photograph of a Yamunā image at

Udayagiri which is clearly a companion piece of the Gaṅgā image under reference (plate 7).

Comparison of this highly eroded Yamunā image with the Yamunā image at Dah Parbatia further strengthens the arguments of Panigrahi. Inspiration for the Gaṅgā image was clearly not a fluke or an isolated one, the same inspiration was working in the case of the Yamunā image also.

The Udayagiri Gaṅgā is preceded by a century by another image in the Paraśurāmeśvara temple at Bhubaneswar (seventh century). The most prominent and unique features of the Dah Parbatia image, viz., an attendant holding a parasol over the head of the deity and two flying birds (geese or swans) in the background are repeated here (plate 8). In fact, these unique features continue for the next two centuries at least as is evidenced by the Gaṅgā and Yamunā images in the Mukteśvara temple at Bhubaneswar belonging to the tenth century (plate 9). Clearly, the contact between the sculptors of Kāmarūpa and Kaliṅga was not a transitory phenomenon but continued for at least four centuries.

Another Gaṅgā image having resemblance with the Dah Parbatia Gaṅgā is in a niche in the Bhṛṅgeśvara Mahādeva temple at Bajrakot.[12] In this ninth century piece the deity's posture and the position of the parasol over her head strongly remind one of the Assam image. There is another image of Yamunā in the Palalesvara temple at Paikpada, again of the ninth century, in which the attendant holding the parasol is of the same type.[13] Another significant example may be added to this list: an image of Yamunā in the Monastery No. 1 at Ratnagiri (plate 10) in which the posture of the deity as well as the attendant figures, the position of the parasol rod (the top not being depicted as it was covered by the *śiropaṭṭikā*), the drapery and ornaments of all the three figures are strikingly similar to those of the Udyagiri Gaṅgā.

The Dah Parbatia Gaṅgā shows all the Gupta features of the Sarnath school, viz., the diaphanous drapery, serene facial expression, suppleness of limbs and, of course, somewhat elongated face and thick lower lip and lack of over-decoration of the stelé. These are continued not only in the specimens noted above but in many other pieces. It would perhaps suffice to mention just three examples from the State Museum at Bhubaneswar. These are, an eighth century Padmapāṇi from Khadipada (OSM no. Ay-28-plate11), an eleventh century Lokanātha from Bhubaneswar (OSM no. Ay 77-plate 12) and a twelfth century Avalokiteśvara from Cuttack (OSM no. Ay 54-plate 13).

The striking similarity between the Gaṅgā images from Dah Parbatia and Udayagiri has given rise to a hypothesis that the Gupta idiom reached Orissa via Assam in the wake of the Bhauma rule, as mentioned above. The discussion in the preceding paragraphs taking notice of other specimens tends to support this hypothesis. But the evidence can hardly be considered conclusive because, (i) we do find some earlier specimens in Orissa betraying Gupta influence[14] and (ii) the Gupta idiom may have reached Orissa directly from the adjoining Magadha country rather than taking the circuitous route via Assam. Then again, it might have reached Orissa in the wake of Śaśāṅka's occupation of the region more than a century prior to the advent of the Bhaumas from Kāmarūpa following the conquest by Harṣadeva. It is not, however, very likely that it may have reached Orissa when the country was under the vassalage of the Guptas in the fourth-fifth cenury because, first, the fact of such vassalage itself has not been conclusively established and, secondly, the Gupta idiom was still in an evolving stage in the Madhyadeśa including Sarnath itself. It could have travelled beyond the region of its birth only after it was fully developed.

In the present discussion, it is not possible to include the Mithilā region because little by way of sculptures relevant for our purpose has been discovered from this region. In the two museums at Darbhanga (Chandradhari museum and Lakṣmishwar Singh museum) as well as in the Patna Museum all the sculptures recovered from the Mithilā region consist of only some typical Pāla-Sena pieces. The author has, however, noticed the photograph of a Sūrya image said to be lying outside the Śiva temple at Kuseshwar-asthan, in the Bhagalpur district, which is clearly in the Orissan style.[15] This is obviously an import from Orissa indicating that images from Orissa used to be brought to Mithilā in the early medieval period as there were perhaps no local productions. In fact, stone is not locally available in Mithilā; the nearest sources of stone are either the Rajmahal hills in the south-east or Chunar in the west, both quite far from Mithilā. Therefore, it seems that Mithilā did not develop the art of stone sculpture and depended on supplies from Orissa and Magadha to meet her requirements. It will, however, not be wrong to consider some specimens from the regions bordering Mithilā, i.e., from Magadha. Thus a sculpture described as Lady with Bird from Sankarigalighat, Rajmahal in the Patna Museum (PM no. Arch. 10346)[16] has a striking resemblance with the Gaṅgā from Ḍah Parbatia at least in respect of the modelling and drapery of the figure.

We must, now, take note of another class of sculptures dateable from the eighth century in which close resemblance between the specimens from Assam and Orissa is perfect inasmuch as similar specimens are not known from any other region except as noted below. Deopani, an archaeological site in the Golaghat district of Assam, has yielded a number of Viṣṇu (ASM no. 8-

plate 39)[17] and Harihara (ASM no. 2454—plate 40)[18] images characterized by the squatness of the figure and a truncated pyramidal headgear A number of these, including two inscribed ones are preserved in the Assam State Museum at Guwahati. The provenance of a large number of images with uniformity in modelling points to the existence of a considerable workshop, almost a school, of sculptures at a time palaeographically dateable to the eighth century AD. Another image of Viṣṇu having some similarity with the Deopani type has been found in western Assam, at Medhipara in the Goalpara district which is kept in the Assam State Museum (ASM no. 3104).[19] It is important tɔ note that the *cakrapuruṣa* is below the left lower hand of the deity and the *gadādevī* below the right lower hand. The image has been dated to the seventh century; the importance of the placement of the *āyudha puruṣas* will be clear from the discussion below. The author has observed a number of Viṣṇu and Harihara images at Jajpur that are stylistically related to the Deopani images. These are seen in the tiny Mukteśvara shrine (plate 42) in the compound of the Jagannatha temple and in the compounds of the Siddheśvara (plate 41), Virāja and Trilocaneśvara temples. The placement of the *āyudhas*, mostly in the anthropomorphic form for the *cakra* and the *gadā* in these images is of exceptional interest. Donaldson has noted that the *Viṣṇudharmottara* prescribes placement of the *gadādevi* on the right side of the deity and that of the *cakra puruṣa* to the left. In the Orissa images, however, this order is found to have been reversed.[20] Some of the images at Jajpur, illustrated by Donaldson, are a late sixth-early seventh century image in the Trilochaneśvara temple compound,[21] a late seventh century image in the Siddheśvara temple compound,[22] a late seventh-early eighth century images in the Rāmeśvara temple compound,[23] a late eighth-early ninth century image in the Siddheśvara temple compound[24] and a late eighth-early ninth century image in the Rāmeśvara temple compound.[25] Interestingly, the placement of the *cakra puruṣa* and *gadādevī* in the Deopani images is of the same pattern as found in the Jajpur images. Donaldson has illustrated a few other similar examples from other sites as well, e.g., Fig. 12 from Mudgala, Fig. 13 from Baripada, Fig. 15 from Uttaresvara, Fig. 17 from Shergarh, Fig. 21 from Turanga, Fig. 22 from Badgaon, Fig. 23 from Simhanatha (Island), Fig. 24 from Simhanatha (Island), etc. – all belonging to the ninth century. Jajpur being the site of Guheśvarapāṭaka or Guhadevapāṭaka, the capital city of the Bhauma-Karas, the provenance of the Deopani type of images there is significant. In more than one Viṣṇu image the *cakra* and the mace (gadā) have been given anthropomorphic representation as *cakrapuruṣa* and *gadādevī* as in the Deopani images. In one Deopani image the front right hand of the deity is shown resting on a *cakra* that has been elongated and a similar features is seen in an image from Jajpur (plate 42); in yet another image from Jajpur the halo behind the deity's head is shown in the form of a *cakra* with spokes, the prototype of which may be seen in a Deopani image.

In connection with these sculptures we should take note of a class of images from Mundeśwari in the Sasaram district of Bihar preserved in the Patna Museum. A Harihara image (PM no. Arch 6008-plate 43)[26] appears to be almost the model for the Deopani Harihara (ASM no. 2454). A Sūrya image (PM no. Arch 6015)[27] and a Pārvati image (PM no. Arch 6005)[28] are also noteworthy for their Deopani-type squatness. The headgear of the Harihara and Sūrya images are particularly noticeable for their likeness to the headgears of the Deopani images. Mundeśwari does not fall within Mithilā but is on its south-western boundry. Needless to say that in the study of art the exact geographical or political boundaries are not very relevant. The epigraphic evidence from Mundeśwari places these sculptures in the seventh century AD. The art of Mundeśwari, therefore, appears to be the link between the Gupta art of Sarnath up to the sixth century and that of Kāmarūpa from the seventh century onwards. In the eighth century a direct communication between Mundeśwari and Deopani seems to have existed. A striking image from Bhojpur, a site not far from Mundeśwari, preserved in the Patna Museum (PM no. Arch 10988-plate 14) may also be noted. In this unusual image, the deity is shown in a *tribhaṅga* posture, wears simple dress and *mukuṭa* and rests his right and left elbow respectively on a *gadā* and a *cakra*. We find the influence of Mundeswari as far as at Benisagar in Singhbhum district in eastern Bihar. A Viṣṇu image (PM no. Arch 64)[29] from Benisagar is in a style that appears to be a transitional stage between Mundeśwari and Deopani. It also has similarities with some Jajpur Viṣṇu images. Significantly, in this image the *cakrapuruṣa* is on the left and *gadādevī* is on the right as in the Orissa and Deopani images. On the basis of the placement of the *āyudhas* it may be said that the Benisagar and Medhipara images show the transition of the Mudeśwari idiom to Deopani and Jajpur. Benisagar is located mid-way between Mundeśwari and Jajpur and Medhipara on the straight line from Mundeśwari to Deopani; it appears that the Benisagar artist had boldly deviated from the Mundeśwari (and the Gupta) convention while the sculptor at Medhipara was still hesitant.

Then, we find resemblances in some isolated examples from Assam and Orissa. In the Rājarāni temple at Bhubaneswar (tenth century), we have a dancing female figure in the *Utkaṭika* pose described by Panigrahi as 'the female counterpart of Naṭarāja'.[30] An identical terracotta plaque from

Guwahati is preserved in the Assam State Museum (ASM no. 2127/2), the only difference being that the Assam image is clearly skeletal (plate 15) and, therefore, may be described as Dancing Cāmuṇḍā. A very similar image may be seen in a niche in the Brahmeśvara temple at Bhubaneswar (plate 44) of the twelfth-thirteenth century.

We have a number of Cāmuṇḍā images from Orissa closely resembling those from Assam belonging to the tenth-eleventh century. I am fully aware that the skeletal Cāmuṇḍā images are more or less similar everywhere but in the case of a few images from Assam and Orissa the similarity is so striking as to warrant a conclusion that they belong to the same sculptural tradition. Among these, the noteworthy are the Cāmuṇḍā at Nabhanga (plate 45) in the Nagaon district of Assam[31] and that from Dharmasala kept in the State Museum at Bhubaneswar (OSM no. AY 66, plate 16). Similarly, two images kept outside a small shrine in the precincts of the Kāmākhyā temple at Guwahati (plates 17 and 18) are very similar to the two images kept outside the Trilocaneśvara temple at Jajpur (plates 19 and 20). Equally striking is an image of Cāmuṇḍā in the court compound at Jajpur (plate 21) of which a prototype found at Borpathar is preserved in Assam State Museum (ASM no. 3569)[32]; the sitting posture of the two is identical and quite different from that of the Cāmuṇḍā images from elsewhere. Both of these are dateable to the eighth century AD.

We may now turn our attention to a class of sculptures for which Orissa has been very famous, viz., the erotic, rather obscene figures placed on the exterior of the temple walls. As to why such revolting practice was introduced in the temple art, no definitive answer has so far been found; nevertheless, the fact remains that from about the tenth-eleventh century AD this became prevalent throughout India. As observed by Panigrahi, obscene or erotic figures ought to be defined as only those "sculptures which represent the different poses of sexual act, as depicted in the *Kāmaśāstra*, or otherwise conceived by the human mind."[33] Naturally, such depictions will be similar everywhere and no regional variations are likely. Yet, we notice one or two characteristics that are peculiar to the sculptures of Orissa and Assam. As already noted, we have no standing monuments of the early period in Assam. But in the architectural fragments found at the various archaeological sites plenty of examples of such art have been discovered. One site is of special interest in this regard. About fifty km north-east from Guwahati there is the temple of Piṅgaleśvara. In the early 1970s while excavating the site for construction of a new temple the villagers found remains of an ancient temple. A large number of erotic images dateable from the eleventh to thirteenth century were found, almost all of them in niches 30 to 50 cm high. Similar figures in niches may be seen at many other places and a few of them are preserved in the Assam State Museum at Guwahati. A notable feature of the erotic figures at Konark, Puri and Bhubaneswar is that in many cases the male is a bearded figure. Interestingly, bearded figures are not seen in Khajuraho and the various other sites known for erotic figures. In Assam, however, in a number of pieces the male has a beard. A typical example may be seen in the sculpture no. ASM 5835 of the Assam State Museum.[34] In the catalogue it has been dated to the ninth century but the present author is inclined to place in it the eleventh-twelfth century because we have really no evidence of the prevalence of this type of art so early as the ninth century. Moreover, the beard in this sculptures is very similar to that of the Brahmā image from Guwahati in the same museum (ASM no. 1985)[35] which has been dated to the tenth-eleventh century.

It is interesting to note that there are certain Purāṇic characters, not deities, whose images are traceable only in Assam and Orissa. Two of such characters are Āstīka and Jaratkāru connected with the legends of the *nāgas*. One image of Āstīka-Jaratkāru found at Bhubaneswar and dated to the tenth century AD is preserved in the Orissa State Museum (OSM no. AY-78—plate 22). Similarly, and image designated as Āstīka-Jaratkāru may be seen fixed to the wall of the *calantā* of the *Kāmākhyā* temple at Guwahati. I am not aware of the existence of an Āstīka-Jaratkāru image anywhere else. In this connection, it is noteworthy that the snake goddess Manasā was very popular in eastern India and the legend of Āstīka-Jaratkāru is also related to the *nāgas.*

Before moving on to the bronze sculpture we must take note of three Naṭarāja images from Assam and Orissa. A beautiful ten-armed Naṭarāja was discovered at Ambari a few years ago and it is now preserved in the Assam State Museum (ASM no. 3384-plate 46).[36] The unique feature of this thirteenth century image is that Śiva is shown dancing on the back of *Nandī.* A similar image in a medallion from Guwahati belonging to the tenth-eleventh century is also in the same museum (ASM no. 1391—plate 47).[37] An exact replica (in miniature) is seen on a wall of the Pāpānaśinī temple at Bhubaneswar built in AD 1449 (plate 48)[38] Śiva standing on the back of his *vāhana* and dancing is certainly an uncommon features; in the Cola bronzes, the most prolific source of the Naṭarāja images, the deity is always shown standing on a supine body. Bhattasali has, however, reported the existence of such images in East Bengal and illustrated two of them that are preserved in the Dhaka Museum.[39] Both of these were found at or near Rampal, the site of the Sena capital, but appear to be of a pre-Sena date because the top of their *ādhāra* is rounded and not conical. Bhattasali has stated that a *dhyāna* of Naṭarāja is found in the *Matsya Purāṇa*, chapter 259; I could not ascertain whether in this *dhyāna*, the god is seen as standing on a corpse as in the Cola bronzes or on the back of the Nandī, as in the examples under discussion. Dr. Satyamurty of ASI has brought to my notice a bronze image from south India having the feature under reference. This image is at Kharkoil in Melakadambur in the Cuddalore district of Tamilnadu (plate 23). It has, however, been held that it was not a local product; it belongs to the Pāla school and was probably brought to the Tamil country from Bengal or Magadha by Rajendra Cola as a war trophy. This bronze image, made in the eleventh century somewhere in eastern India, and the Dhaka Museum images (also of the eleventh-twelfth century), therefore, appear to be the prototypes for the Guwahati, Ambari and the Pāpanāśinī images of the eleventh, thirteenth and fifteenth century respectively. In any case, it does show that the sculptors of Orissa continued to be in contact with those of Assam till the fifteenth century. When we add to this the evidence of the sixteenth century temple at Hajo and the later day temples elsewhere in Assam we come to the irresistible conclusion that the Orissan temple architecture was the main source of inspiration for the temple builders in Assam right from the seventh century for a thousand years and as regards stone sculptures the sculptors of the two regions remained in close contact during this period exchanging art styles and ideas.

Next, we consider the evidence provided by the bronze or copper objects and in doing so it would be worthwhile to consider the objects from Bihar in greater detail.

As regards Assam, the only worthwhile bronze images consist of the collection found at the Kahilipara village near Dispur on the outskirts of Guwahati that is also referred to as the Narakasur bronzes. All these specimens are preserved in the Assam State Museum (ASM) at Guwahati. In Orissa, bronze images were discovered mostly from the Sonepur area in western Orissa. These are preserved in the State Museum (OSM) at Bhubaneswar and have been discussed by Debala Mitra in her book *The Bronzes from Achutrajpur.* Some of the earlier finds from Sonepur may also be seen in the Patna Museum (PM). The specimens from Assam and Orissa may be compared with some objects from Bihar, particularly Nalanda and Kurkihar (Gaya district) that are preserved in PM.

The images from all the three regions represent both Buddhist and Brāhmāṇical deities. Our concern here, however, is not their religious affiliation but their style and technique. Practically all the known specimens from the three regions have been made by the lost wax process and belong to the period from the eighth to the twelfth century AD.

Stylistically, the specimens from the three regions are so similar that all of them may be easily classified as belonging to the same school of art that may be termed as the *Pāla* school or the Eastern Indian school of the early medieval period. It is difficult to determine whether these were manufactured at the respective places of their discovery or were made at some central place and transported to the different places in the three regions. Being portable items, the latter could have been the case. In either case, they do establish a strong cultural affinity between the three regions. Since the Nalanda and Gaya districts have yielded the largest number of bronze objects and of the three regions under discussion it is only here that images of life size or near-life size have been discovered these would appear to be most prominent, if not the only, centres of production of this art.

To consider some of the individual pieces now. First, we take note of two images from the Narakasur hoard (NS) in ASM—one of Tārā in the *Lalitāsana* posture (ASM no. 3009—plate 24) and the other that of a similarly modelled Avalokiteśvara in the *Mahārājalīlāsana* posture (ASM no. 3004—plate 25). Tārā images with identical posture and features are found in the collections from Sonepur (SP) and Kurkihar (KH) in OSM (no. 331—plate 26) and P M (no. 9811)[40] and significantly, these Tārā images are mostly of the Khadiravanī type and their parallels in stone have been found at Ratnagiri and other places in Orissa. Similarly, the standing posture and modelling of Lokanātha and Avalokiteśvara images from the three regions are almost identical, e.g., NS image (ASM No. 3015—plate 27) and KH image (PM no. 9788).[41]

Of greater importance than modelling and posture, however, are certain decorative motifs and conventions. The *ādhār* of the images belonging to the tenth-eleventh century are curved conically at the top as in the stone sculpture of the late Pāla variety. In addition, in a number of specimens we find the conical top surmounted with a *chatra*. An *Indra* images from NS (ASM No. 3000—plate 49),[42] two images from KH (PM no. 9630)[43] and (PM no. 9605—plate 28) and a Tārā from SP (OSM no. 278—plate 29) may be seen for the identical *chatra* design. It is significant that a *chatra* of the same design is seen in a stone image of Vairocana Maṇḍala from Udayagiri.[44] Then there are two bells (*ghaṇṭā*) of a peculiar shape in NS, of which one is intact (plate 30) while the other is broken. The intact piece bears the following three-line inscription:

Śrikumāra-devarājeva-sa-yātmanā-devāsurarāja
hastyantaka-dadhyakābhūttacya pūjā iyaṁ-tena
devatakāryyādikāntaiṣā ghaṇṭakā dattaṁ.[45]

The *kumāra* in this inscription is identified with Kumāravarmādeva, the fourth king of the Śālastambha dynasty, who ruled in the first quarter of the eighth century AD and who was the grandfather of Harṣavarmādeva. The shape of these bells is so peculiar that it immediately attracts our attention. Interestingly, in KH we have eight bells of varying sizes that are identical to these NS bells in their design (PM no. 9647-9653 & 9796–plate 31). Clearly, the NS bells and the KH bells are products of the same school, and may be of the same workshop. A very significant object is a spouted vessel in SP (OSM no. 517–plate 32) of which the lid is of the same design as the *chatras* of the images described above. The spout has a peculiar design with double curves. A Vessel with identical spout design is preserved in ASM (plate 33). Interestingly, a silver vessel with identical spout design was preserved in the Hayagrīva Mādhava temple at Hajo (plate 34).[46] It appears to be a late manufacture (sixteenth–seventeenth century) but the identicality of its design with that of the earlier specimens seem to indicate that it is a copy of some vessel that was used in the original temple of the eighth-ninth century AD.

In the above paragraphs the objects examined or observed by the present author only have been discussed. It may be mentioned that as early as 1931, R.D. Banerji had published his *Eastern Indian School of Medieval Sculpture* and in 1980 B.N. Mukherjee published *East India Art Styles* which is sub-titled as *A Study in Parallel Trends.* The former had made his study essentially from the angle of the Pāla-Sena art. The latter study has a wider perspective but somehow both the works have failed to include Orissa in their discussion. In 1981, a very good study tited *Metal Sculptures of Eastern India* was published by Bimal Bandyopadhyay; it does include Orissa and Assam but, as the title specifies, it deals only with the metal sculptures and does not even take note of their parallels in stone. Moreover, much of its value is reduced because of the rather indifferent quality of the printing of the photographs in the volume. The present author fully agrees with mukherjee's view that from the eighth to the twelfth or thirteenth century eastern India witnessed the emergence of a common school of art that was followed throughout the region but the different sub-regions adopted certain local variations. The Kāmarūpa convention noted by Mukherjee in Chapter 3 of the book cited above is a case in point. I only like to add that Orissa too was a part of this movement and, in fact, greater similarities exist between the art styles adopted in Orissa and Assam than those between the other sub-regions.

PAINTING

The only example of mural painting so far discovered in Orissa is the tempera painting on the ceiling of a rock known as Rāvaṇachāya in the village Sitabhinji in the Keojhar district. This is dateable to the fourth century AD.[47] Of the later periods we get some paintings in the temples of Bhubaneswar and Puri. The earliest of these are the painted ceiling of the Muktesvara temple (tenth century) and the wall paintings inside the Jagannātha temple (twelfth century). However, both of them being worshipping temples these are continually repainted and how far the present paintings represent the original ones is difficult to say and, therefore, it is not possible to study their relationship with the Sitabhinji paintings. In any case, it is also outside the scope of the present study.

In Assam and Mithilā no traces of any paintings of the early periods have survived to enable us to make any comparisons with the surviving Orissan specimens.

So we straightaway come to the manuscript paintings of the late medieval period of which enough are available for a comparative study. A very good study of these paintings was made and published by Rajatanand Dasgupta in 1972 and the observations in the following paragraphs are mainly based on this work.

Orissan painting is a mixture of all India traditions with a great degree of native elements in it.[48] The early examples of these are found in the palm-leaf manuscripts, the earliest being the Vishnupur *Daśavatāra* book cover of AD 1499.[49] These are essentially etchings filled with powdered coal or other dyes. From the early seventeenth century we get manuscripts on paper and on them paintings in the real sense of the term were made. The paintings are, however, characterized by strong lines, reminiscent of the palm-leaf type, though the Rajasthani influence on them is clear. They also absorbed some south Indian influences through Andhra Pradesh. The *Citrapaṭa* or icon paintings of Puri form another class of Orissan painting. Minute delineation of the details is a characteristic of the Orissan miniatures of all ages.[50]

In Assam, the earliest extant manuscript paintings belongs to the Tai-Ahom school, a tradition brought to Assam by the Ahoms in the thirteenth century from Myanmar. *Phung Cin* manuscript dated 1473 is perhaps the oldest of all.[51] Once the Ahoms settled down in Assam, and came into close contact with the neighbouring kingdoms of Bengal, Koch Bihar, Tripura, etc. as well as Orissa and Bihar, their painters were naturally influenced by the schools and styles popular in those regions. These were essentially extensions of the Rajasthani and Mughal Schools. But even before the Ahom court school developed, another school had emerged in the *Satras* of Assam in the wake of the Vaiṣṇava movement in the sixteenth century. A large number of religious texts were illustrated in this style, the earliest being the *Bhāgawata,*

Tenth Book from the Bali Satra in Nagaon[52] which is dated 1539. The *Satriyā* school has a marked similarity with the various north Indian schools of miniatures.[53] This school prevailed from Koch Bihar in the west to the extreme east of Assam and imbibed some influences of the medieval Pāla traditions of the earlier age. In Koch Bihar, a court art developed from the middle of the sixteenth century and lasted for three hundred years. In Assam proper, the *Satriya* school and the Ahom court art, called the Gaṛhgāoñ school had close interaction and from the late seventeenth century for about a hundred years we find great vibrancy in the paintings of Assam. This was the period of the neo-Vaiṣṇava movement initiated by Śaṅkaradeva, close contacts with Orissa, particularly Puri, and, occasionally, of sectarian rivalry between the Śāktas and Vaiṣṇavas. All this is reflected in the paintings of this period. This period also witnessed emergence of a number of a small states like Darrānga, Beltolā and Rānī and their rulers too patronized painters.[54] *Hastividyārṇava* of the year 1734 is an outstanding example of the Gaṛhgāoñ school.[55] Portraits of the royal patrons, of the artists themselves and others are a special features of the Gaṛhgāoñ school, which is sometimes treated to be a provincial style of the Mughal school. A feature common to the *Satriyā* and the Gaṛhgāoñ schools is painting of portraits and sometimes the entire episodes in niches or under cusped arches.[56]

In Assam, the manuscripts were written on *tūlā pāt*, i.e., felted cotton, or, more commonly, on *sāñcī* bark. Some examples of the use of *bhoja patra* are also available but palm leaf was never used. Evidently, the leaf of the local palm tree was not found suitable for the purpose unlike the palm tree in the coastal Orissa. Otherwise, one expects that Śaṅkaradeva must have seen palm leaf manuscripts in Orissa in the fifteenth-sixteenth centuries and would have brought the tradition to Assam. Stylistically, one can find only a general similarity between the paintings of Assam and Orissa during this period and little by way of Orissan influence on the former is discernable.

Nevertheless, Dasgupta has pointed out certain similarities in the late medieval paintings of Orissa and Assam. He observes, "In Orissan reliefs the formula of combined profile and front view is of long standing and appears as a type of a relief by which the figures are made to fit into niches which they occupy or the space between the two pilasters. The figures of the *Amaru Śataka* (late sixteenth-early seventeenth century) are invariably fitted inside a niche composed of pilasters and multi-foiled arches. A similar examples is found in relation to painting and reliefs of the Tuṅgkhuṅgiyā period (AD 1696-1744) of Assamese history. The figures of cavaliers or elephant-riders are exactly similar to those in the *Lava Kuśara Yuddha*[57] manuscript and the reliefs of the

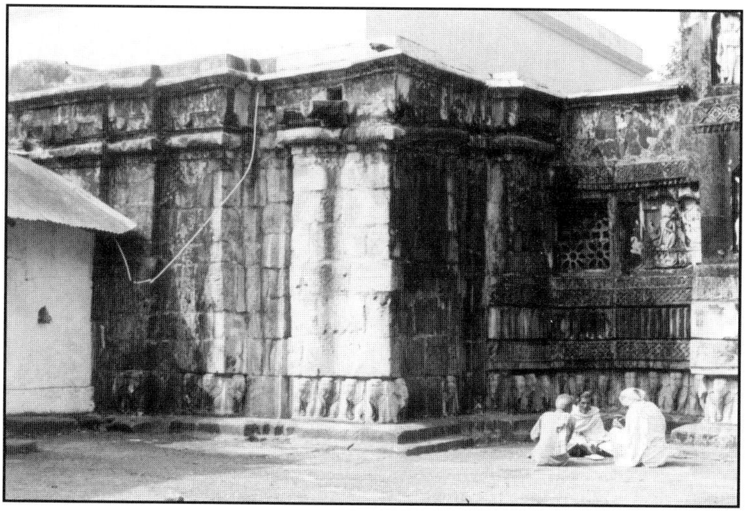

Pl. 1. HM, Lower portion of the temple

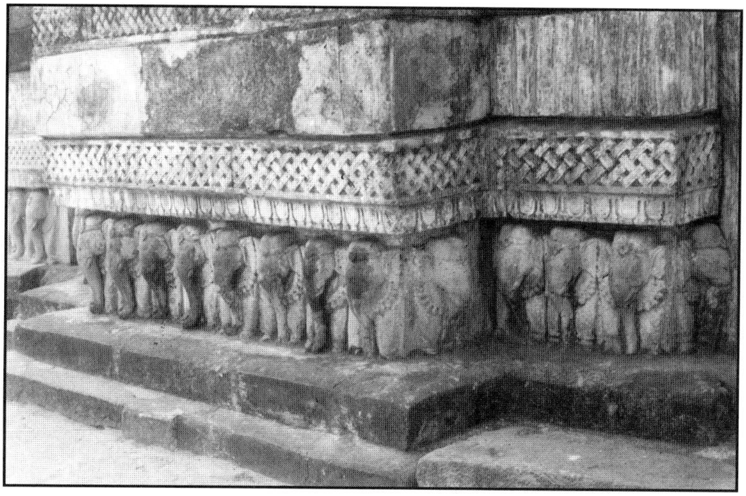

Pl. 2. HM, The lowest moulding, a row of elephants

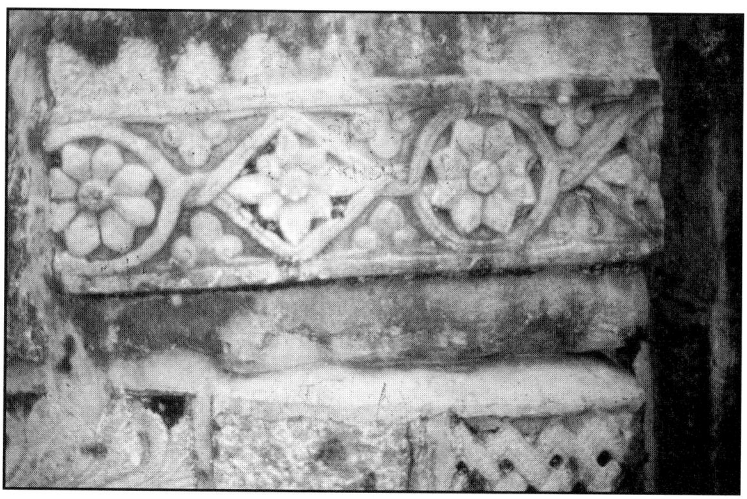

Pl. 3. HM, Kuśa-āsana and padma-āsana mouldings

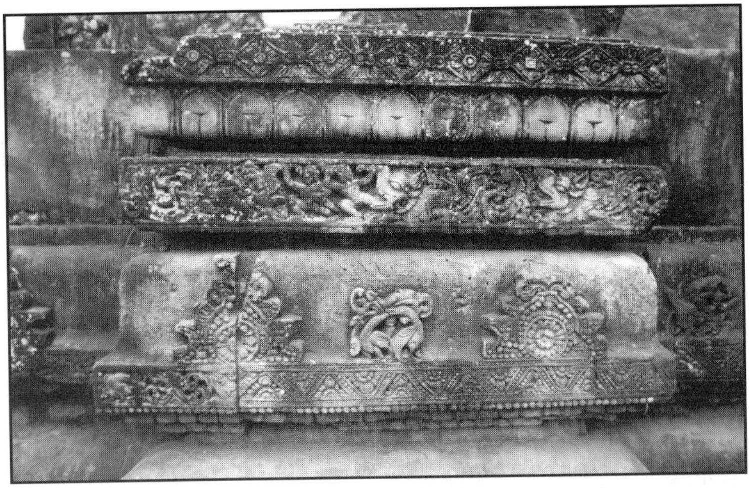

Pl. 4. Bharateśvara group at Bhubaneswar, mouldings

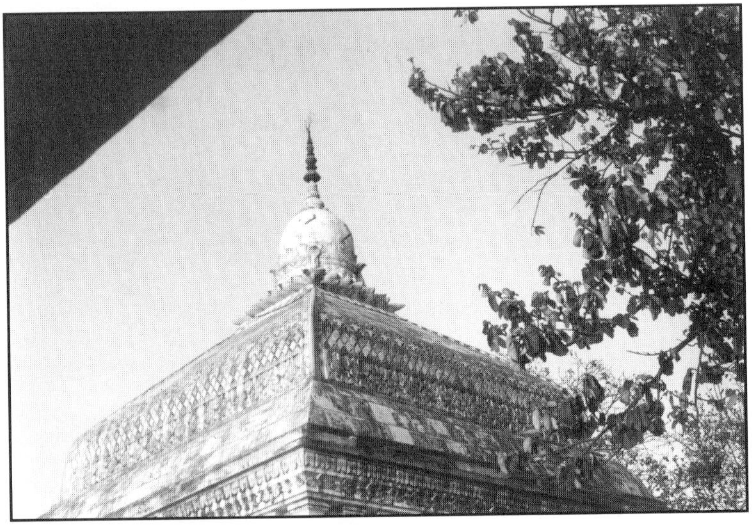

Pl. 6. Dokhar, śikhara of Rajarajeswari temple

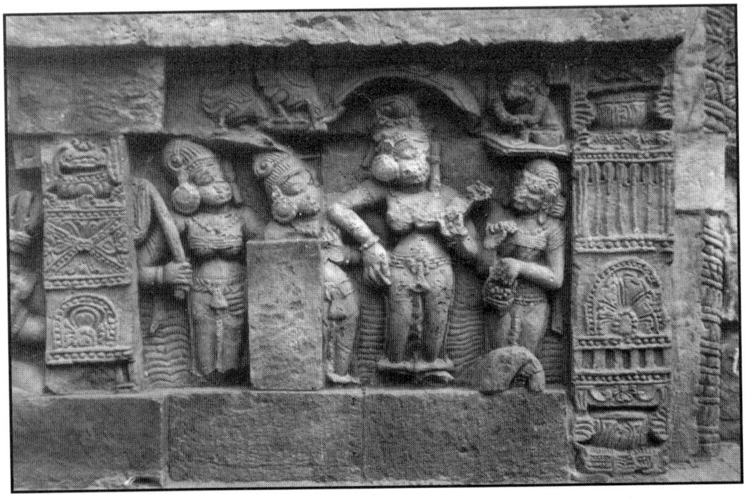

Pl. 8. Paraśurāmeśvara at Bhubaneswar, Gaṅgā

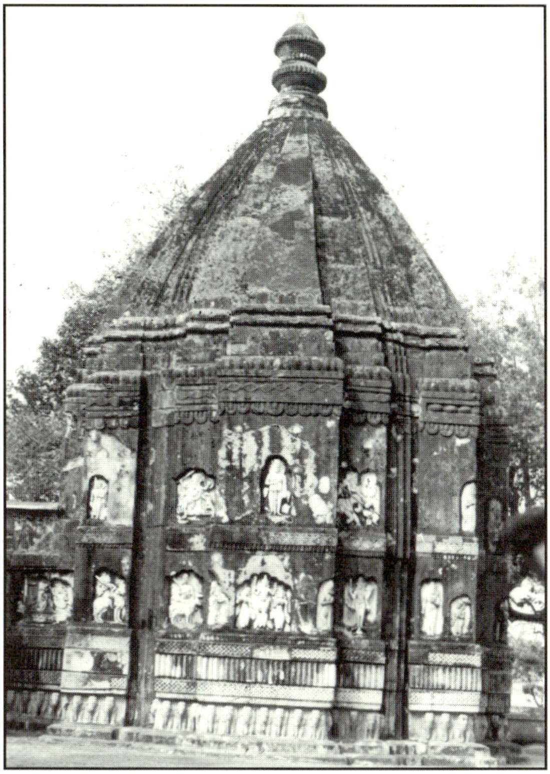

Pl. 5. HM, The śikhara

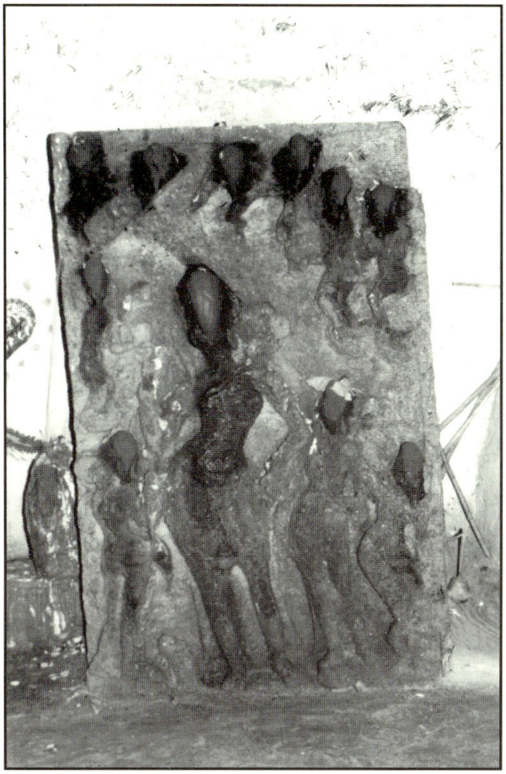

Pl. 7. Udayagiri, Yamunā

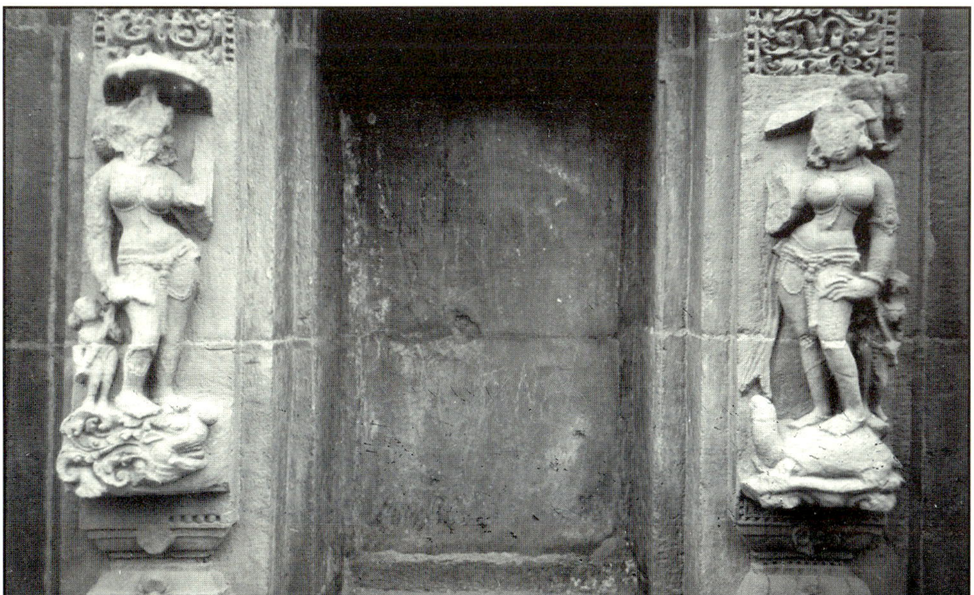

Pl. 9. Mukteśvara at Bhubaneswar, Gaṅgā and Yamunā

Pl. 11. OSM, Padmapāṇi from Khadipada

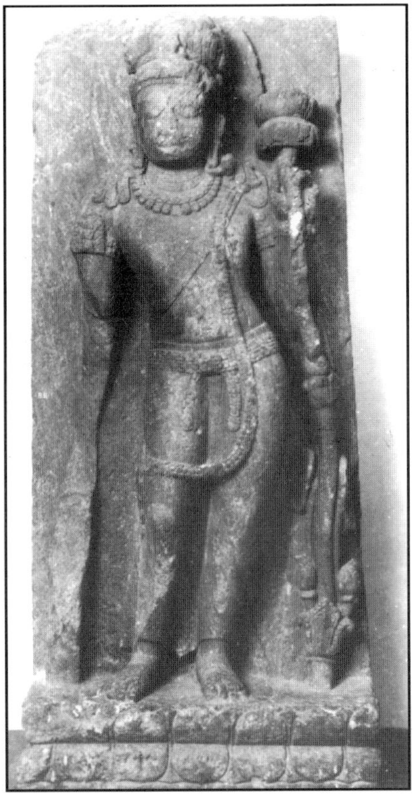

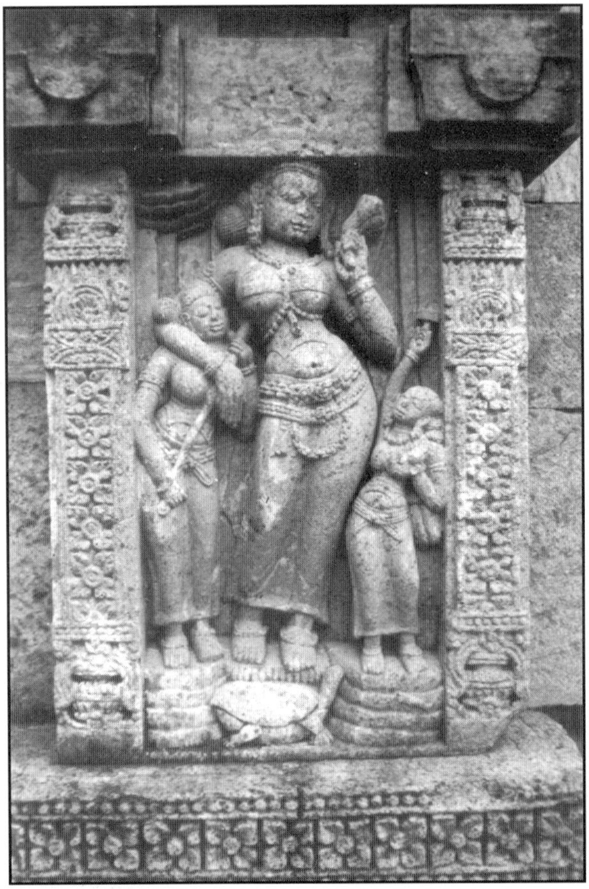

Pl. 10. Ratnagiri, Yamunā

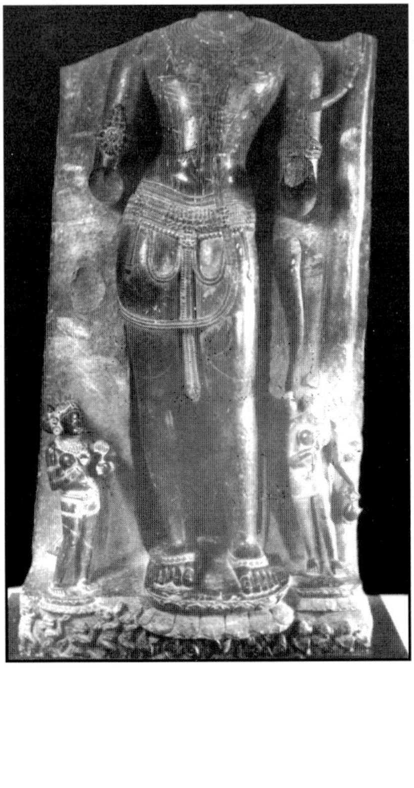

Pl. 12. OSM, Lokanātha from Bhubaneswar

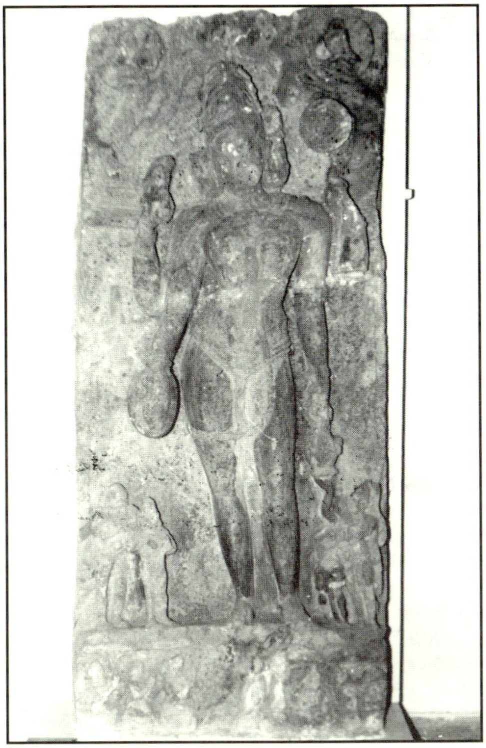

Pl. 13. OSM, Avalokiteśvara

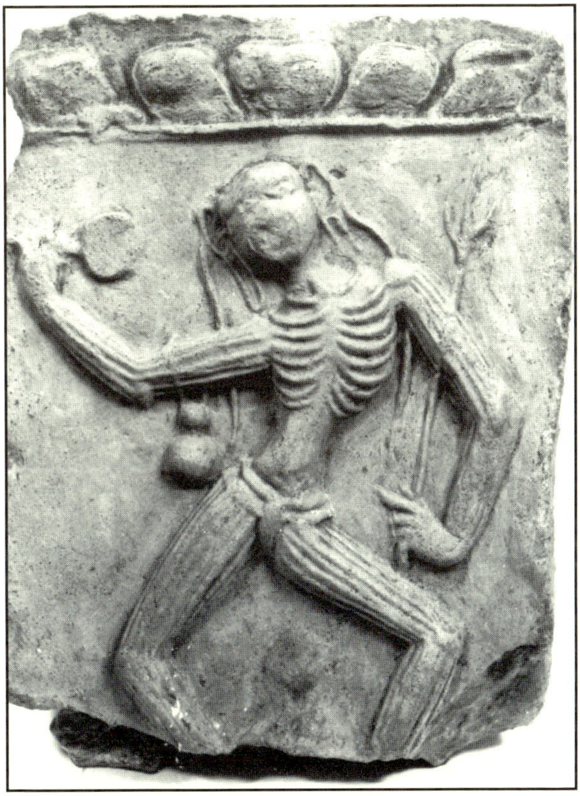

Pl. 15. ASM, Dancing Cāmuṇḍā

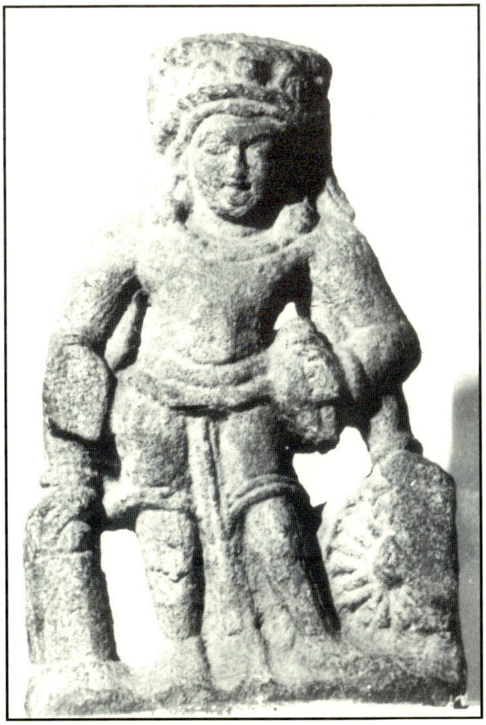

Pl. 14. PM, Viṣṇu from Bhojpur

Pl. 17. Kāmākhyā precincts, Cāmuṇḍā I

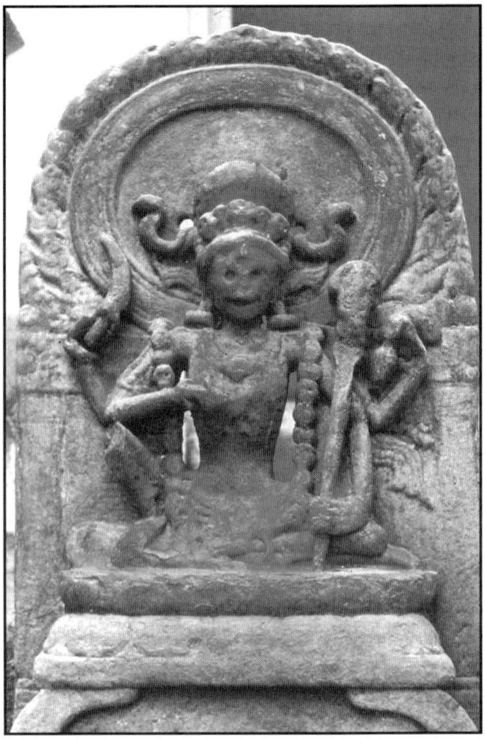

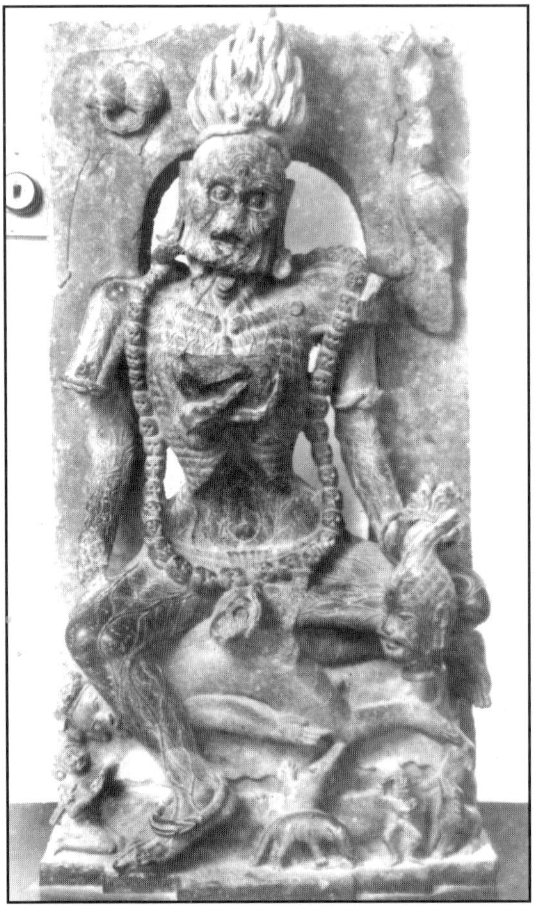

Pl. 16. OSM, Cāmuṇḍā from Dharmasala

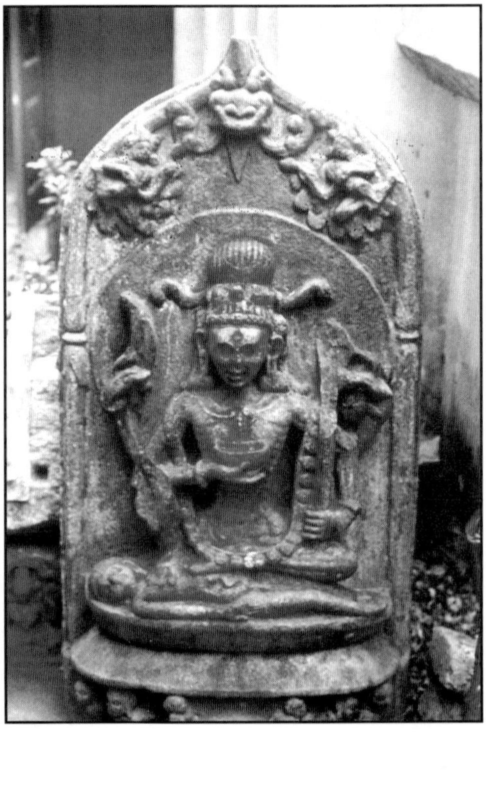

Pl. 18. Kāmākhyā precincts, Cāmuṇḍā II

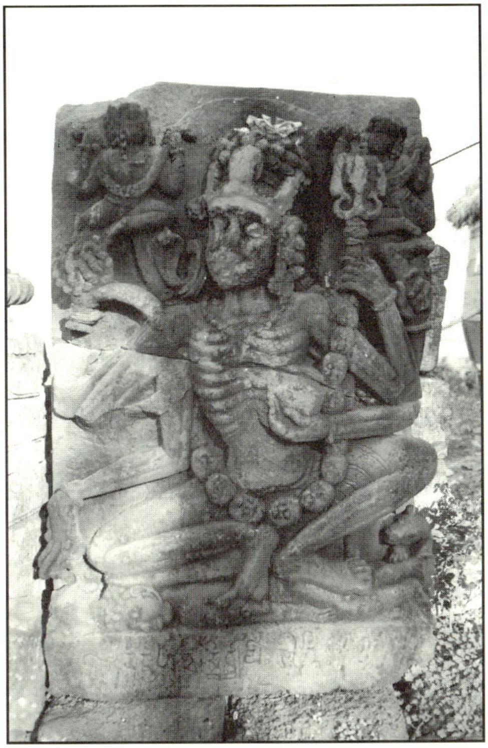

Pl. 19. Jajpur, Trilocaneśvara Compound, Cāmuṇḍā I

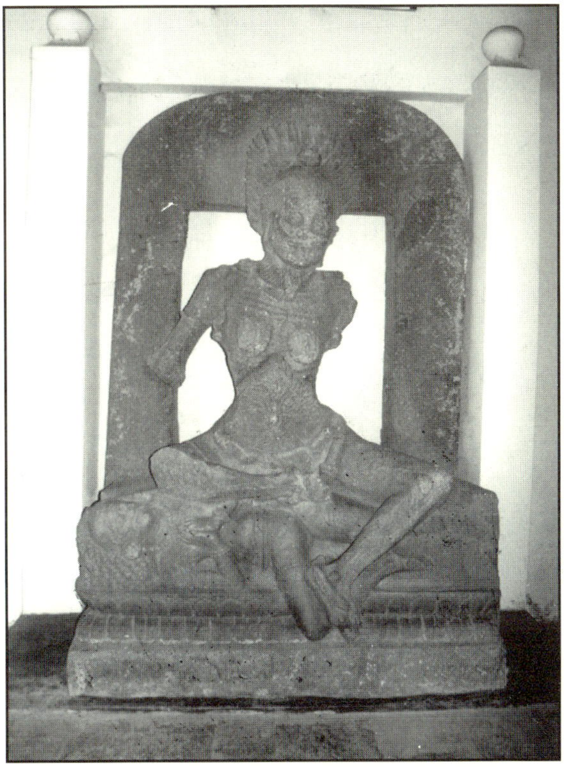

Pl. 21. Jajpur, Court Compound, Cāmuṇḍā

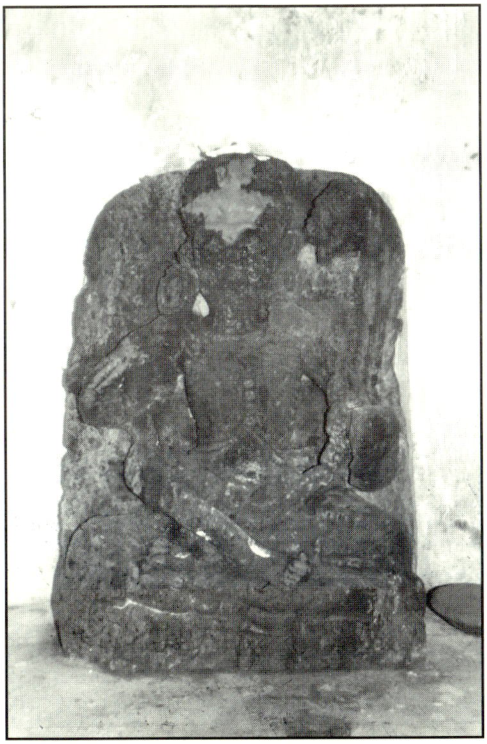

Pl. 20. Jajpur, Trilocaneśvara Compound, Cāmuṇḍā II

Pl. 23. Melakadambur, Naṭarāja (bronze)

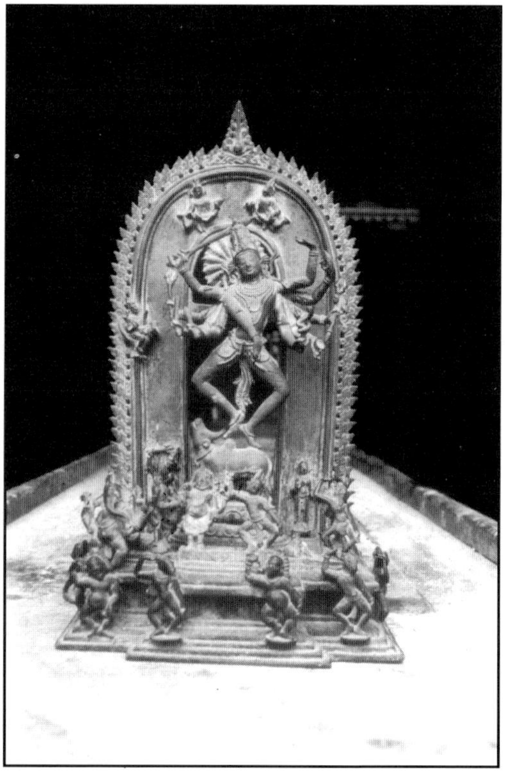

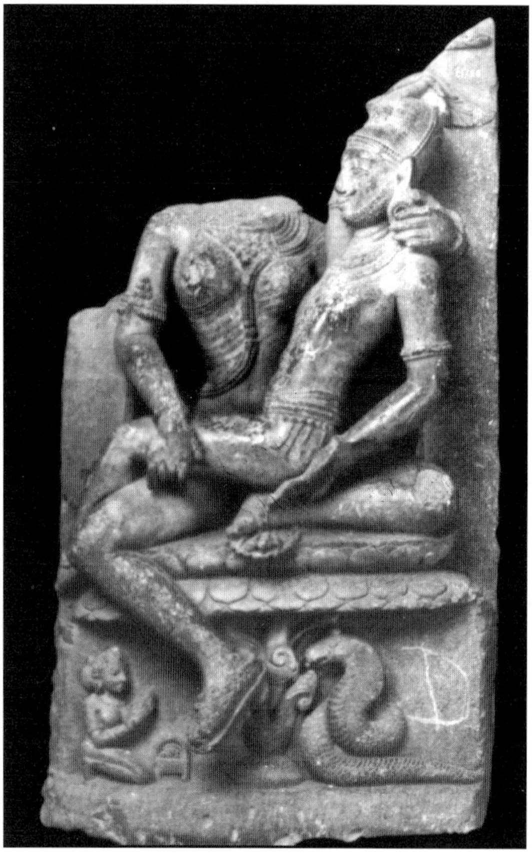

Pl. 22. OSM, Āstīka-Jaratkāru

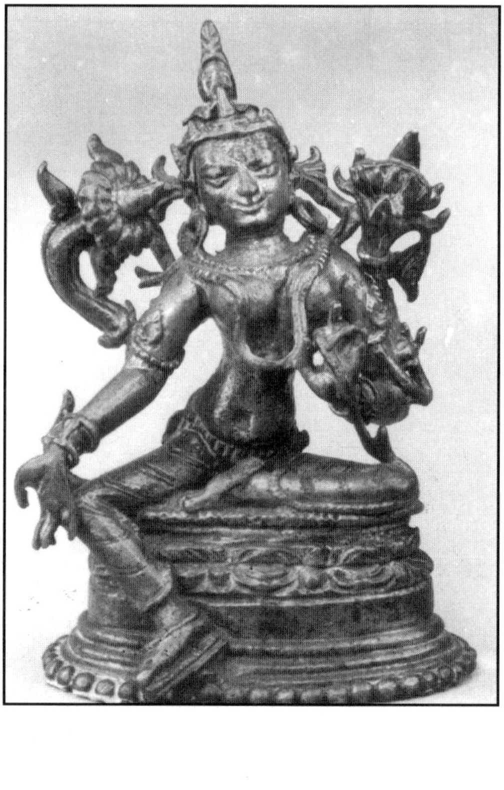

Pl. 24. ASM, Tārā (bronze)

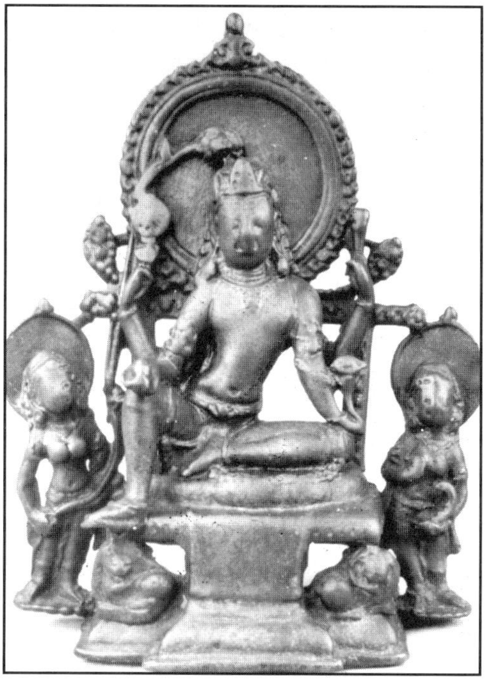

Pl. 25. ASM, Avalokiteśvara

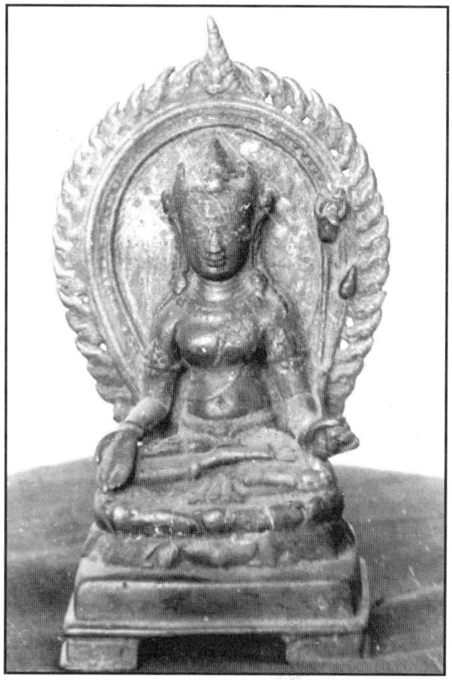

Pl. 26. OSM, Tārā (bronze)

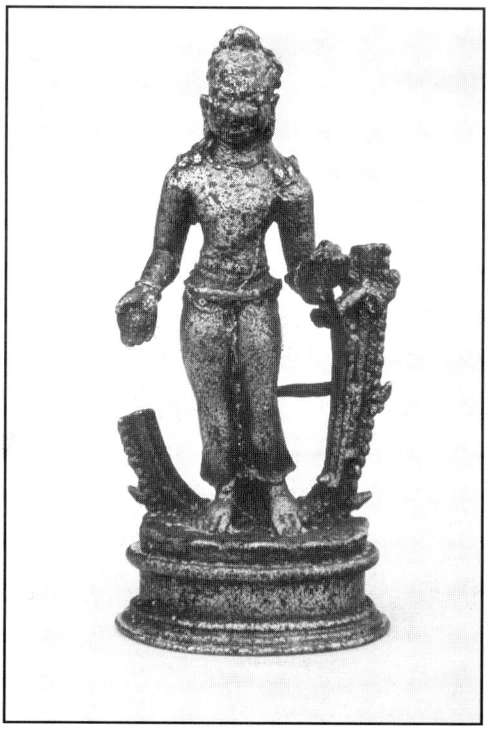

Pl. 27. ASM, Lokanātha (bronze)

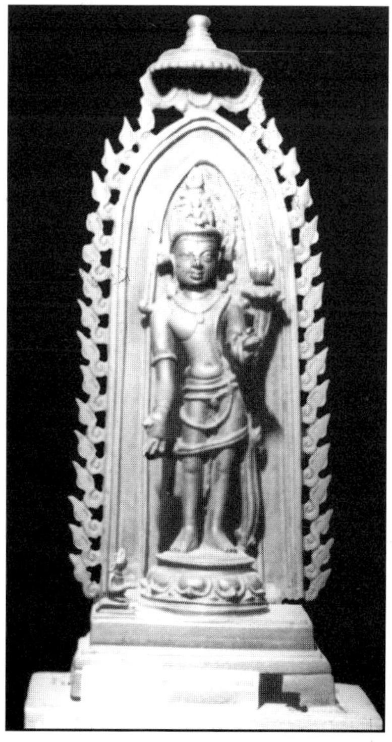

Pl. 28. PM, Lokanātha (bronze)

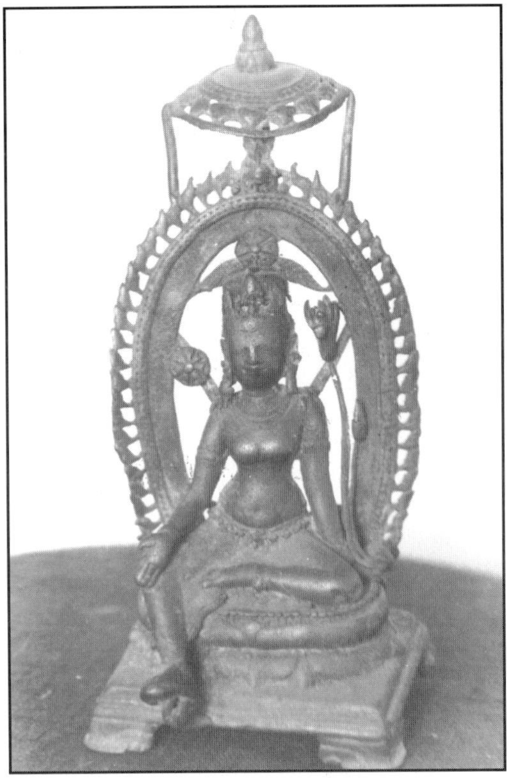

Pl. 29. OSM, Tārā (bronze)

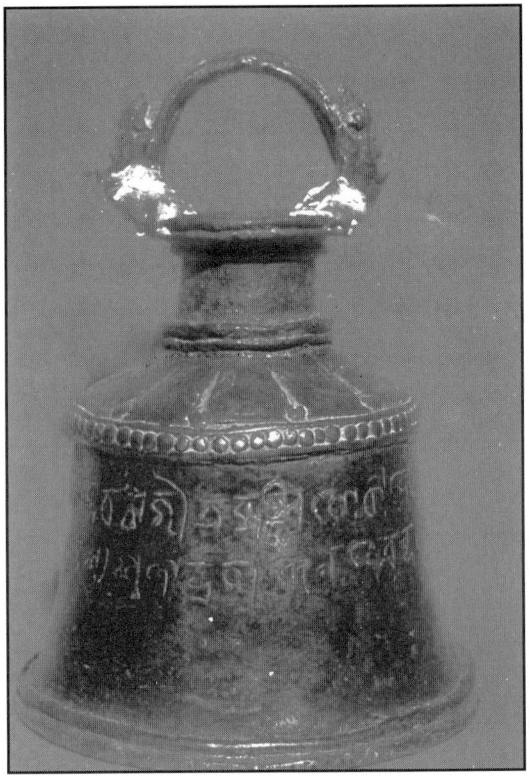

Pl. 30. ASM, Copper bell from NS

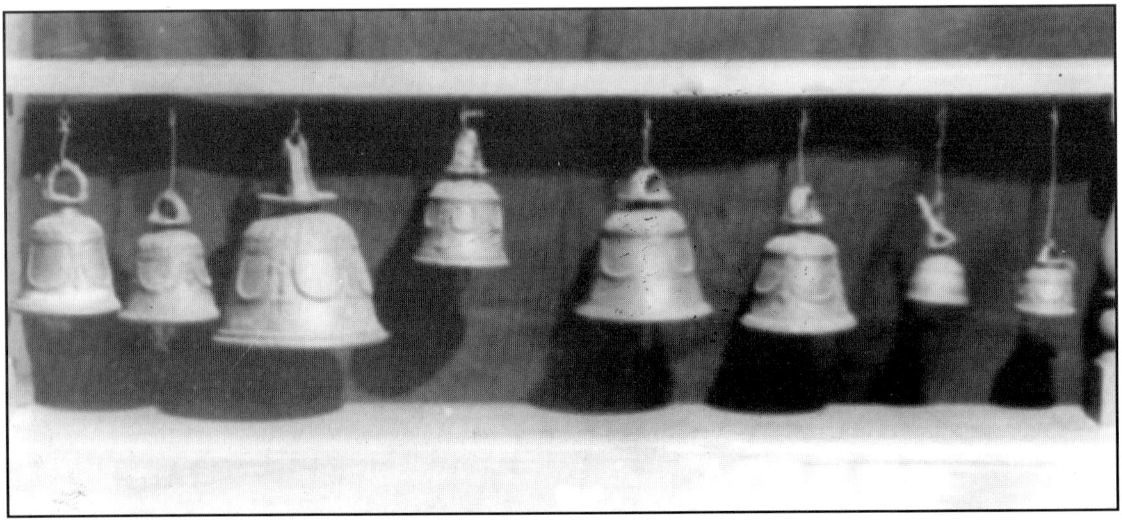

Pl. 31. PM, Eight Copper bells from KH

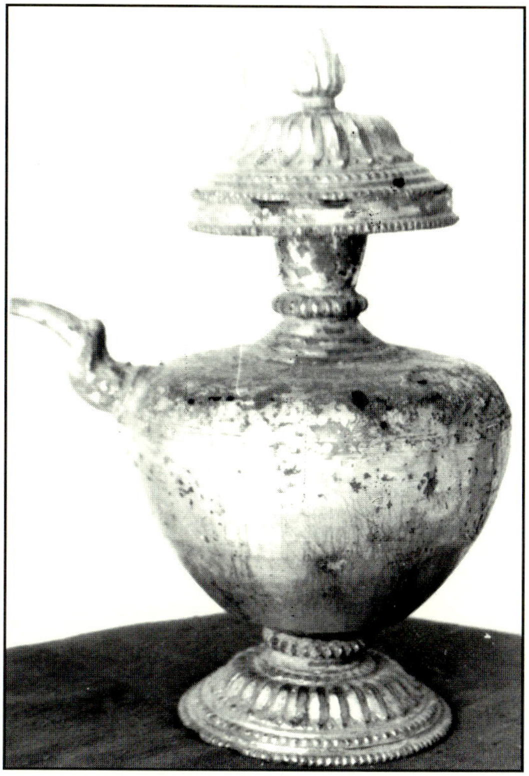

Pl. 32. OSM, Spouted vessel (bronze)

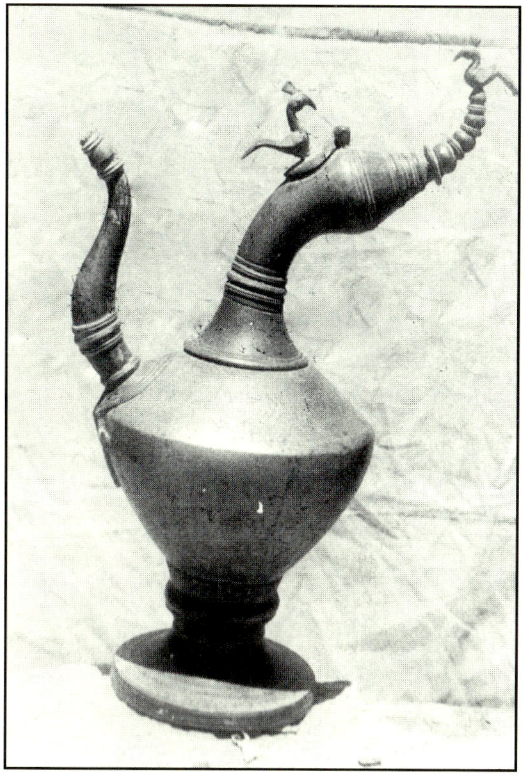

Pl. 33. ASM, Spouted vessel (bronze)

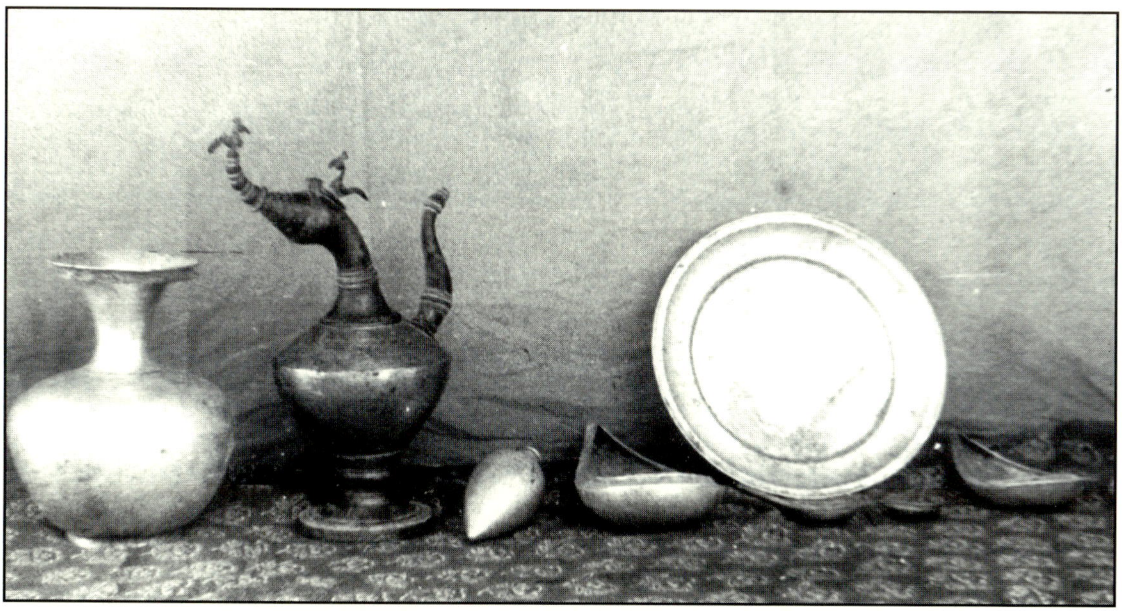

Pl. 34. HM, Silver objects including a spouted vessel

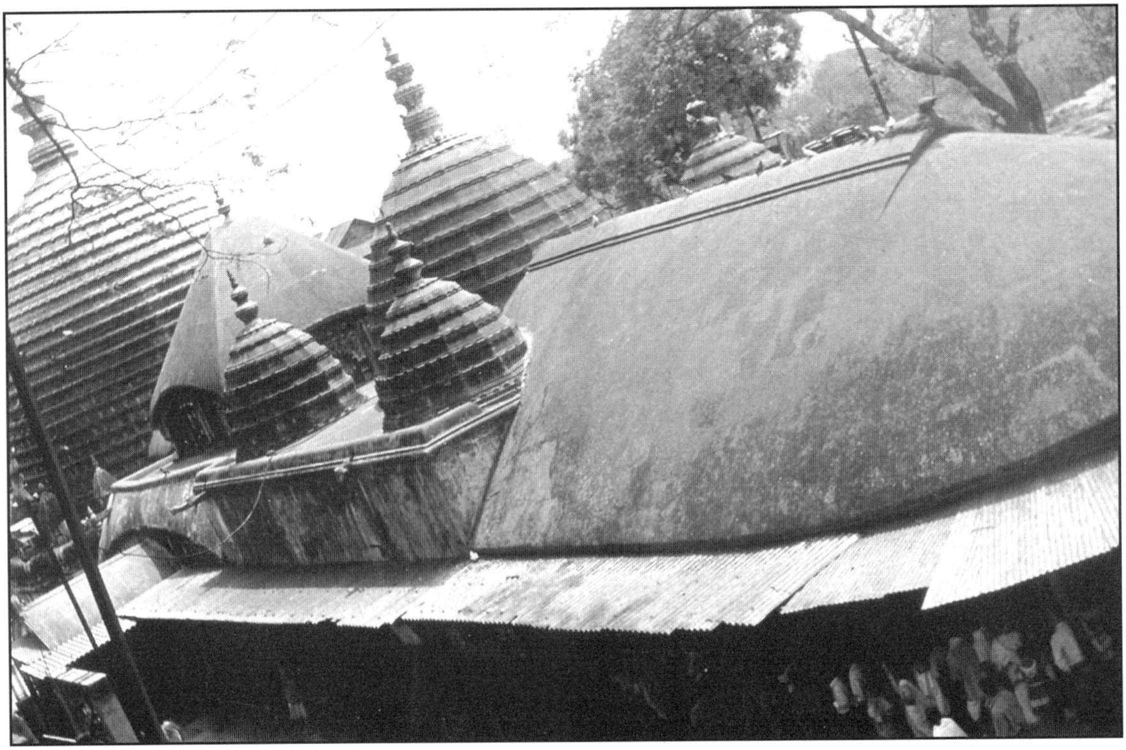

Pl. 35. Kāmākhyā, dome-like śikharas

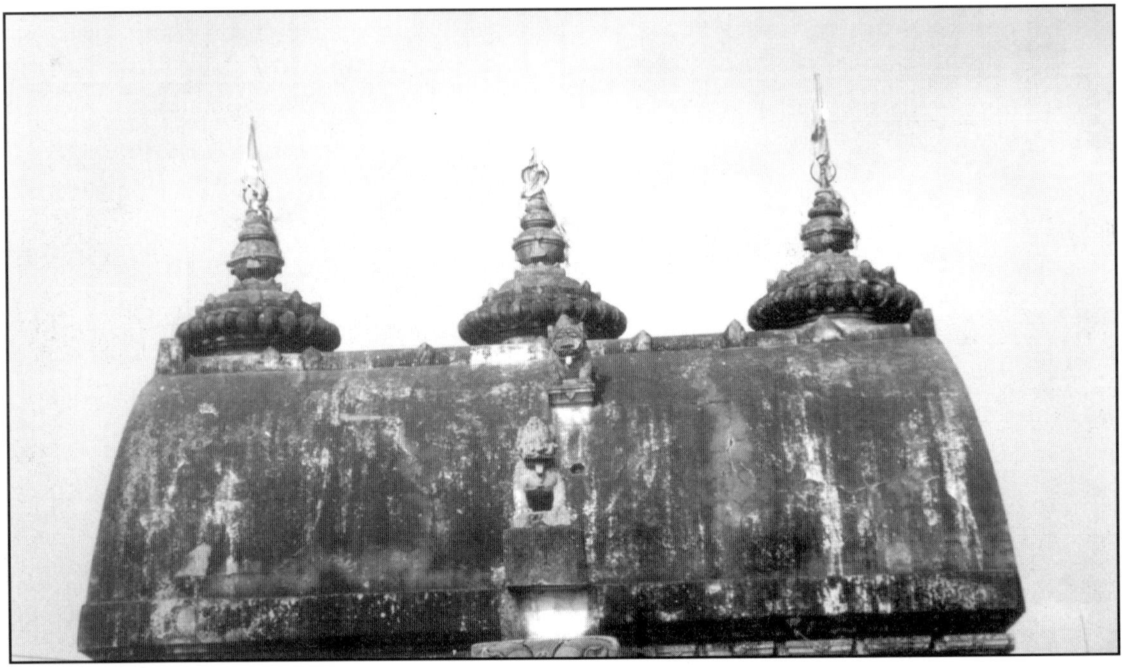

Pl. 36. Vetāla temple, Bhubaneswar, the śikhara

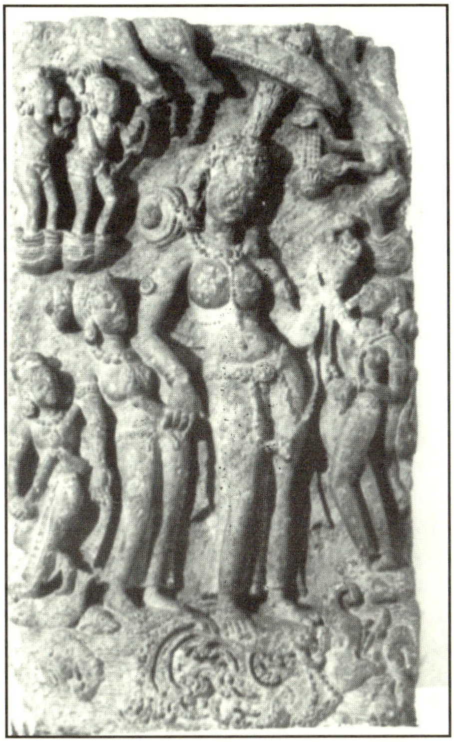

Pl. 37. PM, Gaṅgā from Udayagiri

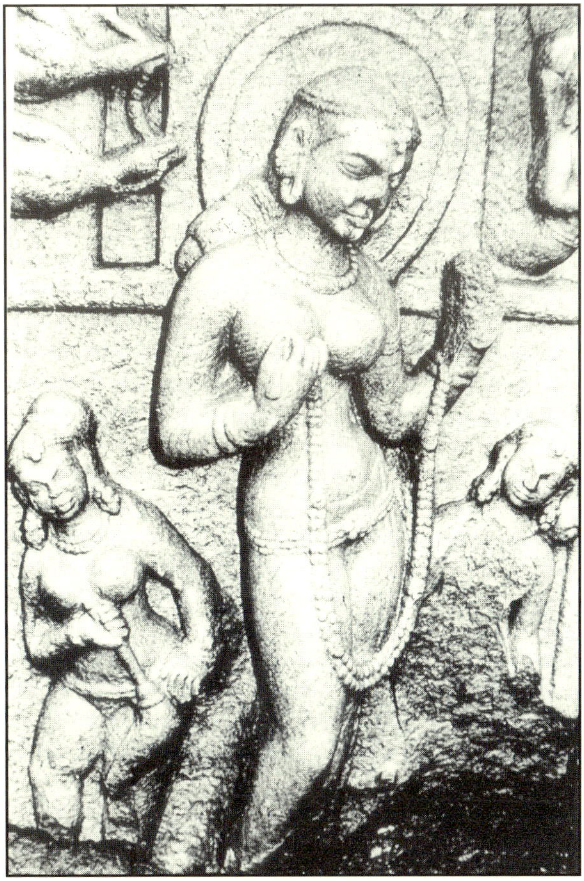

Pl. 38. Dah Parbatia, Gaṅgā

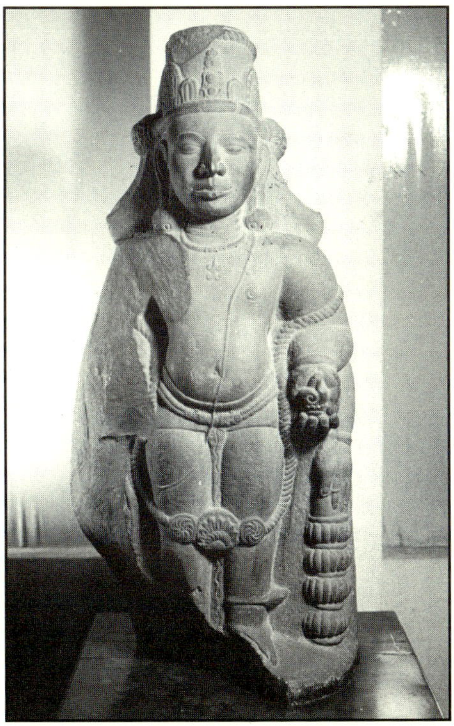

Pl. 39. ASM, Viṣṇu from Deopani

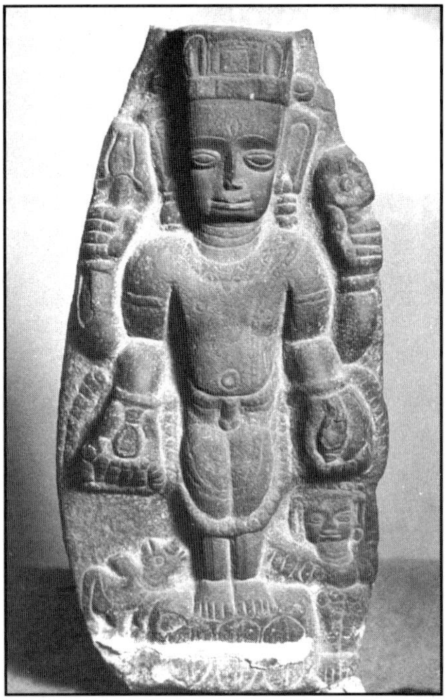

Pl. 40. ASM, Harihara from Deopani

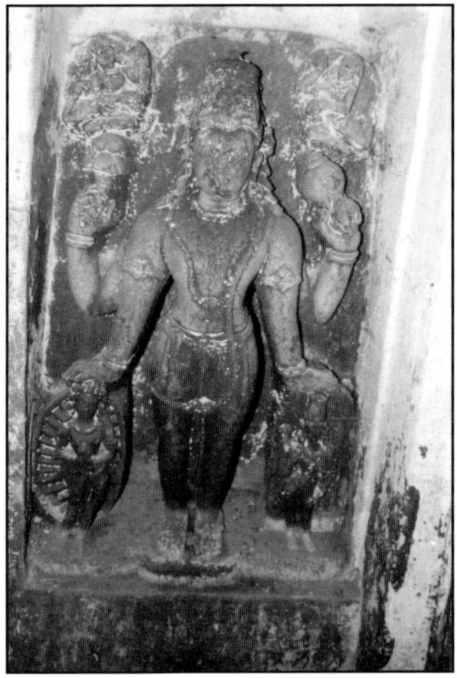

Pl. 41. Jajpur, Viṣṇu in Siddheśvara temple

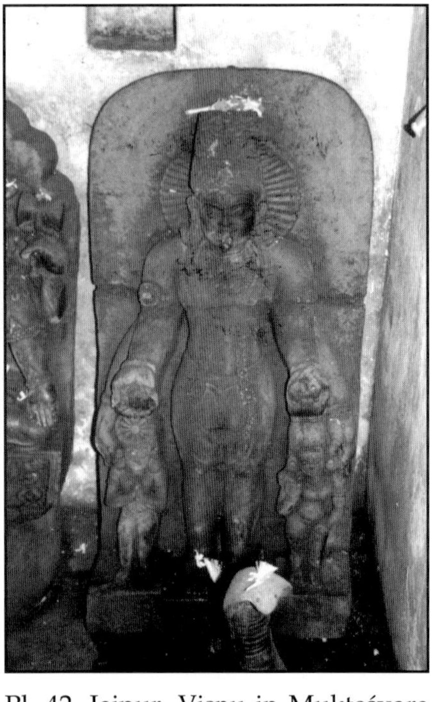

Pl. 42. Jajpur, Viṣṇu in Mukteśvara shrine, Jagannātha temple

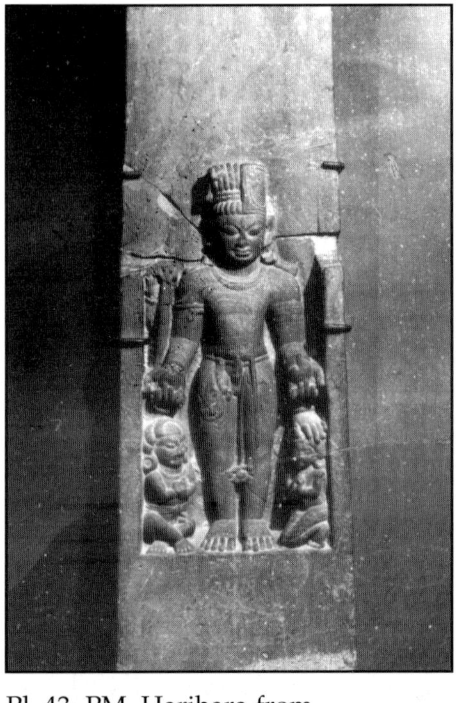

Pl. 43. PM, Harihara from Mundeswari

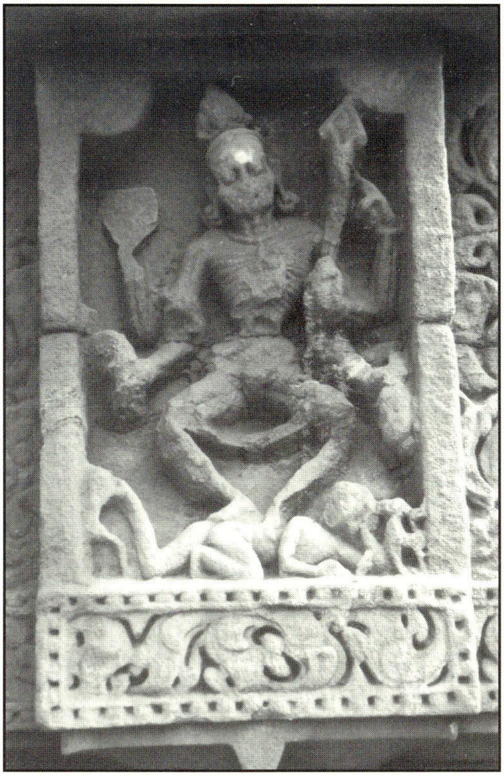

Pl. 44. Brahmeśvara temple at Bhubaneswar, Cāmuṇḍā

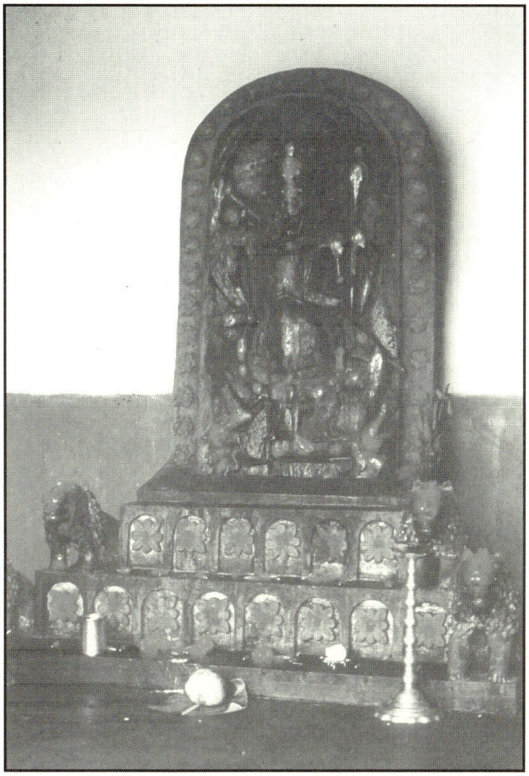

Pl. 45. Nabhanga, Cāmuṇḍā (installed in a modern temple)

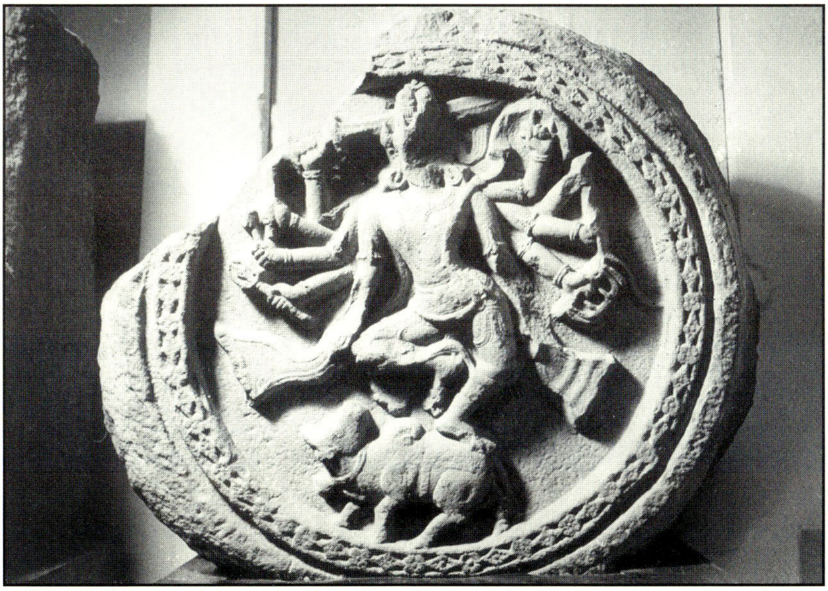

Pl. 47. ASM, Naṭarāja, 10th-11th century

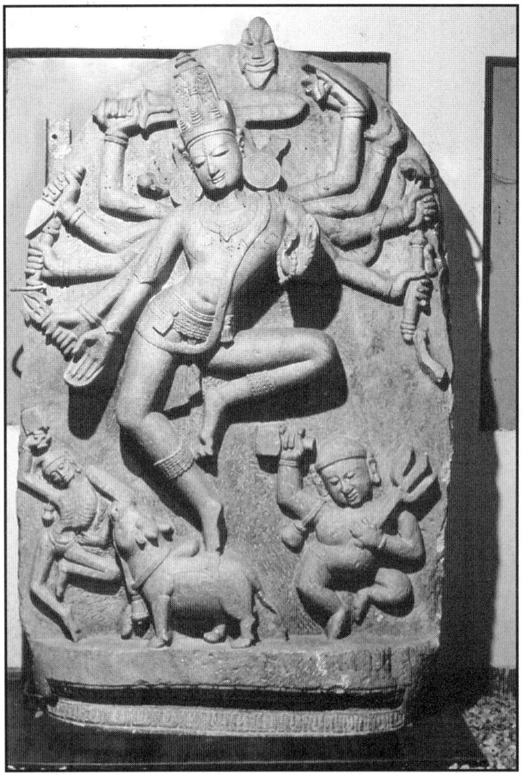

Pl. 46. ASM, Naṭarāja, 13th century

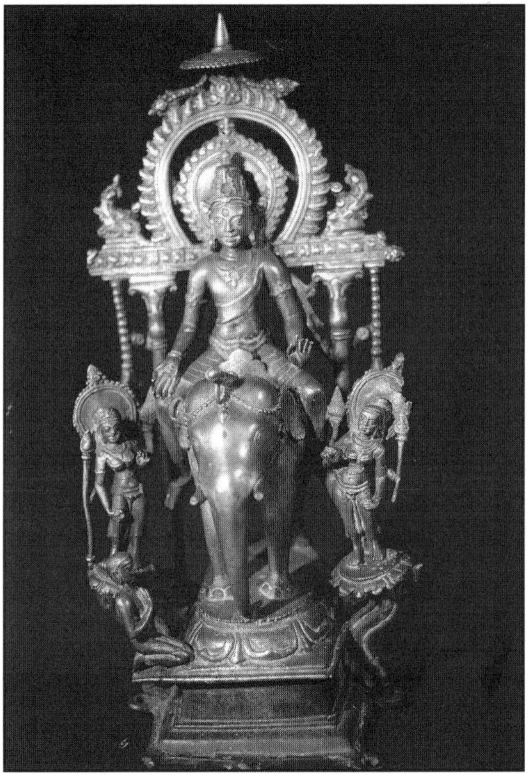

Pl. 49. ASM, Indra (bronze)

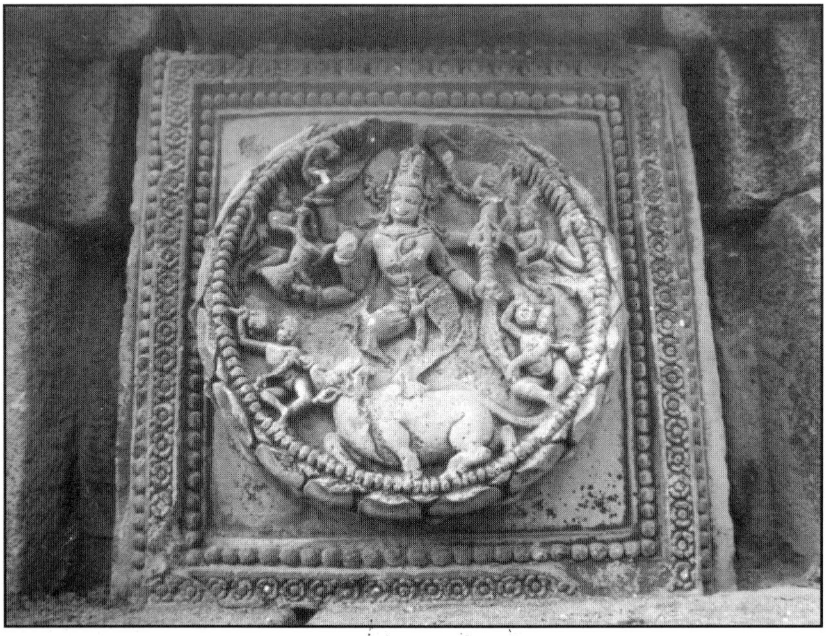

Pl. 48. Pāpanāśinī temple at Bhubaneswar, Naṭarāja, 15th century

Janardan temple of Gauhati. In costume types however they differ from those shown in the *Amaru Śataka* and the reliefs of the Janardan temple of Gauhati and Bhubaneswar."[58] Elsewhere, comparing an Orissan *Gīta Govinda* manuscript with a work of Hyderabad, Dasgupta remarks as follows, "The treatment of diaphanous drapery with stiff and angular ends of the *sārī* or *oḍhanī* also recall a family resemblance with Ruhani paintings from Bijapur. "It is the little stems sinuously embowering the four protagonists, however, the swarm of bees, the air of dazed surrender in the figures, and above all, the prickly treatment of costumes and jewellery which give the picture its Orissan traits." But instead of calling the above traits only Orissan, we can widen the horizon if we term them 'Eastern Indian' for in the *Gīta Govinda* manuscript from Assam, belonging to the early Tuṅkhuṅgiyā period, we find exactly the same treatment of similar items."[59]

The reason for differences in the paintings of Assam and Orissa perhaps lies in the difference in the technique of painting followed in the two regions. While the Orissan painters were following the method of earlier palm leaf painting that was etched by a metal stylus, the Assam painter was using reed pens and brushes like the Mughal and other north Indian artists. However, we do find definite Orissan influence in the paintings of Koch Bihar, an extension of the Assam schools.

It is said that the great saint Śaṅkaradeva was a painter himself and he had presented the king Naranārāyaṇa of Koch Bihar with a manuscript box, the paintings on which were done by the saint himself.[60] This was the beginning of the tradition of painting in Koch Bihar in the mid-sixteenth century. In the following decades the *Satriyā* school made its way to Koch Bihar and in the late eighteenth century a new type of art developed there; it was painting of wooden book covers unlike Assam where the folios themselves were illustrated.[61] By this time Koch Bihar had become a part of the Mughal empire and was having repeated matrimonial alliances with the house of Amer. The book cover paintings of Koch Bihar have, therefore, a general similarity with the Rajasthani schools and are also influenced by the contemporary Patna school,[62] itself a provincial style of the Mughal school. In the eighteenth-nineteenth century Koch Bihar paintings, however, certain similarity with the Orissan paintings is also noticeable. Discussing certain decorative patterns, Dasgupta says, "The same trend where the 'vernacular idiom' takes a pride of place in the post-medieval Indian painting is observed in paintings from Koch Bihar as in Orissa. In the nineteenth century copy of the illustrated *Vaidehīvilāsa* manuscript from Baripada in Orissa, we come across Islamic architecture and European costume in illustrations depicting episodes from the *Rāmāyaṇa.* This had also been a cliche in contemporary Koch Bihar painting."[63] The Koch Bihar art of painting book covers also reached the neighbouring region of western Assam; in the Goalpara and Dhubri districts a number of such specimens are available.[64] In some of them we may detect influence of the folk painting of Mithilā as well as the art traditions of Orissa.

Painting has been an inseparable aspect of Maithila cultural life. They are primarily wall paintings. Archer had styled them as Maithila paintings and nowadays they are usually referred to as Madhubani paintings. However, no specimen of such paintings from an early period has survived. We may only conjecture about their nature from the living art of Madhubani. As remarked by Upendra Thakur, "The paintings dissolve but the sytle goes on."[65] It is interesting to find that this folk art of Mithilā appears to have influenced the painting of Assam in the eighteenth century. Discussing a particular book cover showing the painting of a ceremonial barge, Dasgupta remarks, "It is surprising how in the specimen we find miniature painting turning for help to folk art. The figures of the rowers, with their carelessly treated bodies but intense profiles, with pig-tails and shaven or closely cropped hair, resemble similar figures from folk mural painting of Mithilā. This can only be explained by the long standing contact that existed between Kamarupa and Mithilā from the earliest times."[66] He goes on, "The book covers from Dhubri mentioned above deserve special mention for they represent a continuation of older motifs. These book covers do not antedate the eighteenth century and are painted only in primary colours. But they are calligraphic in treatment in spite of having been painted. A close similarity exists between these and Orissan palm-leaf etchings. The illustrations include the incarnations of Viṣṇu, viz., Matsya, Kūrma, Varāha, Narasiṁha. Vāmana, Paraśurāma, Rāma, Balarāma, Buddha and Kalki. The first four *Avatāras* are in the conventional syncretistic form. The episode of the three steps of Vāmana has been ingeniously depicted by supplying him with an extra leg which is lifted high, for there was no place for him to place it on as he had by taking two steps occupied all heaven and earth. Buddha sits under an architectural niche and Kalki rides high, brandishing his sword. The priests sacrificing at an altar of fire bear the closest resemblance to Orissan figures. The intense eyes, arched eye-brows, pointed beards, and the peculiar shape of the moustaches, all speak of the same tradition."[67] I may add that all the features of the *Avatāras* described here may be seen in the sculptures of Orissa dateable from the early medieval period. In particular, the device of providing a third leg to the Vāmana *avatāra* is a usual feature of the Trivikrama images found in Orissa and South India in which an extra raised leg is shown emerging from the junction of the two normal legs in the lower abdomen.

Before concluding this survey we may take note of some significant works of painting. The *Hastividyārṇava* of the eighteenth century has already been mentioned earlier. Then there is a remarkable work of the time of King Rudra Singha (AD 1696-1714): an illustrated copy of the Assamese rendering of *Gīta Govinda* by Kavirāja Chakravartī.[68] It is remarkable for it contained a series of *Rāgamālā* paintings, of which, unfortunately, only a few have survived.[69]

Rāgamālā paintings take a prominent place in the late medieval paintings of India. In eastern India too, some of the *Rāgas* and *Rāginīs* have been depicted in the manuscript illustrations although a full set is not available in any work. In the *Gīta Govinda* of Rāma Saraswatī (late seventeenth century),[70] we have paintings of a few of them in personified forms even though the book mentions the *Rāga* or *Rāginī* that is to be used for each particular part of the long narrative. A later rendering of this book by Kavirāja Chakravartī during the reign of the King Rūdra Siṅgha (1696-1714) perhaps contained a whole set of such paintings but only a few folios have survived.[71]

The present author is not aware whether any *Rāgamālā* paintings have been found in Orissa; Dasgupta has also not mentioned any. But a whole set of fifty eight *Rāgas* and *Rāginīs* in the Mithilā idiom is preserved in the Chandradhari Museum at Darbhanga.[72]

The above discussion establishes beyond doubt that the old tradition of contact between the sculptors and architects of Kāmarūpa, Kaliṅga and Mithilā continued in the field of painting in the late medieval period, particularly between the artists of Mithilā, Koch Bihar and Orissa. We need not perhaps remind that in the late medieval period it was Koch Bihar and not Assam that was really the successor of ancient Kāmarūpa, both politically and culturally.

NOTES AND REFERENCES

1. K.C. Panigrahi, *Chronology of the Bharma-Karas and the Somavamsis of Orissa*, pp. 22-24.
2. R.D. Choudhary, *The Sculptures of Assam*, Colour Plates I and II.
3. Naseem Akhtar, *Patna Museum Catalogue, Stone Sculptures and Other Antiquities*, Plate XXXVII.
4. The Hayagrīva Mādhava temple inscription in Maheswar, Neog (ed.), *Prācya Śāsanāvalī* (Text, pp. 3-4, Introduction, p. 17).
5. Pradip Sarma, 'Antiquity of the Kāmakhyā Temple on the Nilachala', in *JARS*, vol. XXVI, 1981-82, pp. 46-52.
6. K.C. Panigrahi, *Archaeological Remains at Bhubaneswara*, p. 87.
7. Ibid., p. 159.
8. M. Neog, op. cit., p. 4 (Texts), p. 18 (Introduction).
9. K.S. Behera and and T.E. Donaldson, *Sculpture Masterpieces from Orissa*, Preface, viii.

10. R.D. Banerji, *ARASI, 1924-25,* pp. 92-102.
11. Naseem Akhtar, op. cit., Plate XXXVI.
12. K.S. Behera and Thomas Donaldson, op. cit., Plate 105.
13. Ibid., Plate 106.
14. For example, the Asanpat Naṭarāja image of the 6th (?) century.
15. Illustrated in Makhan Jha, *Civilizational Regions of Mithilā and Mahakoshal.*
16. Naseem Akhtar, op. cit., Plate XVIII.
17. R.D. Choudhury, *Catalogue of Stone Sculptures Assam State Museum,* Fig. 8.
18. Ibid., Fig. 5.
19. Ibid., Fig. 1.
20. T.E. Donaldson, *The Iconography of Vaishnava Images in Orissa,* pp. 266-67.
21. Ibid., Fig. 9.
22. Ibid., Fig. 10.
23. Ibid., Fig. 11.
24. Ibid., Fig. 16.
25. Ibid., Fig. 20.
26. Naseem Akhtar, op. cit., Plate XXI.
27. Ibid., Plate XXI.
28. Ibid., Plate XXII.
29. Ibid., Plate XXIV.
30. K.C. Panigrahi, op. cit., Fig. 64.
31. Illustrated in R.M. Nath, *Background of Assamese Culture.* The image has since been installed in a modern temple and is always covered with vermillion, clothes and flowers making it impossible to study its features or to take its photograph. A very indistinct photograph could, however, be taken and is given at plate 45.
32. R.D. Choudhary, op. cit., Fig. 9.
33. Panigrahi, op. cit., p. 103.
34. R.D. Choudhary, op. cit., Fig. 24.
35. Ibid., Fig. 58.
36. Ibid., Fig. 78; Also R.D. Choudhary, *The Sculptures of Assam,* Colour Plate VI.
37. Ibid., Fig. 36.
38. Panigrahi, op. cit., Fig. 121 and p. 50 for its date.
39. N.K. Bhattasali, *Iconography of Buddhist and Brahmānical Sculptures in the Dacca Museum,* pp. 110-116 and Plates XLII and XLIII.
40. Naseem Akhtar, *Patna Museum Catalogue-Terracottas and Metal Images,* Plate XXV.
41. Ibid., Plate XXIV.
42. R.D. Choudhary, *The Sculptures of Assam,* Colour Plate V.
43. Naseem Akhtar, op. cit., Plate XXIII.
44. K.S. Behera and T.E. Donaldson, *Sculpture Masterpieces from Orissa,* Plate opp. p. 56.
45. D. Sarma, *Kāmarūpa Śāsanāvalī* Part II-texts, pp. 33-35.
46. It was seen and photographed by the author a few years ago in the office of the temple's *doloi* but during his recent visit to the place it was not to be found; the *doloi* does not recollect it!
47. K.C. Panigrahi, *History of Orissa,* pp. 44-45.
48. R. Dasgupta, *Eastern Indian Manuscript Painting,* p. 90.

49. Ibid., p. 92.
50. Ibid., p. 95.
51. Ibid., p. 54.
52. Ibid., p. 57.
53. Ibid.
54. Ibid., p. 64.
55. Ibid., p. 69.
56. See for example, R.D. Choudhury and Naren Kalita, *Manuscript Paintings from Kamarupa Anusandhan Samiti,* p. 6 (Folio 52-B of *Gīta Govinda*) and p. 100 (Folio 20-B of Lava-Kuśara Yuddha).
57. A work of Harihara Vipra (AD 1714-44) in Assamese.
58. R. Dasgupta, op.cit., p. 92.
59. Ibid., pp. 95-96.
60. Ibid., p. 81.
61. Ibid., pp. 81-82.
62. Ibid., p. 81.
63. Ibid., p. 87.
64. Ibid., p. 75.
65. Upendra Thakur, *History of Mithilā,* p. 387.
66. R. Dasgupta, op. cit., p. 78.
67. Ibid., p. 78.
68. Ibid., p. 69.
69. Ibid., p. 109.
70. Ibid.
71. Ibid.
72. Ibid., p. 110.

A Select Inventory of Comparable Stone Sculptures of Assam and Orissa

Sl. No.	Assam	Orissa
1.	Gaṅgā, Dah Parbatia (6th Cent., *in situ*)	Gaṅgā, Paraśurāmeśvara temple, Bhubaneswar (7th Cent., *in situ*) Gaṅgā, Udayagiri (8th Cent., PM) Gaṅgā, Mukteśvara temple, Bhubaneswar (10th Cent., *in situ*)
2.	Yamunā, Dah Parbatia (6th Cent., *in situ*)	Yamunā, Udayagiri (8th Cent., *in situ*) Yamunā, Ratnagiri (8th Cent., *in situ*) Yamunā, Mukteśvara temple, Bhubaneswar (10th Cent., *in situ*)
3.	Viṣṇu, Medhipara (7th Cent., ASM) Viṣṇu and Harihara images, Deopani (8th Cent., ASM)	Viṣṇu and Harihara images at Jajpur in Mukteśvara shrine (Jagannātha temple), Siddheśvara, Virajā and Trilocaneśvara temples (7th-8th Cent., *in situ*)
4.	Cāmuṇḍā, Nabhanga (10th-11th Cent., *in situ*)	Cāmuṇḍā, Dharmasala (10th-11th Cent., OSM)
5.	Cāmuṇḍā, Borpathar (8th Cent., ASM)	Cāmuṇḍā, Jajpur (8th Cent., Court Compound)

6.	Two Cāmuṇḍā images, Kāmākhyā precincts (10th-11th Cent., *in situ*)	Two Cāmuṇḍā images, Jajpur, Trilocaneśvara temple compound (10th-11th Cent., *in situ*)
7.	Dancing Cāmuṇḍā, terracotta plaque (10th Cent., ASM)	Female figure in *Utkaṭika* pose, Rajarani temple, Bhubaneswar (10th Cent., *in situ*) Dancing Cāmuṇḍā, Brahmeśvara temple, Bhubaneswar (12th-13th Cent., *in situ*)
8.	Naṭarāja, Guwahati (10th-11th Cent., ASM) Naṭarāja, Ambari (13th Cent., ASM)	Naṭarāja, Pāpanāśinī temple, Bhubaneswar (15th Cent., *in situ*)

Note 1: This list includes only some of the sculptures actually seen and compared by the Author. A number of other such sculptures not included here have been analysed in the text.

Note 2: A number of pieces with comparable features from different sites in Orissa have been described and illustrated by Donaldson and taken note of at the appropriate places in the present volume, chapter 5.

Chapter 6

Inter-Regional Migration of Brāhmaṇas in the Early Medieval Period

It is well-known that a large number of Brāhmaṇas in Assam, Bengal and Orissa claim to have originally belonged to Kanauj or Kānyakubja. While the claims of all of them can not be substantiated, those in some cases are not devoid of truth. As per popular belief, they must have migrated only in the late medieval period, during the reign of the Koch and Ahom dynasties in Assam, the kings of Nadia in Bengal and Gajapati kings in Orissa. We have, however, definite epigraphic evidence of such migrations much earlier between the sixth and the thirteenth centuries in all the three regions and some oral traditions attesting to the same are also current.

Thus, in the *Kulapañjīs* of the Rāḍha Brāhmaṇas we find references to the migration of Brāhmaṇas from the Madhyadeśa to Bengal during the rule of the Sena dynasty.[1] Not only that, the king Ballālasena is reputed to have sent Brāhmaṇa missionaries from Bengal to Utkala, Aṅga (a part of Mithilā, no doubt), Tibet (or Bhutan) and Mauranga (in Nepal).[2] At Jajpur (ancient Virajā) in Orissa a tradition is current that ten thousand Brāhmaṇas were invited by the king Yayātikeśarī from Kānyakubja when he performed ten *Aśvamedha* sacrifices at Jajpur. The tradition is so strong that the pilgrims, while offering *piṇḍa* to their ancestors at Nābhigayā, a holy place at Jajpur prescribed for such ceremony, they also offer it to these Brāhmaṇas.[3] The present author interviewed some Brāhmaṇas at Jajpur and they told him that the Brāhmaṇas must have come from other places as well like Mithilā, Bengal and Assam.

Coming to the definite epigraphic evidence, the oldest inscriptions in this regard are the Dubi and Nidhanpur copper plates of Bhāskaravarmā of Kāmarūpa, both belonging to the early seventh century AD. Both these inscriptions record the renewal of grants of lands originally made by Bhūtivarmā, an ancestor of Bhāskara, necessitated by the destruction of the original charters by fire.[4] The Dubi plates record the names of two original donee Brāhmaṇas and their twelve descendants at the time of the issue of the renewed plates. The location of the donated land is not known as it was probably inscribed on one of the missing middle plates. The Nidhanpur plates contain no less than two hundred names of the donee Brāhmaṇas. The donated land was located in the Candrapurī *Viṣaya* on the banks of the Kauśikā river. This river has been convincingly identified with the river Kosi and the donated lands between two abandoned beds of this river by K.L. Barua even though the find-place of the plates, viz., Nidhanpur is situated in the Sylhet district of Bangladesh.[5] Barua has shown that this part of Bihar (included in Mithilā, no doubt) was a part of the kingdom of the Varmans of Kāmarūpa at least from the time of Bhūtivarman (early sixth century AD). The following features in these two grants are noteworthy:

1. Most of the donees are described as *Bhaṭṭa* and quite a few as *'Swāmī'* (Some of them, both), e.g., Bhaṭṭa Devaghoṣaswāmī, Śubhadāmaswāmī, Vakulasomaswāmī, Śucipālitaswāmī, etc.
2. Most of the names of the donees end in Ghoṣa, Soma, Datta, Dāma, Pālita, Nāga, etc., the surnames now current amongst the Vaidyas and Kāyasthas of Bengal.
3. In both the grants the lands are donated according to the *Bhūmichidranyāya*.
4. The Veda, its branches, the *Gotras*, the *Pravaras* of the donees are as follows:

i. Kauśika Vājasaneyī
ii. Vājasaneyī Avasarika
iii. Māṇḍavya
iv. Kātyāyana Chāndoga
v. Yāska Bāhvṛcya
vi. Vāhṛcya Gorātreya
vii. Kṛṣṇātreya Vājasaneyī
viii. Bhāradvāja Vājasaneyī
ix. Kauṇḍiñya Vājasaneyī
x. Gautama Chāndoga
xi. Gautama Vājasaneyī
xii. Vātsa Cārakya
xiii. Maudgalya Vājasaneyī
xiv. Kāśyapa Vājasaneyī
xv. Treya Vājasaneyī
xvi. Bhāradvāja Bāhvṛcya

xvii. Vāsiṣṭha Bāhvṛcya
xviii. Sāṅkṛtyāyana Cārakya
xix. Bhāradvāja Taittirīya
xx. Parāśara Bāhvṛcya
xxi. Bāhvṛcya Kātyāyana
xxii. Śāṇḍilya Vājasaneyī
xxiii. Kāsa Vājasaneyī
xxiv. Gārgya Vājasaneyī
xxv. Ālambāyana Vājasaneyī
xxvi. Pracetasa Vājasaneyī
xxvii. Bhāradvāja Chāndoga
xxviii. Kautsa Vājasaneyī
xxix. Pārāśarya Caraka
xxx. Āślāyana Chāndoga
xxxi. Vārāha Vāhvṛcya
xxxii. Kauśika Vāhvṛcya
xxxiii. Kauṭilya Vājasaneyī
xxxiv. Kavestara Vājasaneyī
xxxv. Kauṇḍiñya Vāhvṛcya
xxxvi. Śaunaka Vājasaneyī
xxxvii. Vaisṇavṛddhi Chāndoga
xxxviii. Paurṇṇa Vāhvṛcya
xxxix. Gārgya Vājasaneyī
xl. Pāṅkalya Chāndoga
xli. Kāśyapa Taittirīya
xlii. Agniveśya Vājasaneyī
xliii. Āṅgirasa Vājasaneyī
xliv. Vārhaspatya Vāhvṛcya
xlv. Śaunaka Vāhvṛcya
xlvi. Śakaṭāyana

It is thus seen that the Brāhmaṇas patronized by Bhūtivarman and Bhāskaravarmā in the sixth and seventh centuries belonged mostly to the Yajurveda and Vājasaneyī traditions and to Māṇḍavya, Bhāradvāja, Gautama, Vatsa, Maudgalya, Kāśyapa, Vasiṣṭha, Sānkṛtyāyana, Parāśara, Kāsa, Ālambāyana and Śāndilya Gotras. We do not know whether these Brāhmaṇas belonged to the region of the donated lands or hailed from elsewhere. Here some clue is provided by the term *Bhūmichidranyāya.* D.C. Sircar has explained that the term, literally the maxim of covering up the hole in the land, probably refers to the 'reclamation of fallow land for the first time'.[6] If so, it would be reasonable to presume that these Brāhmaṇas were actually invited from outside, undoubtedly 'Madhyadeśa', and settled on these lands in an effort to 'Aryanize' the kingdom of the donors. This would imply that this was the period when the boundaries of Āryāvarta were being extended beyond Kāśī.

We may also examine the land grants of Kāmarūpa in the post-Varman period, i.e., between the eighth and twelfth centuries AD. The Tezpur[7] and Parvatiya plates of Vanamālavarmadeva (middle of the ninth century AD),[8] Nowgong[9] and Hawraghat[10] plates of Balavarmā (last part of the ninth century AD), the Bargaon[11] and Sualkuchi[12] plates of Ratnapāla (middle of the tenth century), the Gauhati[13] and Guakuchi Grants[14] of Indrapāla (end of the tenth century AD). Gachtal plates of Gopālavarmadeva[15] (early eleventh century), Khonamukhi[16], Śubhaṅkarapāṭaka[17] and Puṣpabhadrā[18] plates of Dharmapāla (end of the eleventh century) reveal patronage to the Brāhmaṇas of the following Gotras, etc.:

Śāndilya *gotra*
Yajurveda
Caraṇa of Sāman
Kapila *gotra*
Kāṇva *śākhā*
Upamanyu *gotra*
Pārāśara *gotra*
Vājasaneya
Bhāradvāja *gotra*
Kāśyapa *gotra*
Maudgalya *gotra*
Mādhyandina *śākhā*
Utathya, Mudgala, Aṅgirā *pravaraḥ*

Coming to Orissa, we find a similar phenomenon taking place from about the same time. In the Chaurasi plate of Śivakaradeva (II) we find the name of only one donee but the Neulpur charter records as many as 204 donees. Both the grants[19] were made in accordance with the *Bhūmichidra* principle as in the case of Bhāskaravarmā's grants. We have already proposed that the Chaurasi plate was issued at the time of the donor's coronation in AD 748. The same may have been the case with the subsequent Bhauma-Kara plates and even the Dubi plate of Bhākaravarman in AD 593-94. It seems that during the period sixth to twelfth century AD it was customary for the kings of eastern

India to invite Madhyadeśa Brāhmaṇas in large numbers and settle them on the newely deforested lands at the time of their coronation. No doubt, in some cases the donation was in favour of only one or two Brāhmaṇas but that really does not affect our hypothesis because in all cases the principle of *Bhūmichidra* has been followed. The practice in Orissa may have been imported from Assam since in the pre-Bhauma Māṭhara inscriptions we find donations to just one or two Brāhmaṇas and that too, the local ones. There are, no doubt, some cases of establishment of *agrahāras*, e.g., in the Madras Museum plates of Anantaśaktivarman (c. fifth century AD),[20] Srungavarapukota plates of Anantavarman (the same period),[21] Baranga grant of Umāvarman (the same period),[22] Takkali plates of Umāvarman (the same period),[23] Chicacole plates of Nandaprabhañjanavarman (the same period),[24] Baranga plates of the same ruler (the same period),[25] Komarti plates of Caṇḍavarman (the same period),[26] etc. It may be noted that all these examples are from southern Orissa, i.e., Kaliṅga proper, where the custom of inviting Brāhmaṇas from Madhyadeśa may not have been in vogue. However, the patronage to learning was undoubtedly an ancient custom as may be seen from the example of donation to Viṣṇusomācārya of Kāmarūpa described below.

An analysis of the Vedic schools to which the donee Brāhmaṇas belonged will be in order at this stage. We have already listed these obtaining in the Dubi and Nidhanpur grants. The schools and branches to which the Brāhmaṇa donees in the Bhauma-Kara charters belong are as follows.

The donee of the Chaurasi plate Jallubhaṭṭa belonged to the Kātyāyana *gotra* and three *pravaras*. The Neulpur plate which has as many as 204 donees saves the space by simply saying that they belonged to *nānāgotra caraṇebhih.* Only with two names the Vāhvṛcya and Vājasaneyī are specifically recorded.

In the charters of the later rulers, however, we get more information in this regard. From the Terundia plate of Śubahakara of the year 100 (AD 836), the Dharakote plate of Śubhakaradeva, of the year 103 (AD 839), the Dhenkenal Grant of Tribhuvanamahādevī of the year 160 (AD 896), Several charters of Daṇḍīmahādevī, e.g., the Santiragrama Grant of the year 180 (AD 916), the Ganjam Grant of the year 183 (AD 919), Kumurang plate of the year 187 (AD 923) and a Grant of Vakulamahādevi of unknown provenance, of the year 204 (AD 940), theAngul and Taltali plates of Dharmamahādevī (clearly of the tenth century AD) we find that the donee Brāhmaṇas belonged to the following *gotras, pravaras, śākhās,* etc.

i. Māṅgalya gotra
ii. Bhāradvāja gotra
iii. Viśvāmitra gotra

iv. Kauśika (or Kuśika) gotra
v. Āṅgirasa pravara
vi. Bhāradvāja pravara
vii. Bārhaspatya pravara
viii. Aurva anupravara
ix. Sāvarṇa anupravara
x. Devarāṭa anupravara
xi. Aṇḍala anupravara
xii. Vājasaneyī caraṇa
xiii. Kāṇva Śākhā
xiv. Mādhyandina Śākhā
xv. Śāndilya gotra
xvi. Asita pravara
xvii. Devala pravara
xviii. Chāndoga
xix. Śāndilya pravara
xx. Kāśyapa gotra
xxi. Kāśyapa pravara
xxii. Avatsara pravara
xxiii. Naidhruva pravara

We may have a similar look at the charter of the Bhañjas. They were minor dynasties during the Bhauma-Kara period and at least some of them were their feudatories. The following list is compiled from the 49 charters included by Snigdha Tripathy in her *Inscriptions of Orissa*, vol. 6:

Śāndilya *gotra*
Śāndilya pravara
Kauśika *gotra*
Viśvāmitra pravara
Aṇḍala pravara
Daivarāṭa pravara
Bāhvṛcya *Caraṇa*
Āśvalāyana *Śākhā*
Vātsa *gotra*
Pañcārṣeya *pravara*
Jamadagni *pravara*
Kauśika *gotra*
Tryārṣeya *pravara*
Vasiṣṭha *gotra*

Vasiṣṭha *pravara*
Yajurveda
Kāśyapa *gotra*
Garga-Apanya-Aṅgirasa *pravarah*
Vāhṛca *caraṇa*
Bhārgava-Abharvya-*Cyavana*
Ātmavana-Yamadagni pravara
Chāndoga *caraṇa*
Kauthuma *Śākhā*
Kāśyapa-Naidhruva
Vātsyāyana *pravara*
Yajurveda *Śākhā*
Kṛṣṇātreya *gotra*
Ātreya-Arcanansa-Savasma *pravarah*
Maudgalya *gotra*
Bhākramyasva *pravara*
Āṅgirasa *anupravara*
Rohita *gotra*
Rohita *aṣṭaka*
Viśvāmitra *pravara*
Kaṇva *gotra*
Āṅgirasa-Ajāmīḍha-Kaṇva pravarah
Āśvalāyana *śākhā*
Bābhṛca *caraṇa*
Kauṇḍinya gotra
Kauṇḍinya-Vasiṣṭha-Maitrāvaruṇa *pravara*
Upamanyu *gotra*
Bāhvṛca *śākhā* of Ṛgveda
Atri-Ātreya-Arcanaṅśa *pravarah*
Gautama *gotra*
Autathya *pravara*
Āṅgirasa *anupravara*
Bhārgava *anupravara*
Vaidhṛte *pravara*
Taittirīya *Śākhā*
Vārhaspatya *anupravara*
Piṅgala *gotra*
Jātakarṇṇa *pravara*
Taittirīya *śākhā*
Ariṣṭasena *gotra*

It is noteworthy that the donee Brāhmaṇas in the Bhauma-Kara as well as the Bhañja plates almost invariably have the epithet *Bhaṭṭa* and often also *Swāmī*. For instance, in the Neulpur plate, out of the 204 names there is not even one without either the prefix *Bhaṭṭa* or suffix *Swāmī* and about half of them have both. This is just like the Nidhanpur plate of Assam of a century earlier. The practice remained in full force in the Bhañja plates of Orissa but in Assam, in the post-seventh century period it appears to have become weaker. As to the significance of the term *Bhaṭṭa*, it appears that it only meant a man of great learning and has no other implication.

An in-depth analysis of the data assembled in the above paragraphs is likely to reveal that the Brāhmaṇa scholars of certain Vedic schools, i.e., *gotras*, *caraṇas* and *śākhās* were being particularly patronized by the rulers of Kāmarūpa and Kaliṅga-Utkala during the seventh to twelfth century AD. *Prima facie*, majority of these Brāhmaṇas appear to be Yajurvedīs and Sāmavedīs. Such preference must have resulted in exchange of scholars between the two regions.

One of the earliest of such instances is met with in a copper plate inscription found at Gurandi near Parlakemudi in the Ganjam district in Orissa. By this charter a Brāhmaṇa named Viṣṇusomācārya was donated some land by Jayavarmā, brother of king Anantavarmā in the year 204. The donee is stated to have been a resident of Śṛngāṭika *agrahāra* in the Kāmarūpa *viṣaya* belonging to the Parāśara *gotra* and well-versed in the *Veda-vedāṅga*. Scholars have held the era used in the charter to be the Gaṅgā era that commenced in AD 496 and Śṛngāṭika has been identified with the village Singri near Tezpur in Assam.[27] Might not this Viṣṇusoma ācārya have belonged to the family of one of the Nidhanpur donees with Soma-ending name? This inscription thus conclusively establishes that as early as AD 700, i.e., even before the advent of the Bhauma-Kara dynasty, the Kāmarūpa Brāhmaṇas were being patronized in countries far beyond their homeland, in the far away Kaliṅga region. Evidently, it was because of their great scholarship. Were they originally from the Madhyadeśa?

That the Brāhmaṇas and other scholars from the Madhyadeśa were migrating to eastern India right from the Gupta period is a well-established fact. The Paharpur copper plate[28] of the Gupta era 159 (AD 479) records a gift of land to the disciples of the Jaina Ācārya Guhanandin living at the village Vaṭagohālī but originally from Kāśī. A number of copper plate grants of the fifth century have been found at Damodarpur in the district of Dinajpur (Bangladesh), which record donations of lands in the Koṭivarṣa *viṣaya* in Puṇḍravardhana *bhukti*. This Koṭivarṣa was evidently situated in the Himalayan foothills adjoining the region of Mithilā in the west and that of Kāmarūpa in the east. In the plate dated G.E. 214 (AD 534) there is mention of Amṛtadeva, born of a noble family of Ayodhyā to whom land was allotted on payment of the usual fee in connection with the worship in the shrine of Śvetavarāhasvāmin, an *avatār* of Viṣṇu.[29] The places from where the donee Brāhmaṇas migrated is rarely mentioned in the inscriptions of the Pālas of Bengal and the same is true of the early rulers of Kaliṅga like the Māṭharas and Vasiṣṭhas.[30] In the copper plates of the Śalastaṁbha and Brahmapāla rulers of Kāmarūpa and those of the Bhañjas of Khiñjalīmaṇḍala of Orissa, however, we find many such references. These records belong to the period from the eighth to twelfth century AD. One of the important places from where these Brāhmaṇas migrated was Śrāvastī in ancient Uttara Kośala, included in the empire of the Guptas and, subsequently, that of Kānyakubja. Some families from Śrāvastī seem to have migrated and settled in certain tracts of land in eastern India from where they moved on to the different kingdoms of Bengal, Assam, Orissa and Mithilā in search of patronage. The region where the Brāhmaṇas from Śrāvastī were concentrated was given the name Śrāvastī *maṇḍala* after their original home. It was located in north Bengal and was most probably a part of the Kāmarūpa kingdom. One of the central villages in this *maṇḍala* was Takārī. One of the earliest mentions of Takārī is found in the Baud plates of Raṇabhañjadeva of the year 58 (AD 794).[31] From this we learn that Bhaṭṭa Śubhadāma, son of Vṛṣabhadāma, an emigrant from the Takārī village in the Śāvaṭhideśa was now resident in Bhaṭataralā village in the Oḍra viṣaya and by this charter he was donated land in the Turallā village. Incidentally, we are again reminded of the Dāma-ending names in the Nidhanpur charter. This Takārī again finds mention four centuries later in the Antirigrama plates of Jayabhañjadeva[32] in which the donee Śri Jagadhara, son of Paṇḍita Dharādhera is described as *Madhyadeśīyā Ṭākārīvipra Samudbhava* and hailing from Paṭavāḍapāṭaka in Dakṣina Tośalī. This donee has been identified with the donee of the Kapoteśvara plate of Aniyaṅkabhīma III and, therefore, the record is dateable to the early thirteenth century AD.[33]

Śrāvastī finds mention in the charters of Kāmarūpa as well. Thus, the Guakuchi Grant of Indrapāla (late tenth century)[34] records the donation of land to the pious Brāhmaṇa, Devadeva of the Vaināma village in Sāvathī. The donated land is obviously in Sāvathī proving that Sāvathī was located within the domains of Indrapāla, i.e., Kāmarūpa. In the Śubhaṅkarapāṭaka plates of Dharmapāla (late eleventh century),[35] the great grandson of Indrapala, we again get a mention of Śrāvastī. The donated land was located in the Dijjinā *viṣaya* which is identified with Dinajpur district in Bangladesh. Then we have the Silimpur inscription which speaks of the tract of land named Śrāvastī and refers to Jayapāla, a king of Kāmarūpa. This record informs us that the Brāhmaṇa Prahāsa migrated from Tarkkarī in Śrāvastī and to him the land was donated in the village Bālagrāma in Puṇḍra.[36] The Kāmarūpa king Jayapāla under reference was probably the son of Dharmapāla and the last ruler of the Brahmapāla dynasty. It is probably this king who was vanquished by Rāmapāla, the Pāla king of Bengal. Tarkkarī of the Silimpur inscription is clearly the same as Tarkārī which is named in the Orissan epigraphs mentioned above. Another important centre of the learned Brāhmaṇas of Śrāvastī was Krosañja mentioned in the charter of Dharmapāla. As observed by D.C. Sircar, the same place seems to have been referred to in several other epigraphs with slight variations in spelling lilke Kroḍañja, Kolañca, Kolaṅga, Koḍañjī, etc; he has, if fact, discussed the importance of this place in detail.[37] This place is named as Kolañcha in the tenth century Taltali plate of Dharmamahādevī, one of the rare Bhauma-Kara records specifying the place from where the donee had migrated.[38] D.C. Sircar has also surmised that Takārī and Kroḍañja were originally villages in the original Śrāvastī and the migrants from those villages carried those names to their settlements in the new Śrāvastī in north Bangal.

While Śrāvastī *maṇḍala* in north Bengal was named after the original Śrāvastī, we find mention of a Pāñcāla *viṣaya* in Uttara Tośalī where the lands donated by the Neulpur charter were located.[39] No doubt, this *viṣaya* was so named because of concentration of Brāhmaṇas migrating from Pāncāla in Madhyadeśa. Another place of Madhyadeśa that finds mention in some records is Kauśambī. The Nalanda Stone slab inscription of the time of Mahīpāladeva (early eleventh century)[40] records a gift from Bālāditya, a migrant from Kauśambī and now settled in the village Tailaḍhākā, who was a Mahāyana Buddhist. Another mention of Kauśambī is found in the Belava copper-plate of Bhojavarman of the twelfth century.[41] In this record the donated land is described as situated in the Kauśambī Aṣṭagacchakhaṇḍala of the Adhaḥpatana *maṇḍala* in the Puṇḍra *bhukti* and the donee, Romadevaśarman, as an immigrant from Madhyadeśa.

Then, there are a few more records in which the donees are described simply as emigrants from Madhyadeśa without specifying the place in Madhyadeśa. An early record of this type is the undated Baud plate of Rāṇaka Raṇabhañja[42] by which Bhaṭṭaputra Devahara, son of Bhaṭṭaputra Kāchila, an emigrant from Madhyadeśa—*madhyadeśavinirgata*—and now resident of Mahiṣipadraka, evidently somewhere in Khiñjalīmaṇḍala, was granted some lands. In Orissa we also come across migration from Vārendrī. Thus, in the Orissa Museum Plates of Mahārāja Neṭṭabhañjadeva[43] the donee Ivadattaka is said to be an immigrant from Tribhuvanapura in Vārendrī. It is reasonable to presume that this Brāhmaṇa originally came from Madhyadeśa and settled in Vārendrī before moving to Orissa. In yet another record, the Ganjam plates of Vidyādharabhañja,[44] the donee Bhaṭṭa Purandara is said to have migrated from Taḍisamā *viṣaya* in Vārebdhī. The date of this record is the year 174 (=910 AD?) and Vārebdhī appears to be the engraver's error for Vārendrī.

It has been observed earlier that the Pāla records generally do not mention the original home of the donees. The Bangaon plate of Vigrahapāla III, however, seems to be an exception. This inscription records the grant of land in a locality called Vasukavarta in the Hoḍreya *viṣaya* of Tīrabukti to the Brāhmaṇa Ghaṇṭukaśarman who originally came from Kolañca.[45] This inscription thus gives us a clue to the settlement of Madhyadeśa Brāhmaṇas in Mithilā. Another reference to Kolañca is found in the Panchobh copper plate of Saṅgramagupta. The donee, Kumārasvāmin, is stated to be a grandson of Bhaṭṭa Śrīrāma who hailed from Kolañca and is said to have visited Tīrabhukti. The donor appears to be a feudatory of the Karṇāta kings of Mithilā and the record is dateable to the twelfth century AD.[46] The find place of the epigraph is in the Darbhanga district.

The facts brought together in the above paragraphs amply demonstrate that between the sixth and thirteenth centuries large scale movement of Brāhmaṇa scholars was taking place in eastern India between Kāmarūpa, Kaliṅga, Mithilā and, Gauḍa or Vaṅga. This was thus the period when the eastern India was experiencing the last and most intense phase of 'Aryanization'. The most prominent among these Brāhmaṇa ambassadors of culture were the ones who originally belonged to Śrāvastī. This seems to be the origin of the belief amongst the Brāhmaṇas and some other high castes in Bengal, Assam and Orissa that they came from Kanauj. After all, Śrāvastī was a part of the Kanauj empire during this period!

Before concluding this discussion it may be pointed out that the donees in the Bhauma-Kara as well as the Bhañja plates are almost invariably given the title *Bhaṭṭa* just as we find in the Kāmarūpa plates. There is, however, little justification in considering the Bhaṭṭa Brāhmaṇas as a class as has been done by Biswarup Das when he states "The Bhaṭṭa Brāhmaṇas also enjoyed the patronage of the Gaṅga monarch Anantavarman Coḍagaṅga. Mahāśivagupta Tīvaradeva, the Somavaṁśī King of Kośala, granted villages to Bhaṭṭa Brahmans named Bhaṭṭa Bhavadeva, Bhaṭṭa Haradatta... etc."[47] Nowhere in the *smṛtis*, or in the works of the *nibandhakāras* do we find any mention of this class of Brāhmaṇas; *Bhaṭṭa* appears to be only a title added to the name of a person to indicate that he was a great scholar just as the title *Paṇḍita* is used. Preponderance of Bhaṭṭas amongst the donees in Kāmarūpa and Utkala only shows that the rulers were trying to raise the level of education, particularly the Vedic knowledge, in their kingdoms by settling these scholars. It is also noteworthy that almost all land grants have been made according to the *Bhūmichidranyāya.* This was so in the case of Bengal also during the Pāla and Sena rules. All this cumulative evidence goes to show that between the sixth and twelfth centuries AD the rulers of all east Indian states were making great efforts to 'Aryanize' their kingdoms by inviting learned Brāhmaṇas from the Madhyadeśa and settling them on large tracts of land. These migrants from the Madhyadeśa settled in Mithilā and Puṇḍravardhana in the first instance and from there moved on to new locations in Kāmarūpa, Vaṅga and Utkala. The efforts of these rulers bore fruit very soon as the next few centuries witnessed great intellectual activity in the entire eastern India. Mithilā, Bengal, Kāmarūpa and Utkala produced some of the greatest poets and philosophers as well as commentators on the Dharmaśāstra during the eighth to twelfth centuries and the tradition continued right up to the eighteenth century.

It has not been possible to make a detailed study of the *Veda, Śākhā, caraṇa, gotra,* etc., of the donee Brāhmaṇas as found in the epigraphs under notice. A through statistical analysis of their distribution and relating them to the position obtaining today will surely lead to interesting inferences. Just a couple of hints for further research may be made at this stage. Kolancha was a seat of Yajurvedī Brāhmaṇas of the Śāndilya *gotra.* Is it possible to trace their descendents at present in Assam, Bengal, Orissa and Mithilā? A casual look at the list of *Śākha, Carana,* etc. given in the above paragraphs shows that the most common *śākhā* is the Vajasaneyī; with a few exceptions all the donees belong to the *Yajurveda* and *Sāmaveda.* It is significant to note that the Maithila Brāhmaṇas today belong to these two Vedas only. The majority of the Yajurvedīs are adherents of the Mādhyandina *śākhā.* Again, the Maithila Brāhmaṇas are divided into two categories, viz., Bācasnaī (=Vājasaneyī) and chāndoga and each group is strictly exogamous.[48]

NOTES AND REFERENCES

1. D.C. Sircar, 'Aryanism in Bengal' in *Studies in the Society and Administration of Ancient and Medieval India,* chapter I, pp. 1-30.
2. N.N. Vasu, *Archaeological Survey of Mayur-bhanj,* p. lxiv.
3. Snigdha Tripathy, 'The Unique Neulpur Charter of Subhakara II of the Bhaumakara Dynasty and a Local Tradition of Viraja Kshetra' in *OHRJ,* vol. XLII, No. 1 to 4, pp. 35-46.

4. D. Sarma, *Kāmarūpaśāsanāvalī Part II,* Texts, pp. 7-18 (Dubi) and pp. 19-32 (Nidhanpur).
5. K.L. Barua, 'Kausika and Kusiara' in *Indian Culture,* vol. I No. 3, January 1935, pp. 421-32.
6. D.C. Sircar, *Indian Epigraphy,* p. 398.
7. D. Sarm*a,* op. cit., pp. 43-50.
8. Ibid., pp. 51-55.
9. Ibid., pp. 71-78.
10. Ibid., pp. 65-70.
11. Ibid., pp. 78-87.
12. Ibid., pp. 88-90.
13. Ibid., pp. 91-98.
14. Ibid., pp. 99-102.
15. Ibid., pp. 103-118.
16. Ibid., pp. 119-123.
17. Ibid., pp. 124-131.
18. Ibid., pp. 132-139.
19. Snigdha Tripathy, *Inscriptions of Orissa,* vol. II, pp. 105-109 (Chaurasi) and pp. 110-115 (Neulpur).
20. Snigdha Tripathy, *Inscriptions of Orissa,* vol. I, pp. 98-99.
21. Ibid., pp. 102-103.
22. Ibid., pp. 104-105.
23. Ibid., pp. 106-107.
24. Ibid., pp. 114-115.
25. Ibid., pp. 116-117.
26. Ibid., pp. 124-125.
27. Jogendra Chandra Ghosh, 'A Kamarupa Brahman in Kalinga in AD 700' in *JARS,* 1936, pp. 113-15. P.C. Choudhary in *The History of Civilisation of the People of Assam to the Twelfth Century* AD., p. 384 has taken the date of this grant to be AD 922, the basis of which is not clear. Further, R.D. Banerji in *History of Orissa,* vol. I, p. 239, holds that the Ganga era commenced in the year AD 741 which will yield AD 945 as the date of our record. All these variations, however, do not affect our contention.
28. Ramaranjan Mukherji and Sachindra Kumar Maity, *Corpus of Bengal Inscriptions bearing on History and Civilization of Bengal,* pp. 53-58.
29. Ibid., pp. 70-75.
30. Snigdha Tripathy, op. cit., p. 25.
31. Snigdha Tripathy, *Inscriptions of Orissa,* vol. VI, pp. 112-18.
32. Ibid., pp. 209-214.
33. Ibid., p. 214.
34. D. Sarma, op. cit., pp. 99-102.
35. Ibid., pp. 124-131.
36. Ibid., Part I-General Introduction, p. 80.
37. D.C. Sircar, 'Aryanism in Bengal' in *Studies in the Society and Administration of Ancient and Medieval India,* Chapter I, pp. 22ff.
38. Snigdha Tripathy, *Inscriptions of Orissa,* vol. II, pp. 216-21.

39. Ibid., pp. 110-115.
40. Mukherji and Maity, op. cit., pp. 208-09.
41. Ibid., pp. 234-44.
42. Snigdha Tripathy, *Inscriptions of Orissa*, vol. VI, pp. 119-24.
43. Ibid., pp. 156-161.
44. Ibid., pp. 132-37.
45. D.C. Sircar, op. cit., pp. 21-22.
46. Upendra Thakur, 'Samgramagupta of the Panchobh Copper-plate' in *Some aspect of Ancient Indian History and culture*, chapter III, pp. 29-33.
47. Biswarup Das, *Orissa Social Cultural and Religious Aspects*, p. 96-97. In this work the author has also discussed a number of land grants, the names and titles of the donee Brahmaṇas and the places of their origin at pp. 20-36. These discussions appear to support the findings of the present study.
48. Makhan Jha, *Civilizational Regions of Mithila and Mahakoshal*, p. 38.

Chapter 7

Religious Traditions and Legends

JAGANNĀTHA AND MĀDHAVA CULTS IN ORISSA

Jagannātha Puri, or simply Puri, or the Puruṣottama Kṣetra and its presiding deity, Puruṣottama Jagannātha and the stories of his origin are too well known to be described afresh.[1] We shall, however, take note of certain facts that are strictly relevant for the present study.

The present temple of Jagannātha was built in the early twelfth century by Coḍagaṅgadeva but the antiquity of the cult of Jagannātha is decidedly much older. The legends in the Purāṇas, particularly in the *Brahma Purāṇa* and the *Utkala Khaṇḍa* of the *Skanda Purāṇa*, tell us that originally in a forest on the sea-shore there was a blue stone that used to be worshipped by Viśvavasu, a chief of the Śavara tribe and Indradyumna, the king of Avantī, made attempts to procure it. The king did not succeed in this and was instructed by a divine voice to have the image of the Lord carved out of a log of wood that he would find floating in the sea. Accordingly, he got three images carved and installed them in a temple. The blue stone worshipped by Viśvavasu got metamarphosed as the god Nīlamādhava and finally Jagannātha on the blue hill, the Nīlācala. It appears that all religions prevailing in Orissa at different periods of history appropriated this deity into their respective systems.[2] The local tribal origin of the deity is clear from the Purāṇic account itself. Then, the scholars have traced a Buddhist origin of Jagannātha and even Tāntrik elements in his cult. No doubt, all these elements are traceable in the all-pervasive Jagannātha as he has evolved over the centuries and as he exists today. In the twelfth century he became synonymous with Viṣṇu and later with Kṛṣṇa. The triad of images in the temple was given a completely Vaiṣṇava identity; they are known as Balarāma, Subhadrā and Kṛṣṇa from left to right. Not only that, the fourth object, a pillar-like image, came to be identified as the *Sudarśana cakra.* The following facts about Jagannātha as found in the Purāṇic legends and current practices are of special interest for our study:

(i) The original tribal deity was a piece of blue stone; this came to be known as Nīlamādhava in the formal Hindu system.

(ii) Jagannātha is normally conceived of as a triad but, if and when, an image of his alone, i.e., the third image of Viṣṇu-Kṛṣṇa is made, it is called Dadhi Vāmana.[3]

(iii) The three images were carved out of a log of wood that had come floating to the sea-shore and which the king Indradyumna was ordered in a dream to collect and from which to have the images carved.

(iv) Indradyumna got the images carved and then built a temple for them; he also got a tank dug out nearby.

(v) Some divine tortoises carried on their backs stone blocks used for construction of the temple and, in a later age, testified to having done so when the buildership of the temple was disputed. The descendents of those tortoises inhabit the Indradyumna tank up to this day; no one is allowed to hurt them as they are considered sacred.

(vi) No caste distinction is recognized in any matter relating to the deity; people of all castes are expected to sit together and partake the Lord's *prasāda.*

(vii) Cooked cereal food—rice, *dāl* and vegetables—comprise the *prasāda* of the Lord unlike in other Vaiṣṇava shrines all over India where the food offered to the Lord consists of fruits, dry fruits, milk and milk products only. Of course, there are some exceptions too, particularly in the south and on occassions like Kṛṣṇa Janmāṣṭami when *Pañjīrī*—wheat flour fried in ghee with sugar—is eaten. Another exception is *besan laddoos* but that again is a sweet and not a cereal meal.

(viii) The wooden images of the deities are replaced by new ones during the *nava kalevara* every few years, when certain stellar configurations take place, and the old ones are consigned to flames at a spot near the temple known as 'Koilī Baikuṇṭha', i.e., solitary or unique heaven. The practice is clearly a residue of some ancient *tāntrik* ritual; in any case, it does suggest the original Jagannātha's connection with some event, ritual or cult involving the corpse or the *śmaśāna.*

(ix) The dust from the Koilī Baikuṇṭha, supposed to be mixed with the ashes of the past images, is collected by (in practice, sold to) the pilgrims who believe that burying it into the foundation while building a new house will bring good luck.[4] A connection with the Buddhist practice of building *Caityas* or *stupas* over the ashes and other remains of the dead is clearly discernible here.

(x) Inside the image of Jagannātha a secret object called the *Brahma* is kept and every time the image is replaced it is transferred to the new image in a secret ritual by the specially authorized priest. Some skeptics believe that the *Brahma* is nothing but a tooth of the Buddha that had reached the Kaliṅga country soon after his *parinirvāṇa* and is said to have been taken away later to Śri Lanka. These people believe that the story of the tooth's transit to Śri Lanka is fictitious.

(xi) There is another legend saying that when Kṛṣṇa passed away his dead body was placed on a pyre by Arjuna and Jarā whose arrow had killed him but it was not fully consumed by the fire and the navel portion remained unburnt. The two cremators then dumped the remaining portion into the sea and it is this object that came floating to the Puri sea-shore. Some believe that the *Brahma* is really the navel portion of Kṛṣṇa.[5] In this legend too, the Buddhist element may be seen as it is only in Buddhism that the relics of a dead body are venerated; the orthodox Hinduism does not allow any such practice.

(xii) The custom of employing *devadāsīs* in the Jagannātha temple was strongly in vogue till very recently. This custom is perhaps of the south Indian origin.

(xiii) Finally, the annual *ratha yātrā* of Jagannātha is one of the most spectacular religious events of India. The custom of such ceremonial procession of the deities is prevalent mostly in south India.

The relevance of picking out these few points from the hundreds of significant aspects of Jagannātha will become clear in the following paragraphs. Between the twelfth and the sixteenth centuries, i.e., from the time of Rāmānuja to Caitanya, the Vaiṣṇava character of Jagannātha attained perfection and the spread of his cult in and outside Orissa henceforth was only the Viṣṇu-Kṛṣna cult. An authority on Jagannātha has stated that after the Lakṣmaṇāvatī war (1245-46) "the spread of the cult of Jagannatha came to be facilitated by the construction of Jagannātha temples in east Madhya Pradesh, Assam, Manipur and the whole of Bengal."[6]

The above statement does not appear to be accurate as far as Assam is concerned. As we have noted in Chapter 5, supra, in Assam no temple or any other building antedating the sixteenth century is extant. The present author is not aware of the existence of any Jagannātha temple of even the post-sixteenth century; no ruins purporting to be those of a Jagannātha temple are found anywhere in Assam either. The only two exceptions, as far as I could ascertain, are the Baguan Jagannātha Mandir in the Goalpara subdivision of the district of the same name and the Jagannātha Devalaya in the Guwahati subdivision of the Kamrup district.[7] The former is said to be a Viṣṇu temple established by the people of the Nāth community but nothing is known about its antiquity. The other one is a modern temple less than two hundred years old. It is indeed somewhat surprising because Jagannātha Puri has always been one of the most popular places of pilgrimage for the people of Assam. However, in the legends and practices of the Hayagrīva Mādhava temple at Hajo we come across a number of aspects highly suggestive of its connection with the Jagannātha of Puri. These will be discussed in the following section of this chapter.

Before turning our attention to the Mādhava cult in Orissa, we may take note of a couple of further facts about Jagannātha. First, the antiquity of the *ratha yātrā* festival goes back to at least the eighth century because we find the ninth century poet Murāri stating in the prologue of his drama *Anargha Rāghava* that it was being presented before an elite gathering during the *yātrā* of Puruṣottama.[8]

Then there is an anecdote relating to the tenth century Maithila philosopher, Udayanācārya, in which the story of his visit to Puri is related. It is said that when he reached the temple, its doors were closed as he had reached beyond the hours prescribed for *darśana*. The scholar was furious and gave vent to his anger by addressing the Lord from outside as follows:

Aiśvaryamadamattosi māmavajñāyatiṣṭhasi
Punarbauddhāḥ samāyāte madādhīnā tava sthitiḥ

This *śloka* is well-known amongst the scholars of Mithilā. From this anecdote we may draw the following inferences, viz., (i) even in the tenth century the temple of Jagannātha was a glamorous place, (ii) Jagannātha's sanctity was recognized in Mithilā and (iii) disputes between the Buddhists and followers of some Brahmaṇical faith, possibly Vaiṣṇavas, had taken place in the past for appropriating Jagannātha and, it is likely that the support of the scholars from Mithilā was instrumental in ensuring victory for the latter.

After Jagannātha, we take up the cult of Mādhava. A number of shrines in Orissa are dedicated to Mādhava. As noted above, Jagannātha was earlier worshipped as Nīla Mādhava. It appears that the worship of Viṣṇu under the name of Mādhava was in great vogue before his appellation Jagannātha acquired popularity. A number of places where the Viṣṇu images are worshipped as Mādhava are located in the Prachi Valley;[9] some of them are enumerated below:

(i) Nīla Mādhava image at Chahata or Chhabati.
(ii) Viṣṇu image in the Mādhavānanda temple at Adaspur called Mādhava.
(iii) Eight Viṣṇu images known as Mādhavas kept outside the Śobhaneśvara temple at Niali.

(iv) Mādhavānanda image in a thirteenth century temple at Mādhava, eight km from Niali.
(v) A Viṣṇu image designated as Mādhava in the Amareśvara temple very close to the Nimapara-Astaranga Road, about two km from Chahata.
(vi) Mādhavānanda at Nilakanthapur.
(vii) Nīla Mādhava at Mudgala Mādhava, about five km from Jiunti.
(viii) Mādhava at Sudarśana Tīrtha.

Besides these, there are a number of Viṣṇu images at the various other places in the Prachi valley dateable from the seventh to the thirteenth century. It appears that in this region the four-armed Viṣṇu images as a class were named as Mādhava during this period. It will be interesting to study their iconographic features in detail to ascertain whether all of them belong to the Mādhava form of the *caturviṁśati mūrtis* of Viṣṇu as described in the various *Śilpa* texts.

Outside the Prachi valley, the tradition speaks of twelve Mādhava shrines in the Virajā *Kṣetra*, i.e., the Jajpur area. These have been named as Ādi Mādhava, Varāha Mādhava, Ananta Mādhava, Gadādhara Mādhava, Purṣottama Mādhava, Narakāṇtaka Mādhava, Bhoga Mādhava, Vāsudeva Mādhava, Yoga Mādhava, Campaka Mādhava, Harihara Mādhava and Siddha Mādhava.[10] Of these, only the temple of Varāha is still extant in Jajpur while even the sites of the other eleven are not traceable. The name Narakāṇtaka Mādhava appears to be significant. It is not a common or popular name of Kṛṣṇa even though it is included in th *Viṣṇu Śatanāma Stotraṁ*. Does it not point to some connection with Kāmarūpa?

TRADITIONS AT VIRAJĀ

Virajā (modern Jajpur) is one of the most ancient places of pilgrimage. Located on the Vaitarani river in the Cuttack district, Virajā as a place of pilgrimage finds mention in the *Mahābhārata* and the *Brahma Purāṇa*. In the latter, as many as twelve *ślokas* are devoted to the Virajā *kṣetra*. These were elaborated in *Kapila Saṁhitā*, a fourteenth century text composed in Utkala. Further, a late medieval work titled *Virajākṣetramāhātmya* embodies all the early and late traditions about the *kṣetra* current in the fifteenth-sixteenth century when it was compiled.[11] The presiding deity of the *kṣetra*, Virajādevī is none other than the Mahiṣāsuramardinī. The image being worshipped in the Virajā temple is that of a two-handed Durgā that is dateable to the Gupta period.[12] For the purpose of the present study, however, the more noteworthy is the legend of Nābhigayā. It is a small well in the premises of the Virajā temple in which the pilgrims offer *piṇḍa* to their ancestors. The tradition is quite ancient since it is mentioned in the *Brahma Purāṇa.* The legend says that in the ancient days there lived a virtuous demon—an *asura*—named Gayāsura whose severe austerities greatly alarmed the gods. Responding to their pleas, Lord Viṣṇu went to the *asura* and extolling his virtues advised him to surrender his pure body for the purpose of sacrifice. Gayāsura agreed to do so on the condition that the places where his head, feet and the navel fell at the time of his death would become great *tīrthas* on the earth and people offering *piṇḍa* to their ancestors at these places would become immune to the tortures of hell. Viṣṇu accepted. Gayāsura's head fell at Gayā, the feet at the Mahendra mountain and his navel at Virajā. This spot at Virajā thenceforth came to be known as Gayā-nābhi or Nābhigayā.[13]

In the historical times we find many references to the Virajā *maṇḍala* and Virajā *nagara* in the epigraphs from the sixth century. Guhadevapāṭaka, later called Guheśvarapāṭaka, the capital of the Bhauma-Karas was located in the vicinity of this city. The city of Virajā continued to exist alongside Guhadevapāṭaka as we find its mention in the Dhauli Cave Inscription of Śāntikara, of the year 93 (AD 829)[14] and the undated Ganeśgumpha Inscription[15] of the time of the same ruler. Then, there is at least one epigraph, viz., the Bada Khimedi Plates of the Gaṅga Mahārājā Jayavarman, of Śvetaka, issued in Saṁvat 20 (AD 756) implying that the seat of the Bhauma-Kara sovereign Unmaṭṭakeśarin (i.e., Śivakara II) was at Virajā.[16] It appears that Guhadevapāṭaka and Virajā were sometimes treated as synonymous because of their close proximity.

HAYAGRĪVA AND OTHER MĀDHAVAS IN ASSAM

About 22 km west-north-west of Guwahati in Assam is situated the small town of Hajo which is famous for the temple of Hayagrīva Mādhava; from the later part of the sixteenth century for a few decades Hajo was the capital town of Koch-Hajo as the eastern half of the partitioned Koch kingdom was called. Hajo is surrounded by a number of hillocks, each of which is topped by a temple or a mosque of the Ahom period. The most famous of these hillocks is named 'Maṇikūta' on which the temple of Hayagrīva Mādhava (HM) is situated. At the northern foot of the fifty metres high hill, there is an ancient tank called '*Apunarbhava*' from which a roughly-paved causeway leads to the gateway of the temple at the hill-top.

Regarding Hayagrīva and how his name got associated with Mādhava there are a number of Purāṇic accounts that, like all legends, are not logically correlated. To begin with, Hayagrīva is one the twenty four *avatāras* of Viṣṇu.

The *Mahābhārata* and the *Devī Purāṇa* state that Viṣṇu had adopted the form of Hayagrīva for killing certain demons; the former names these demons as Madhu and Kaitabha while the latter names the demon also as Hayagrīva.[17] In the *Brahma Khaṇḍa* of the *Skanda Purāṇa*, however, a completely different story involving rivalry between Viṣṇu and Brahmā is narrated in which certain circumstances resulted in substitution of the Viṣṇu's head by the head of one of the horses of the Sun-god's chariot.[18] The *Bhāgavata Purāṇa* says that Hayaśira is one of the *avatāras* of Viṣṇu; it also says that Viṣṇu in his *matsya* incarnation had killed the demon Hayagrīva who had stolen the Vedas.[19] The *Brahma* and *Viṣṇu Purāṇas* tell us that Śrikṛṣṇa killed five *asuras* led by Muru and Hayagrīva before entering the city of Prāgjyotiṣapura for destroying Narakāsura.[20] The *Kālikā Purāṇa* follows the same story and adds that Hayagrīva was the guardian of the northern gate of Prāgjyotiṣapura.[21] The *Garuḍa* and *Matsya Purāṇas* also speak of the Hayagrīva *avatāra* of Viṣṇu and describe his iconography. The features of Hayagrīva described in the former correspond to those of the *Vāmana* form of the *Caturviṁśati mūrtis* given in the same text.[22] The connection between Hayagrīva and Vāmana is, however, not made clear. The iconography of Hayagrīva according to the *Matsya Purāṇa* is most interesting: his head is that of a horse, in his four hands he holds *Śaṅkha, cakra, gadā* and *Veda*, his left and right foot are placed respectively on *śeṣanāga* and a tortoise.[23] The present author has not seen such an image anywhere and there is little chance to ascertain if the HM image corresponds to this description. Significantly, even a *Pāñcarātra* text, still extant, goes by the name *Hayaśīrṣa Pāñcarātra*. More interesting than the said Purāṇic accounts is a popular legend based on the *Kālikā Purāṇa* (78.76-81) which is narrated in an eighteenth century Assamese poem *Maṇikūṭa* (unpublished) by an obscure poet named Sri Rama Chandra. According to this legend, once upon a time, there lived on the Maṇikūṭa hill, a demon named Jvarāsura—the Fever demon—who was also called Hayāsura—the Horse demon— and who used to torment all people. At a nearby place, was the *āśrama* of Aurva Muni, constantly practicing severe austerities. He prayed to Viṣṇu and telling him of the atrocities of Jvarāsura, requested him to destroy the demon and make Maṇikūṭa his abode. The Lord accordingly appeared on the scene and proceeded to kill Jvarāsura. Before dying the demon prayed to Viṣṇu that now that he was ready to depart from this world would the Lord be pleased to reside at the Maṇikūṭa hill for ever in the guise of Hayāsura, so that whoever worshipped Viṣṇu at this place would automatically remember the demon who had obtained *mukti* at the hands of the Lord. Viṣṇu accepted the prayer and hence the Mādhava at Maṇikūṭa is in the form of Hayagrīva.[24] It is also stated that after killing Jvarāsura, Viṣṇu suffered from fever, so he took bath in the Apunarbhava tank and was cured.

Architectural features of the HM temple have already been dealt with in Chapter 5, supra, and we have noted that the original temple at HM dates back to the eighth or ninth century. This was the period of close cultural contacts between Kāmarūpa and Kaliṅga-Utkala following Harṣadeva's conquest of the Orissan lands.

In the sanctum of the HM temple, five stone images are installed in a row on a platform. The arrangement is strongly reminiscent of the Jagannātha triad installed on the *ratnavedī* in the temple at Puri, particularly for the fact that there are no steps leading to the platform. There is no way to know how the images in the original temple were installed but in the reconstructed sixteenth century temple (the present temple), it seems, the model of Puri was consciously adopted. The five images are collectively called *Pañca Mādhava* and individually named, from the left to right, as Vāsudeva, Govinda Mādhava, Hayagrīva Mādhava, Dvitīya Mādhava and Garuḍa Viṣṇuvāhana. The principal deity HM has the largest image and appears to be in the sitting posture. The interior of the sanctum is quite dark and the images are always heavily covered with clothes and garlands of flowers; it is, therefore, impossible to study their iconographic features or to take their photograph. In 1934, K.L.Barna had published a paper on Hajo[25] in which he had extensively quoted from Dr. Waddell's book *Lamaism* (described as a rare book by Barua). It appears that Dr. Waddell had visited the HM temple towards the end of the nineteenth century when he recorded quite different names for the images except HM and Dvitīya Mādhava; in fact it appears that the images have been given different names from time to time according to the whims and fancy of the priest in charge, called the *Doloi.* Only HM and Dvitīya Mādhava have retained their names for over two centuries; for, the name of HM is found in the dedicatory inscription[26] of the year 1583 itself and that of Dvītīya Mādhava also occurs in an inscription of the Śaka year 1721 (AD 1799) in which a grant of land in favour of Dvitīya Mādhava by the Ahom king Kamaleśvara Siṁha[27] is recorded.

HM is also worshipped by the Buddhists of Bhutan whose border is barely a hundred kms away. They come down to Hajo every winter for worshipping HM; earlier, even pilgrims from Tibet used to come. They call the main image as *Munirmuni Mahāmuni,* or simply *Mahāmuni.* Similarly, the other images have also been given Buddhist names by them. The Lama informant of Dr. Waddell had given the names of the four images as Ugyan Guru, Dorje Dolo, Sakya Thuba and Sencha Muni. My informant, being a Brāhmaṇa from Hajo was not quite comfortable with the Tibetan names or language and could not tell me the Buddhist names of the Pañca Mādhava. Hajo is a sacred place for the followers of Tibetan Buddhism. The sanctity of the place is, however, not derived from the temple of Mahāmuni; it is really the other way round, for the Buddhists of Tibet and Bhutan identify Hajo with Kuśinagara, the place where the Buddha attained *parinirvāṇa.* The details of this belief and how a replica of the spot at Hajo where the Buddha is said to have been cremated has been made at least at four places in Tibet have been recorded in the paper of K.L.Barua under reference. The pilgrims from Bhutan still collect the dust from this spot in Hajo. It is interesting that the belief of Hajo being Kuśinagara is endorsed and entertained by the people of Hajo as well. It is significant that a Buddhist Tāntrik deity is also named Hayagrīva.

Now we come to the most interesting legend about the making of the HM image as current among the local people and also contained in the *Yoginī Tañtra,* a sixteenth century work composed in Kāmarūpa. According to this legend, when the king Indradyumna collected the log of wood that had come floating to the sea-shore at Puri, he got seven images made out of it; three were installed as Jagannātha at Puri, two were installed in Śvetadvīpa (unidentified) and two were brought to Hajo. One of them was the HM image and the other was of Viṣṇu in his *matsya avatāra* and both were installed on the Maṇikūta. The *Yoginī Tantra,* however gives a more elaborate description of the distribution of the images: the main (*mūla*) portion in the Oḍradeśa, the torso (*kabandha*) portion in Kaśmīradeśa as Āditya, the top (*ūrdhva*) portion as Āditya at Śoṇa, two top-most portions in Kāmarūpa and the lower portion on the Malayagiri. It further says, "On the *Maṇikūṭa* are installed the deities called Haya and Mādhava."[28]

I am inclined to think this second image is the one named Dvitīya Mādhava. In any case, the entire legend might really mean that the images in the HM temple were imported from Orissa. It is likely that the whole legend was fabricated around the time of the reconstruction of the HM temple in AD 1583 because it is not found in the *Kālikā Purāṇa* of the late ninth century. Significantly, the *Kālikā Purāṇa* does mention Maṇikūṭa as the abode of Viṣṇu in the form of Matsyadhvaja.[29]

The close resemblance between certain aspects of Jagannātha and HM are unmistakable. *Vaiṣṇava* character of the two deities, their association with Buddhism as well as with the cult of Death or a corpse, the tradition of Koilī Baikuṇṭha of Jagannātha and the Buddha's cremation ground at Hajo surely point to an exchange of traditions. Carving out of the images at Jagannātha and Hajo from the same log of wood puts the final seal of confirmation to the evidence of such exchange. I may also mention that on the south of the Maṇikūṭa hill there is a vast depression in the land which is called as Varāha Kuṇḍa but more often as *Kekorā Sāgara,* or simply as *Sāgara.* This depression is clearly the dried up bed of some ancient natural lake. It appears that to make HM's analogy complete with Jagannātha the people named this lake as Sāgara, i.e., the Sea. This depression could even be the old abandoned bed of the Brahmaputra which is believed to have been flowing in the ancient days by the Maṇikuṭa hill. It is pertinent to note that on account of its vastness this great river was often called a *sindhu* or *sāgara* (as for example, in the tenth Century Bargaon plates of Ratnapāla). Another significant aspect of HM is that his *prasāda* consists of cooked cereal food—clearly a practice imported from Jagannātha. The Apunarphava tank near the HM temple is clearly the counterpart of the Indradyumna tank near the Jagannātha temple. The Hajo tank contains a large number of big fishes; like the tortoises of the Indradyumna tank these fish are also considered sacred and no one is allowed to hurt them in any way. All these may have been in vogue in the original temple or may have been started only when the new temple was built. In Chapter 5, supra, we have proposed that the builder of the HM temple, King Raghudeva, might have invited architects from Orissa to build a flawless temple. The Orissan legends and practices may have come at the same time. Very significantly, the code of worship of HM contained in the *Yoginī Tantra* is modelled on the *Pūjā Vidhi* of Jagannātha of Puri as found in the *Brahma Purāṇa.*[30]

There is a distinct possibility that the exchange of legends and practices commenced in the eighth-ninth century. In addition to those noted above, another practice apparently borrowed from Orissa is the *devadāsī* system. The HM temple is one of the very few temples in Assam where the system was prevalent till very recently. In Assam the *devadāsī* was called *naṭī.*[31] The present author is inclined to think that the system was imported from Utkala during the time of Vanamālāvarmadeva, the fifth in descent from Harṣavarmādeva, in the ninth century. In his Tezpur as well as Parvatiya Plates we find the temples and beautiful dancers and courtesans mentioned in the same breath.[32] True, the inscriptions do not overtly connect the two but the general tenor of the description suggests that these dancers belonged to the temple of Kāmeśvara-Mahāgaurī named in the epigraph. It is of interest to note that Karṇāṭī damsels are mentioned in particular. May we be pardoned for imagining that when the *devadāsī* system was introduced into Orissa from the south of India, some dancers were also imported from the Karṇāṭadeśa and, in course of time, some of them found their way to Kāmarūpa? After all, it must have taken some time, a couple of centuries say, to recruit local women for the new and strange system. The tradition of *ratha yātrā* at Jagannātha was also imported from south India. In an abridged form it existed at the HM also. Temple chariots are not found in any temple of Assam. At HM also it is no more extant but the remnants of an ivory *siṁhāsana* on which the ceremonial image of HM used to be placed luring the procession can still be seen in the office of the *Doloi.*[33] At the time of Dr. Waddell's visit, however, a wheelless car was still there on which the ceremonial images used to be taken out in a procession.

With the traditions of Jagannātha, those of Virajā also got mixed up somewhere on their way to Kāmarūpa. That the legend of Jvarāsura or Hayāsura is clearly the Kāmarūpa version of the Virajā legend of Gayāsura needs hardly any convincing. Yet, it is pertinent to note that about twelve km to the south of HM is the village of Sualkuchi on the bank of the Brahmaputra. The place is famous as an old centre of silk production but, significantly, it is also recognized as a very suitable place for offering *piṇḍa* to one's ancestors. Shades of Nābhigayā, undoubtedly!

We may now turn to certain other shrines in Assam associated with the name Mādhava.[34] These are as follows:

(i) Kūrma Mādhab Devālaya in the Guwahati sub-division.
(ii) Saubhāgya Mādhab Devālaya in the Nagaon sub-division.
(iii) Gopāl Mādhab Devālaya in the same sub-division.
(iv) Mādhab Gosāin in the same sub-division.
(v) Saubhāgya Mādhab Mandir in the Tezpur sub-division.
(vi) Dulāl Mādhab Devālaya in the same sub-division.
(vii) Sūrya Mādhab Devālaya in the same sub-division.

All these shrines are either in utter ruins or of very recent origin. For example, the last-named is known to have been built by the Ahom king Gadādhara Siṁha (late seventeenth century)[35] and about the first one, which does not exist any more, the only known fact is that the king Śiva Siṁha (early eighteenth century) granted some lands to it.[36] The author, however, believes that the origin of all these temples goes back to the early medieval period. The belief is based on what I found at the Saubhāgya Mādhab and Gopāl Mādhab Devālayas in Nagaon. Both of them are located near Kaliabor, a large village about forty km east of the district town of Nagaon.

The only trace of the temple that survives in both cases is the brick-made plinth of their *garbhagṛha* (measuring about 5m x 5m) to a height of thirty to forty cm. The original image in both cases is kept in these *garbhagṛhas* by the local villagers. Both the images are of the four-armed Viṣṇu in the sitting posture; made of black basalt these are easily dateable to the ninth-tenth century AD.

Besides the above Mādhava shrines and images, dozens of Viṣṇu images may be seen at the various sites in the lower and central Assam; majority of them are of the *sthānaka* variety and dateable from the eighth to the thirteenth century. Quite a few of them have been shifted to the Assam State Museum at Guwahati or to the various district and site museums.[37] A detailed typological study of these images and their comparison with their counterparts in the Prachi valley of Orissa is likely to be very rewarding. As a matter of interest, it may be observed that the images of the Deopani type (cf. Chapter 5, supra) are rather rare in this region.[38]

BĀṆĀSURA, PARAŚURĀMA AND VASIṢṬHA LEGENDS

Of the various Purāṇic legends, those connected with Bāṇāsura, Paraśurāma and Vasiṣṭha are conspicuous by their association with events and places in both Assam and Orissa.

First, Bāṇāsura. Bāṇa, son of the great *asura*, Bali, was the ruler of Śoṇitapura, a kingdom adjacent to that of Prāgjyotiṣapura. In the Purāṇic accounts, Bāṇāsura's name gets mentioned in two stories: first, he was a friend of Naraka of Prāgjyotiṣa and it was under his influence that the latter developed demonic tendencies and appointed Hayagrīva and other *asuras* as his generals. Further, according of the *Kālikā Purāṇa*, it was on the advice of Bāṇa, that Naraka practised severe penance for one hundred years to propitiate Brahmā for getting relief from the curse of Vasiṣṭha.[39] The second story relates to Bāṇa's daughter, Uṣā. She got enamoured of Aniruddha, a grandson of Śrī-kṛṣṇa on seeing a picture of the prince drawn by her companion, Citralekhā. Coming to know of her infatuation, Kṛṣṇa came to Śoṇitapura from Dvārakā and, overpowering Bāṇa, took the princess away to Dvārakā where she was married to Aniruddha. This is a well known story and finds a place in many Purāṇas.

The legend of Uṣā and Aniruddha is a prominent part of the folk-lore of Assam and many poems and dramas have been written on this theme. The popular belief identifies Śoṇitapura with the modern town of Tezpur where a number of ancient ruins and natural features are connected with Bāṇāsura. To establish the connection between Śoṇitapura and Tezpur, it is pointed out that *tez* in Assamese means blood, i.e., *śoṇita.* This etymology is no doubt fanciful and quite recent in origin because 'Tezpur' is probably derived from some Austric formation like *ti+ja+pur.* In the Austric tongues *ti* or *di* means water or river and there are hundreds of places and rivers in Assam with names having *ti* or *di* as prefix or suffix. For our present purpose, however, the only relevant point is that Tezpur is connected with Bāṇāsura.

It is interesting to note that in the Puri district in Orissa there is a place named Banpur which is connected with Bāṇāsura by the common folk. Near Banpur, there is a place known as Ghantasilā on the bank of the rivulet Salia. This place has some ancient ruins that the local tradition considers to be of Bāṇa's fort.[40]

A copper-plate inscription of Daṇḍīmahādevī, of the year 187, was found at this place[41] in which the grant of a village named Kansaranagarī to certain Brāhmaṇas has been recorded. This village has been identified with Ghantasila but here we are not concerned with such aspects of the matter. Of interest to us is the only fact that Ghantasila was a noted village in the Bhauma-Kara kingdom in the early tenth century (736+ 187 = AD 923). During this period the region of Tezpur in Assam was under the Śālastaṁbha rulers and there were regular cultural contacts between the two regions. Either the Tezpur region or the Banpur region got connected with the legend of Bāṇāsura and from there the legend travelled to the other region. Interestingly, certain places in Himachal Pradesh are also connected with the legend of Bāṇa. Sarahan in the Kinnaur district is the site of ancient Śoṇitapura according to the local belief. How has the legend of Bāṇa and the romance of Uṣā and Aniruddha travelled over the long distances between Himachal Pradesh, Assam and Orissa will certainly be a fascinating study. There is a hypothesis that the original Prāgjyotiṣa was located somewhere in the northern Himachal Pradesh or southern Kashmir from where the inhabitants migrated *en masse* to western Assam.[42] While migrating they also carried their language, legends and traditions with them and named their new settlements after their original places. This hypothesis needs extensive research to be established. For our present purpose we may presume that it was the Tezpur area that got connected with the legend of Bāṇāsura—either imported from Himachal Pradesh-Kashmir or otherwise. There is every likelihood that some persons from the Tezpur area migrated to the Ghantasila area in Orissa and carried the legend of Bāṇāsura with them and this may have happened in the late ninth- early tenth century AD. Regarding the donees of the Kumrung plate we have no particulars except their names and that they belonged to the Bhāradvāja and other *gotras.* The donated village was located in the Koṅgoḍa *maṇḍala.* In the Santiragrama Grant of the same queen, of the year 180 (AD 916),[43] however, we find that the village Santiragrama in Dakṣiṇa Tośala was donated to Bhaṭṭa Makyadeva of the Bhāradvāja *gotra*, Vājasaneya *caraṇa* and Mādhyandina *śākhā* who hailed from Takari. We should recall that Koṅgoḍa *maṇḍala* was also a part of Dakṣiṇa Tośalī. Another grant of land in the Koṅgoḍa *maṇḍala* is recorded in the Arabala Grant of the same queen, of the year 183 (AD 919) in which the donee is said to belong to the Bhāradvāja *gotra*, Vājasaneya *caraṇa* and Kāṇva *śākhā* and to have migrated from Puṅḍravardhana. From these examples one may be justified in inferring that in the ninth-tenth centuries a large number of Brāhmaṇas migrating from Puṅḍravardhana, a part of the Kāmarūpa kingdom, were settled in the Koṅgoḍa *maṇḍala* by the Bhauma-Kara rulers. These settlers carried with them their legends and traditions like the legend of Bāṇāsura and transplanted them at the new settlements.

Then there are places connected with the story of Paraśurāma. The Purāṇic story in which Paraśurarāma is said to have killed Reṇukā, his mother, with his axe, on the order of his father, sage Jamadagni, is well-known. The legend current in Assam is the one contained in the *Kālikā Purāṇa*. According to this account, Paraśurāma, on the advice of his father, went to Brahma Kuṇḍa in the valley of Kailāśa and took bath there to get rid of the sin of matricide. He then cut the banks of the sacred lake and made the river Brahmaputra flow through it.[44] Brahmakuṇḍa, also known as Paraśurāmakuṇḍa is situated in the eastern corner of Arunachal Pradesh. The popular legend adds that the axe with which Paraśurāma had beheaded his mother had got stuck to his hand due to his sin and it is only when he washed it in the Brahmakuṇḍa that it got unstuck and fell in the kuṇḍa. In Orissa, a place called Jhankad in the Cuttack district has close association with Paraśurāma. At this place there is an image of the goddess Sāralā, the local name of Saraswatī, which is said to have been engraved by Paraśurāma with his arrow.[45] What is the connection between the legend of Paraśurāma in Assam and that in Orissa is difficult to fathom. Nevertheless, it is interesting to note that the legend of Paraśurāma is quite current in Himachal Pradesh too. Lake Reṇukā and the nearby Jamadagni peak in the Sirmaur district represent a very strong tradition. However, the Paraśurāma connection with Orissa is perhaps the strongest because the sage is said to have practised penance on the Mahendra mountain which is identified with the hills of the same name in the Ganjam region.

Another Purāṇic figure that has exercised considerable influence on the minds of the people of Kāmarūpa and Utkala is the sage Vasiṣṭha. In the case of Assam, in the words of Banikanta Kakati, "The figure of Vasiṣṭha is made to stand at the cross-roads of political and social changes in Assamese legends. His curses cause changes in religious and social customs and the birth of new dynasties. His curses caused the downfall of king Naraka and the result was the initiation of *Vāmācara* (left hand) rites in ancient Kāmarūpa. In a later legend he is found to curse god Indra and cause the emergence of a new dynasty of kings. This legend occurs in the chronicles of the Ahom (Shan) kings."[46] Dr Kakati's surmise is that the Vasiṣṭha legend goes back to the Buddhist Taṅtras and thence it was introduced into the *Kālikā Purāṇa* and from there it ramified into later works. In the Buddhist Tantras, *Brahma Yāmala* and *Rudra Yāmala*, Vasiṣṭha is said to have meditated on the goddess Buddheśvarī according to the Atharvedic process. According to the former he went to the Kāmākhyā hill to meditate while the *Rūdra Yāmala* says he went to the sea-shore.[47] Thus in the Vasiṣṭha motif we clearly see the connection between Kāmākhyā and the sea-shore or, between Kāmarūpa and Utkala, the two principal seats of devī worship and Vajrayāna.

The *Tārā Tantra* and *Yoginī Tantra* say that Vasiṣṭha meditated on a *mantra* related to the goddess Tārā. It may be mentioned that the *Kālikā Purāṇa* establishes the oneness of Tārā and Cāmuṇḍā.[48] A number of images of Cāmuṇḍā belonging from the ninth to the twelfth century have been found both in Assam and Orissa (see, Chapter 5, supra). It is also worth mentioning that just outside Guwahati there is a place known as Vasiṣṭhāśrama, or simply Vasiṣṭha, and within the city there is a temple of Ugratārā. While the present temple is only of the Ahom period, its site shows evidence of a much earlier temple, possibly of the tenth or eleventh century.

It seems that the legend of Vasiṣṭha playing a significant role in the polity and society of Kāmarūpa was carried to Utkala by the migrating Brāhmaṇas during the Bhauma-Kara period; when the Bhañjas felt a need to present themselves as belonging to an ancient and holy lineage the Brāhmaṇas obliged them by fabricating the myth of the *Aṇḍaja Kula*. In the copper-plate inscriptions of the Ādi Bhañjas of Mayurabhanja, it is stated that the progenitor of the dynasty, Gaṇadaṇḍa Vīrabhadra was born of a pea-hen's egg and nursed by the sage Vasiṣṭha.[49] This tradition is not found in the inscriptions of the Bhañjas of Khiñjalīmaṇḍala but in those of the earlier ones, viz., the Bhañjas of KhijjiṅgaKoṭṭa, the first person of the dynasty is invariably mentioned as *mayūrāṇḍabhītvā* and *Vasiṣṭha munipālito.*[50] The tradition continued in the late medieval period since the descendents of the ancient Bhañjas continued to rule in a number of small principalities in Orissa. Thus, the great Oriya poet, Upendra Bhañja, a scion of a royal Bhañja house, while introducing his family uses the words *Viśiṣṭa Vasiṣṭha Pālakā, Śrirāmedatta rājaṭikā.*[51] In these royal families this tradition is current even now. It is indeed significant that when the Paṇḍitas were faced with the task of naming a patron sage for the Bhañjas they selected Vasiṣṭha out of the hundreds of the Purāṇic figures available to them. Was it not because they were aware that Vasiṣṭha was known to have performed such functions in Kāmarūpa? We shall not be unjustified in surmising that the Paṇḍitas who created the legend of mythical origin of the Bhañjas around the ninth-tenth centuries were well-versed in the traditions of Kāmarūpa. Indeed, they might have been the Brāhmaṇas who had migrated from Kāmarūpa. We have already noted in Chapter 6 that the Bhañjas of KhijjiṅgaKoṭṭa like Raṇabhañjadeva, etc. had settled a number of Brāhmaṇas from Ṭakarī, Vārendrī, etc. in their kingdom; these grateful Brāhmaṇas perhaps easily obliged their benefactors by declaring that they had been brought up by the great sage Vasiṣṭha.

It is significant to note that even Vasiṣṭha has some association with the region of Himachal Pradesh. The *Kālikā Purāṇa* narrates the story of the birth of Arundhatī and her marriage to Vasiṣṭha.[52] These happened on the bank of the river Candrabhāgā, evidently the river of the same name in the Sivalik hills. In the same context, the story of Candrabhāgā's birth is also given in which she is made to flow by the lake Vṛhat Lohita—a reminder of connection with the river Lauhitya of the north-east! In the Sivalik foothills there is also a place called Vasiṣṭhāśrama.

NOTES AND REFERENCES

1. Reference may be made to (i) Kulke, Eschmann and Tripathy, *The Cult of Jagannatha and the Regional Tradition of Orissa;* (ii) K.C. Misra, *The Cult of Jagannatha*; (iii) Himanshu S. Patnaik, *Lord Jagannath—His Temple, Cult and Festivals*; (iv) Ramesh Prasad Mohapatra, *Temple Legends of Orissa*, Chapter II—*The Temple of Lord Jagannatha of Puri*, pp. 19-48 and (v) Pandit Nilakantha Das, 'Hints on the Significance and History of Jagannatha', in *OHRJ*, Vol.VIII, Part 1, April 1958; pp 1-36.
2. Himanshu S. Patnaik, op. cit., pp. 7-10.
3. Ibid., p. 23 refers to the Dadhivāmana's temple erected by the widow of Coḍagaṅga. Dadhivāmana's popularity has continued through the ages as may be inferred from the legend of Paramandanda Sahu who built a Dadhivāmana temple in the eighteenth century in the village Bhatli near Baragarh town in the Sambhalpur district. See Mohapatra, op. cit., pp. 103-04.
4. This was observed by the author.
5. Mohapatra, op. cit., pp. 29-30. This version is found in the Oriya *Mahābhārata* of Sāralādāsa of the sixteenth century.
6. Himanshu Patnaik, op. cit., p. 23.
7. P.D. Chaudhury, *Archaeology in Assam*, pp. 33 and 40.
8. Shailendra Mohan Jha, *Brajabolī Sahityā* (in Hindi), pp. 251-52.
9. This list is compiled from P.K. Ray, *Prachi Valley*, being the Archaeological Survey Report 1974 -75 of the Orissa State Archaeology.

10. R.P. Mohapatra, op. cit., pp. 66-67.
11. Upendra Nath Dhal, *The Glory That was Virajākṣetra or Virajākṣetramāhātmya*, Chapter I, Introduction.
12. K.C. Panigrahi, *History of Orissa*, p. 331.
13. R.P. Mohapatra, op. cit., p. 64.
14. Snigdha, Tripathy, *Inscriptions of Orissa*, Vol. II, pp. 116-17.
15. Ibid., pp. 118-19.
16. Ibid., Introduction, pp. 20-22; also, U.N. Dhal, op. cit., pp. 4-8.
17. *Śānti Parva*. 347.
18. *Devī Purāṇa*. 1/5.
19. *Bhāgawata Purāṇa*, 6.6.30; Also refer to Banikanta Kakati, *Viṣṇuite Myths and Legends*, p. 110.
20. *Brahma Purāṇa*, Chapter 202 and *Viṣṇu Purāṇa*, 5.29.
21. *Kālikā Purāṇa*, 40.6-8.
22. Thomas E. Donaldson, *The Iconography of Vaishnava Images in Orissa*, p. 5 refers to *the Garuḍa Purāṇa, I. 34. 11-13* as giving the iconography of Hayagrīva. The table given by him at p. 4 indicates that the *Padma Purāṇa* also gives the same alignment of the *āyudhas* for the Vāmana form.
23. Mamata Chandra Majumdar, *Hājo āru Dhopgurī Satrar Camū Itivritta* (booklet in Assamese), p. 11.
24. Ibid., p. 10.
25. K.L. Barua, 'Was there a Buddhist temple at Hajo?' in *JARS*, Vol. II, No. 2, July 1934, pp. 39-44.
26. Maheswar Neog, *Prācya Śāsanāvalī*, Introduction, p. 143, Texts, p. 3.
27. Ibid., Introduction p. 180, Text, p. 80.
28. *Yoginī Tantra*. II. 9.242.
29. Banikanta Kakati, op. cit., p. 110.
30. Maheswar Neog, op. cit., Introduction, p. 143.
31. P.C. Choudhury, *The History of Civilisation of the People of Assam to the Twelfth century A.D.*, p. 326.
32. D. Sarma, *Kāmarūpaśāsanāvalī*, Part II- Texts, pp. 43-49 (Tezpur) and pp. 50-55 (Parvatiya).
33. Seen by the author.
34. This list has been extracted from P.D. Chaudhury, op. cit., pp. 31-60.
35. Ibid., p. 48.
36. Ibid., p. 38.
37. For example, see Figs. No. 50 (ASM 2872), No. 54 (ASM 2871), No. 55 (ASM 3508), No. 63 (ASM 3256) and No. 66 (ASM 1486) in R.D. Choudhury, *Catalogue of Stone Sculptures Assam State Museum*; all these belonging to the eleventh-twelfth centuries were found at the various sites in the lower and central Assam.
38. Some of the Deopani-type images in the above catalogue are Figs. No. 1 (ASM 3104), No. 5 (ASM 2454), No. 8 (ASM 8) and No. 11 (ASM 3568), all belonging to the seventh-eighth centuries.
39. *Kālikā Purāṇa*, Chapter 39.
40. Pandit Binayak Misra, *Orissa Under the Bhauma Kings*, Section I (Inscriptions), p. 60.

41. Ibid., p. 60. Even though this plate was actually found at Ghantasila, it is known as the Kumrung Plate because it was in possession of a certain gentleman, inhabitant of the village Kumrung which is nearby.
42. C.D. Tripathy, *Aspects of the Medieval History of Assam*, p. 7-10.
43. Snigdha Tripathy, *Inscriptions of Orissa*, Vol. II, pp. 173-177.
44. *Kālikā Purāṇa*, 83.25-29.
45. Booklet on Cuttak published by Orissa Tourism.
46. Banikanta Kakati, *The Mother Goddess Kamakhya*, p. 30.
47. Ibid., pp. 31-32.
48. *Kālikā Purāṇa*, 61.95.
49. Snigdha Tripathy, *Inscriptions of Orissa*, Vol. VI, Introduction, p. ii.
50. For example, see the Bamanghati Plate of Raṇabhañjadeva in ibid., pp. 1-5 and Ukhunda Plate of Pṛthvībhañja in ibid., pp. 39-42.
51. Ibid., Introduction, p. iii.
52. *Kālikā Purāṇa*, Chapter 22.

Chapter 8

Some Relevant Medieval Texts

PURĀṆA AND DHARMAŚĀSTRA TRADITIONS

Dr. M.A. Mehendale has rightly held that in the 'original' Purāṇas considerable changes were introduced in the different regions by the local temple priests "helping themselves by adding to the Purāṇas a great deal of new matter which served their ends."[1] He further added, "Some of these additions have a local tinge so that the *Brahma Purāṇa* may represent the Orissa version of the original work, just as the *Padma* may give that of Puṣkara, the *Agni* that of Gayā, the *Varāha* that of Mathurā, the *Vāmana* that of Thaneswar, the *Kūrma* that of Banaras and the *Matsya* that of Brahmaṇas on the Narmada."[2] The present *Brahma Purāṇa* is indeed a work of the Brāhmaṇas of Orissa as is evident from the large space it devotes to the descriptions of the Puruṣottama Kṣetra,[3] Ekāmra Kṣetra,[4] Virajā Kṣetra;[5] and Koṇāditya Kṣetra;[6] not only that, it even has sections on *samudrasnānamāhātmya*[7] and *Oṇḍradeśastha brāhmaṇa praśaṁsā.*[8]

It is significant that the *Brahma Purāṇa* narrates not only the legends about the holy places in Orissa, but also those about Kāmarūpa and Videha. Thus a major portion of one chapter is devoted to the legend of the burning of Kāmadeva by Śiva[9] and one whole chapter is written on the episode of the killing of Naraka of Prāgjyotiṣapura by Śrīkṛṣṇa[10] and many *ślokas* are devoted to the episode of the Kṛṣṇa's taking away the *pārijāta* tree from the garden of Indra when he visited the *devaloka* after killing Naraka.[11] These legends have found a place in very few other Purāṇas. Their inclusion in the *Brahma Purāṇa* by its compilers in Utkala clearly indicates their contact with the Purāṇic scholars of Kāmarūpa.

Not only of Kāmarūpa, some legends from the land of Mithilā also find a place in the *Brahma Purāṇa.* For example, the story of Gautama's curse to his wife Ahalyā and a description of the Gautamī or Indra tīrtha occupy a whole chapter.[12] This *tīrtha* is located in Mithilā and has received scant attention in the other Purāṇas. Similarly, one whole chapter is devoted to the Janasthāna tīrtha and the dialogue between Janaka and Yājñavalkya.[13] Even more noteworthy for us is the detailed description of the Kokā tīrtha that covers a whole chapter.[14] It is the place where Viṣṇu in his Varāha incarnation rescued the divine *pitṛs* who had been engulfed in the waters of the Kokā, a stream that dashed through the Himalayan rocks (*śiśirādri*).[15] It is also the place where Viṣṇu-Varāha rescued the earth and impregnated her who eventually gave birth to Narakāsura, the *Bhauma.*[16] The *Brahma Purāṇa* speaks of the place as *Viṣṇoh Kokāmukhe divyavarāharūpaṁ.*[17]

It is interesting that from the Damodarpur copper-plate Inscription of the time of Budhagupta[18] we learn that the shrine of Kokāmukhasvāmin as Śvetavarāhasvāmin was located in the Kotivarṣa viṣaya of Puṇḍravardhana bhukti. In describing its location this epigraph uses the word *himavacchikhare* which is almost identical with *śiśirādri* used in the *Brahma Purāṇa.*

The connection of Kokāmukha with both Mithilā and Kāmarūpa through Narakāsura is thus established by the *Brahma Purāṇa.* Being the birth-place of Narakāsura, this place must have exercised a special fascination and sanctity in Kāmarūpa whose rulers traced their descent from him. Could this have been an additional (sentimental) reason for the kings of Kāmarūpa to occupy Puṇḍravardhana towards the end of the fifth century, i.e., soon after the date of the said epigraph?

That the composers of the *Brahma Purāṇa* in Utkala had close links with Kāmarūpa and Mithilā is also testified to by some other passages dealing with *śrāddha.* The *Brahma Purāṇa* not only sanctions but extols the value of offering fish and meat as *piṇḍa* to one's ancestors.[19] Clearly, it was in deference to the tribal customs in eastern India, particularly Kāmarūpa and possibly Utkala. The enormous popularity of fish-eating in Mithilā, Kāmarūpa, Vaṅga and Kaliṅga-Utkala and use of fish in all auspicious ceremonies even amongst the Brāhmaṇas is well known.

It appears that the *Brahma Purāṇa* that perhaps took shape around the fifth-sixth centuries was considerably influenced by the legends and practices prevailing in Utkala, Mithilā and Kāmarūpa on the one hand and, on the other, it had a profound influence on the scholars of these regions in the subsequent centuries. The composers of the texts like the *Kālikā Purāṇa* (late ninth century) and the *Yoginī Tantra* (sixteenth century) in Kāmarūpa seem to follow the *Brahma Purāṇa* traditions in a substantial way and for the *nibandhakāras* of all the three regions from the early to the late medieval period *Brahma Purāṇa* is usually the most-quoted authority, next only to the *Mahābhārata.* For instance, Siddhāntavāgīśa Bhaṭṭācāryya, a late sixteenth century digest-writer of Kāmarūpa, in his *Tīrtha Kaumudī* cites the authority of the *Brahma Purāṇa* as many as eighteen times.[20] Of course, the most-quoted authority is the *Kālikā Purāṇa*, a work of Kāmarūpa itself. The other Purāṇas whose frequency of quotation exceeds that of the *Brahma Purāṇa* are the *Skanda* (35 times) and *Garuḍa* (24 times).[21] This is clearly because the *Garuḍa Purāṇa* was also very popular in eastern India and the list of Kāśī and other *tīrthas* of northern India is the most exhaustive in the *Skanda Purāṇa*. It may be noted that the *Garuḍa Purāṇa* is believed to have been composed in Mithilā[22] which explains its great popularity in Kāmarūpa. Incidentally, it may also be mentioned that the *Garuḍa Purāṇa* explicitly states that it narrates the *dharma* formerly promulgated by Yājñavalkya whose association with Videha and its king Janaka is well-known. He is also credited in the *Mahābhārata* and the various Purāṇas with having promulgated the White Yajurveda[23] or the *Vājasaneyī saṁhitā*. These systems thus appear to have originated in Mithilā. In this light it is significant to recall that the majority of the Brāhmaṇas who were donated lands in Kāmarūpa and Utkala were the Yajurvedīs or belonging to the *Vājasaneyī śākhā* (see Chapter 6, supra).

The religious, social, domestic and personal life of the Hindus have always been regulated by *dharma* and for defining and elaborating *dharma*, a vast body of literature known as the Dharmaśāstra developed since the Vedic times. The *Manusmṛti* lays down five different sources of *dharma*: the whole Veda is the foremost source of *dharma* and next, the tradition and the practice of those that know it, i.e., the Veda; and further the usages of virtuons men and self-satisfaction.[24] Similar dicta are found in the *Yājñavalkya* and other *smṛtis*. P.V. Kane summarizes the position by saying, "These passages make it clear that the principal sources of *dharma* are conceived to be the Vedas, the *Smṛtis*, and customs."[25] Next to the Vedas, the earliest works of Dharmaśāstra are the *Śrautasūtras* and *Dharmasūtras* and the two epics. These are followed by the *Smṛtis*, and the Purāṇas, all of which appear to have been composed between the second century BC and ninth century AD. Towards the end of this period, commentaries on the earliest *Smṛtis* of Manu and Yājñavalkya were also written by Medhātithi and Viśvarūpa respectively.[26] From the eleventh century we find the development of a new class of Dharmaśāstra literature known as *Smṛtinibandhas* or, simply *nibandhas*, or digests. Mm. Har Parsad Shastri has attributed this development to the establishment of the rule of the iconoclastic Turks which gave a rude shock to the Hindus and "they began, from time to time, to regulate more rigidly their social and domestic affairs. . . . That led to the system of writing digests of law in different kingdoms of India."[27] In several matters of Hindu Law such as marriage, adoption, inheritence, partition and recovery of debts various schools of *nibandhas* developed over a period of time and under the British rule five main schools came to be identified, viz.; (i) the Vārāṇasī School, (ii) the Mithilā School, (iii) the Western (or Bombay) School, (iv) the *Dākṣinātya* or Southern School and (v) the Bengal School. The *Mitākṣarā*, a famous commentary on the *Yājñavalkya saṁhitā* composed by Vijñāneśvara towards the end of the eleventh century in the Calukyan country is the source of the writings of the first four schools while the Bengal school follows the rules laid down in the *Dāyabhāga*, a digest compiled by Jīmūtavāhana in Bengal around the same period. Though the modern Assam at present is governed by the *Dāyabhāga* system of the Bengal school, there is ample evidence to show that a separate school of Dharmaśāstra existed in the ancient Kāmarūpa. However, the earliest known *nibandhakāra* of Kāmarūpa, Nīlāṁbarācārya is placed between AD 1240 and 1300 by P.V. Kane.[28] *Śrāddhaprakāśa*, *Kālakaumudī* and *Candraprabhā* are his known works. Vedācārya, son of Viṣṇu Upādhyāya, the author of *Smṛticandrikā* is another early *nibandhakāra* of Kāmarūpa whose period has been determined as AD 1250-1350.[29]

We do not know which system was followed in Kāmarūpa before the thirteenth century but it is reasonable to presume that after the fall of the Brahmapāla dynasty and establishment of the hegemony of the Pālas of Bengal in Kāmarūpa in the early twelfth century the law prevailing in Bengal must have been introduced in Kāmarūpa. It was the law that was being codified by Jīmūtavāhana around that time. It is likely that before this time the legal system of Mithilā was prevalent in Kāmarūpa but here again, unfortunately, no work of a *nibandhakāra* of Mithila antedating the thirteenth century has survived. Śrīdatta Upādhyāya and Harinātha, both of the late thirteenth century[30] are the earliest Maithilā digest-writers whose works are available today although they mention the names of some of their predecessors. It is, however, certain that the Mithilā school did have some differences with the Bengal school; thus, Harinātha has challenged the authority of the *Gauḍīya* school at some places in his *Smṛtisāra*.[31] It will indeed be interesting to make a detailed comparative study of the works of Harinātha, Nīlāṁbarācārya and Jīmūtavāhana; such a study will reveal whether the Kāmarūpa school in its early phase was inclined towards the Bengal school (*Dāyabhāga*) or towards the Mithilā school (presumably, *Mitākṣarā*).

It is significant to note that there is some evidence of digest-writing in Kāmarūpa even before the thirteenth century. Manoranjan Sastri has reported the existence of a book *Svalpa-matsya-purāṇa*, a work of the Dharmaśāstra nature that was probably compiled in the ancient Kāmarūpa earlier than the eleventh century.[32] If so, it would be earlier than both *Dāyabhāga* and *Mitākṣarā*.

A few other works believed to be of a date earlier than the thirteenth century are *Smṛti-mīmāṅsā, Dhavala-saṁgraha, Smṛtisamuccaya* and *Tātparya-nibandha.* The authorship of these works except *Smṛtisamuccaya* is not known but these have been quoted by the *nibandhakāras* of Kāmarūpa as well as Bengal such as Śūlapāṇi and Raghunandana. The author of *Smṛtisamuccaya* is Satkavi Viśveśvara about whom nothing except his name is known. *Dhavala-saṁgraha* has been quoted even by the great Jīmūtavāhana, so it must be a work compiled earlier than the twelfth century. Tradition in Assam informs us that in the ancient days commentaries on *Manu-saṁhitā* and *Yājñavalkya saṁhitā* were written by Nārāyaṇa Sarvajña and Ācārya Vimalabodha respectively. Unfortunately, none of these texts is available now and their names are known only from their referecnes in the works of the later *nibandhakāras* of Kāmarūpa, Bengal and even other regions.[33]

The later *nibandhakāras* of Kāmarūpa no doubt followed the *Dāyabhāga* system but there are many differences between their opinions and those of the writers of Bengal. Manoranjan Sastri says, "This is somewhat similar to the differences of opinion that exist among the followers of the *Mitāksharā,* which led to form different schools in western India."[34] The most prominent amongst the later *nibandhakāras* are Dāmodaramiśra, the author of *Smṛtisāgarasāra,* who flourisshed in the first half of the fifteenth century and Pītāṁbara Siddhāntavāgīśa, of the sixteenth century who is credited with the writing of eighteen (twenty-eight, according to another view) digests on different topics called *Kaumudīs.* Among the post-thirteenth century works mention may be made of *Dharmapurāṇa* (quoted by Dāmodaramiśra in 1434), *Yoginī Tantra* (sixteenth century), *Hara-gaurī-saṁvāda* (fifteenth century), *Gṛhyaparaskara* (later than the fifteenth century), *Āngirasa-saṁhitā* (not later than the fourteenth century), *Pūrṇacandra* written by Ripuñjaya Bhaṭṭācārya between AD 1610 and 1660.[35]

In the sixteenth century the Bengal school was dominated by Raghunandana whose twenty eight works with names ending with *tattva* are epoch-making contributions to the *Smṛti* literature. In Kāmarūpa, it was the age of Pītāṁbara Siddhāntavāgīśa who adorned the court of Naranarayaṇa and later that of his son Lakṣmīnārāyaṇa. Pītāṁbara has refuted the views of Raghunandana on many issues. Manoranjan Sastri has shown how the two great writers differ from each other by citing their views on the question of inheritance of the *strīdhana* of a lady who dies without an issue.[36]

To illustrate the differences between the Kāmarūpa and Bengal schools Manoranjan Sastri has mentioned that, "All *nibandhakāras* of Kāmarūpa except Nīlāṁbarācārya are supporters of the *sauravāda* (the theory of solar month).

Jīmūtāvahana, the earliest and most prominent *Smṛtinibandhakāra* of Bengal also supported this theory which definitely shows that during this time the solar month traditionally prevailed in Bengal as well as in Assam.... Nīlāṁbarācārya was the first to have introduced the *cāndravāda* or the theory in which lunar month is assumed to be the direct meaning (*śakyārtha*) of the word *māsa.* His view was not welcomed by people and the later *nibandhakāras* of Kāmarūpa but in Bengal some prominent *nibandhakāras* like Śūlapāṇi and Raghunandana accepted Nīlāṁbara's views and established it on a stronger basis by raising more vigorous arguments against the theory of Jīmūtāvahana and others. . . the *sauravāda* was later replaced by *cāndravāda* in Bengal."[37] The same author cites the case of observance of the Kṛṣṇa Janmāṣṭamī. He says, "Another strange rule found in Kāmarūpīya system is that the Janmāṣṭamīvrata is observed here, even now, during the *saura bhādra,* while it is observed in lunar *bhādra* in other parts of India. . . . All the Kāmarūpīya *nibandhakāras* (except Nīlāṁbarācārya and Pītāṁbara Siddhāntavāgīśa) and the Vaiṣṇava saints of Assam prescribe this practice quoting some ancient dicta which are not mentioned by other *nibandhakāras* anywhere."[38] It would be instructive to ascertain the system followed in Mithilā and Utkala in the earlier days; the present author has not been able to do so but there is a strong likelihood that it was the same as the Kāmarūpa system.

The Bengal *nibandhakāras* right from the time of Jīmūtavāhana have profusely quoted the authority of the Kāmarūpa writers using expressions like *Kāmarūpīya nibandha* or *Kāmarūpa-nibandha.* This was naturally reciprocated by the *nibandhakāras* of Kāmarūpa. But from the sixteenth century onwards we notice greater opposition to the views of the Bengal writers. So much so, that in the words of S.K. Bhuyan, "...Pītāṁbara Siddhāntavāgīśa set up in Assam a rival school to combat the influences of Raghunandana."[39] It is rather difficult to agree with this view which has clear political undertones; Pītāṁbara's efforts are more likely to have resulted from his free intellectual exercise.

We may now have a brief look at the *smṛtinibandhas* of Mithilā and Utkala. While the Maithila *nibandhakāras* constitute a full-fledged school following the *Mitākṣarā* system, those of Orissa are surely not so prominent.

As noted earlier, no work of a Maithila writer earlier than the thirteenth century has survived. After the thirteenth century, however, Mithilā produced some of the greatest *nibandhakāras* like Caṇḍeśvara Ṭhakkura (early fourteenth century), Vidyāpati (late fourteenth-early fifteenth century), Vardhamāna Upādhyāya (end of fifteenth century) Śaṅkaramiśra (mid-fifteenth century), Vācaspati Miśra (late fifteenth century), Rudradhara (early fifteenth century)

Misarūmiśra (early fifteenth century), Maheśa Ṭhakkura (sixteenth century) and Gonḍīmiśra (seventeenth century).[40]

The *nibandhakāras* of Mithilā and Bengal are known to have exercised considerable influence on each other. The authors of one school referred to by those of the other have been exhaustively listed by S.C. Banerji[41] and some of the issues on which their views tally or differ have also been briefly discussed by him.[42] Only a detailed study will show how the followers of the different systems have influenced each other; in all probability, the points of their agreement are the issues not coming strictly under the domain of *Dāyabhāga* and *Mitākṣarā.* These might be the questions relating to observance of festivals or *pūjāvidhis,* etc.

It may also be mentioned that we get references to at least one very early *nibandhakāra* of Mithilā, viz., Śrīkara, who probably lived between AD 800 and 850 and has been mentioned several times by Jīmūtavāhana and Bhavadeva Bhaṭṭa, the earliest *nibandhakāras* of Bengal.[43]

Turning our attention to Orissa, we are told that "it is known that more than sixty numbers of authors of Dharmaśāstra have taken birth in Orissa and almost one hundred and fifty nos. of volumes on various aspects of *Smṛti* scriptures have been written by them."[44] The information about the earliest *nibandhakāras* is, however, rather hazy. The earliest name of a *Smṛti* writer of Utkala that we know is that of Śatānanda, whose known date is AD 1099. While he is very well known as an astronomer, not much about him as a *Smṛtikāra* is known except that his work *Śatānanda Saṁgraha* was definitely a work on *Smṛti.*[45] He appears to have been totally ignored by the *nibandhakāras* of Utkala as well as other regions. Śridhara Ācārya and Nīlāṁbara Ācārya appear to be the earliest of the *nibandhakāras* of Utkala. Both of them have been assigned to the twelfth century by K.N. Mahapatra but K.C. Panigrahi is inclined to consider them to be of a later date.[46] Another early writer is Śaṅkhadhara, assigned by K.N. Mahapatra to a period before AD 1300, whose work *Smṛti Samuccaya* was accepted as an authority by the *smriikāras* of Utkala, Gauḍa and Mithilā.[47] Panigrahi says that he has been frequently quoted by Jīmūtavāhana.[48] If so, he should be assigned to a period prior to the twelfth century. Two writers of the late thirteenth century are Śaṁbhukara Vājapeyī and his son, Vidyākara. The former is said to have been "frequently quoted in the *smṛti* works of other parts of India"[49] and the latter is famous for his work *Nityācāra Paddhati.*[50]

Amongst the writers of the post-thirteenth century period,[51] mention may be made of Gadādhara (late fifteenth century), Godāvarī Miśra (fifteenth century), King Pratāparūdradeva (1497-1539), Narasiṁha Vājapeyīn (early sixteenth century) who is famous for his *Nityācāra Pradīpa* and *Sadācāra Pradīpa*, Śridhara Śarma (eighteenth century), Kṛṣṇa Miśra (eighteenth century), Kṛṣṇa Dāsha, Gopala Nanda, Bṛhaspati Sūri, Basudeva Nanda, Raghunātha Dāsha, Divyasiṁha Mahāpātra and Yogeśwara Pātra (all of the eighteenth or ninteenth century).

For our study the more important than the listing of the *nibandhakāras* is the fact that the earlier ones amongst them are said to have been quoted by the authors of Bengal and Mithilā. S.C. Banerji has noted Vidyākara Vājapeyīn and Narasiṁha Vājapeyīn as the only *nibandhakāras* of Orissa who had influenced the writers of Bengal. Both of them have been quoted by Raghunandana.[52] As noted above, Śaṅkhadhara and perhaps some others had influenced the writers in Mithilā too. Since Utkala and Mithilā belong to the two different systems it will be interesting to study in what matters they influenced each other. As observed above in respect of Mithilā and Bengal, in the case of Utkala and Mithilā too, these must be the matters not strictly covered by the *Dāyabhāga* and the *Mitākṣāra.* It is, however, relevant to note that Kaliṅga is really regarded as a part of the ancient *dakṣināpatha* and Utkala is known to have absorbed many influences from south India, for example, in the sphere of art and architecture. It is, therefore, conceivable that in the earlier period, the *nibandhakāras* of Utkala followed the school of Vijñāneśvara and thus there should have been close affinity between the Utkala and Mithilā schools.

S.C. Banerji has made a useful study of the inter-relation among different schools of the Navya Smṛti. It is, however, limited to the study of relation between the Bengal school on the one hand, and Mithilā, Kāmarūpa, Orissa, South Indian and Benares schools on the other. No one has so far made any attempt to study the inter-relation between the Dharmaśāstra schools of Mithilā, Kāmarūpa and Utkala which will really be relevant for the present study. The present author has also not been able even to make a beginning as the resources required for such a comprehensive study have just not been available to him. Majority of the *nibandha* works relevant for such a study are either not traceable or available only in the manuscripts on palm leaf (in case of Orissa), *sāñcīpāt* (in case of Assam) or paper (the late copies). It need not perhaps be stated that such a study is likely to reveal a close affinity between the systems of Dharmaśāstra prevailing in the three regions in spite of the fact that after the twelfth century Kāmrūpa and Utkala came under one system (*Dāyabhāga*) and Mithilā under another (*Mitākṣarā*). The Brāhmaṇas of the same Vedic schools—Sāmavedin and Śukla Yajurvedin or followers of the Vājasaneyī *śākhā*—inhabited all the three regions from the sixth century onwards (see Chapter 6, supra); therefore, the existence of common elements in the *nibandhas* written by them in the three regions is most likely. B.K. Barua has stated that "the Brahmaṇas of Assam today follow the Mithilā school in matters of social law, such as inheritance, gift, will and marriage."[53] It is difficult to accept this observation since, under the British dispensation, it is the *Dāyabhāga* of the Bengal school that came to be applied to Assam.[54] Moreover, the *nibandhakāras* of Kāmarūpa who command unreserved respect of the Brāhmaṇas of Assam, also belong to the *Dāyabhāga* school notwithstanding their differences with their Bengal counterparts on specific issues. The statement of Dr. Barua perhaps does contain some grain of truth but it seems to have been made primarily to be politically correct by distancing the Assam system from the Bengal school. The real and whole truth can be established only by a study of the type indicated above.

INTER-REGIONAL SIGNIFICANCE OF CERTAIN WORKS

Kālikā Purāṇa

As noted in earlier chapters, the *Kālikā Purāṇa* is clearly a work written in Kāmarūpa towards the end of the ninth century.[55] It describes in great detail the geography of Kāmarūpa from its western boundary of the river Karatoyā to the eastern boundary of the river Dikkaravāsinī.[56] Of the regions outside Kāmarūpa noticed in this text, the most prominent is Mithilā. We have already discussed the legend of Naraka, the son of Varāha-Viṣṇu and Pṛthvī, who was brought up by Janaka, the king of Videha.[57] In the description of this legend throughout the term 'Videha' has been used. It, therefore, appears that the name Tīrabhukti had not become popular in Kāmarūpa up to the ninth century.

Oḍra also finds significant mention in *KP*. *KP* is an important *Śākta Āgama* and it describes the four main *pīṭhas* as follows:

> "*Oḍrākhyaṁ prathamaṁ pīṭhaṁ dvitīyaṁ Jālaśailakaṁ tṛtīyaṁ Pūrṇapīṭhaṁ tu Kāmarūpaṁ caturthakaṁ*"[58]

In the next verse there is a further elaboration of the Odrapitha as follows:

> "*Oḍrāpīṭhaṁ paścime tu tathaivoḍreśvarī śivāṁ*
> *Kātyāyanīṁ Jagannāthamoḍreśaṁ ca prapūjayet*"[59]

While in this verse the geography is a bit confused' in another verse the writer of *KP* shows a better and correct knowledge of the location of Oḍra as follows:

*"Jālandharaṁ likhet pīṭhamuttare paścime likhet.
Oḍrāpīṭhaṁ dakṣiṇe tu Kāmarūpaṁ tu pūrvataḥ."*[60]

A significant point to be noted here is the mention of Jagannātha. In the above verse the goddess at the Oḍra pīṭha is named as Kātyāyanī and her *Bhairava* is Oḍreśa Jagannātha. We have noted earlier that Jagannātha had already acquired renown by the eighth century, if not earlier. By the time of the composition of the *Kālikā Purāṇa*, Jagannātha or Puruṣottama was recognized as the Supreme God in Kāmarūpa. He was so important that the *Kālikā Purāṇa* offers salutation to him in the very beginning. It is all the more significant since this text was composed for extolling the greatness of Kāmākhyā; it would be expected to offer salutation to the goddess in the *maṅgalācaraṇa*. Instead, the book starts with three verses saluting Hari,[61] and the third of these mentions him as Puruṣottama as follows:

*"Īśvaraṁ jagatāmādyaṁ praṇamya Puruṣottamaṁ
nityajñānamayaṁ vakṣye purāṇaṁ Kālikāhvayaṁ"*[62]

It is significant that the *KP* very frequently uses the name Jagannātha and Mādhava for Viṣṇu. We know that the name Jagannātha as a synonym of Viṣṇu became popular only after the Lord of Nīlācala made his entry into the Puraṇic Hinduism and Jagannātha was earlier being worshipped as Mādhava in Orissa. These traditions of Orissa are very extensively adopted in *KP*. Just two examples may be cited:

*"Etānhatvā mahākāyān mahāviryān durāsadān
āsāsāda Jagannāthaḥ puraṁ Prāgjyotiṣahvayaṁ"*[63]
*"Tathaiva vāruṇaṁ chatraṁ garuḍopari Mādhavaḥ
āropya Satyayā sārdhamāsīnaḥ sumanā Hariḥ"*[64]

There are dozens of verses in *KP* in which the identity of Jagannātha, Mādhava, Keśava and Kṛṣṇa has been established.

The *Kālikā Purāṇa* also knows a deity who does not exist outside Orissa, viz., Dadhivāmana. We have noted earlier (Chapter 7, supra) that if and when an image of Kṛṣṇa alone out of the Jagannātha Triad is made and worshipped it is called Dadhivāmana and in Orissa there are temples dedicated to this deity. To the best of my knowledge, this deity is not known anywhere outside Orissa; not even at Vārāṇasī, where perhaps all gods and goddesses of the Hindu pantheon have their abode! The *KP* is one of the rare texts that is not only familiar with Dadhivāmana but describes his iconography in detail.[65] It will be interesting to examine the Dadhivāmana images in Orissa in the light of the description in *KP*.

The above references clearly establish that the composers of *KP* were fully conversant with Oḍra as a *Śākta pīṭha* and as the abode of Jagannātha.

Yoginī Tantra

Yoginī Tantra is a renowned Tantra text that was composed in Kāmarūpa in the sixteenth century. This is also a *Śākta* work and describes the various *tīrthas* in Kāmarūpa in detail. Regarding the places outside Kāmarūpa, *YT* exhibits considerable familiarity with the places in Orissa. We have already discussed the story of the carving of the Hayagrīva Mādhava images from the same log of wood from which the Jagannātha images were carved. The distribution of the seven images is as follows:

> "*Oḍradeśe mūlabhāgaṁ kalpayāmāsa vai vibhuḥ*
> *tadūrdhvaṁ Kāśmīre Kabandhakarameva ca*
> *Ādityaṁ taṁ vijānīyādrāmeṇa sthāpitaṁ purā*
> *Śoṇādityaṁ tadūrdhvaṅgaṁ śukrena sthāpitaṁ priye.*
> *Śilārūpaṁ maheśāni sthāpitaṁ guruṇā tataḥ*
> *bhāgadvayaṁ Kāmarūpe bhāgaikaṁ malaye girau*"[66]

In this description reference to one part being installed as Śoṇāditya is interesting. It perhaps refers to some Sun temple on the river Śoṇa which will place it in Magadha or the borders of Mithilā. Could it be referring to Muṇdeśwari, the site noted in Chapter 5, supra? In the *YT*, Virajā of Orissa also finds very respectful mention. Being a Tantra text, it rates the *Śākta Kṣetra* of Virajā much higher than Kāśī and Puruṣottama:

> "*Kāśīvāsaṁ yugānyaṣṭau dinaikaṁ Puruṣottame*
> *tadeva koṭiguṇitaṁ Virajāmukhadarśane.*" [67]

In a number of verses the merits of offering *piṇḍa* at Virajā have been extolled.[68] *Mantrajāpa* at Virajā is also said to bring great merit.[69]

Yoginī Tantra is also familiar with the traditional *Śākta pīṭhas* like Jālandhara, Uḍḍiyāna and Śrīhaṭṭa. Mention of the name Uddiyana[70] shows that even as late as the sixteenth century this name had not gone out of use, at least in the *Śākta* circles. *YT* also shows familiarity with the Ekāmra *Kṣetra* and prescribes it as a place for *mantrajāpa*.[71] In fact, *YT* refers to Ekāmra Kānana at many places.[72] The author of *YT* exhibits accurate knowledge of the Orissa region when it speaks of Someśvara, Virajā, Ekāmra, Bhāskara Kṣetra and Daṇḍaka vana in the context of Uḍḍiyāna and Oḍrapīṭha.[73]

The *Yoginī Tantra* shows familiarity with the Mithilā region too as it refers to Gaṇḍakī [74]and Kauśikī.[75]

Varṇa Ratnākara

Varṇa Ratnākara is considered to be the oldest book in the Maithili language. "It is a sort of lexicon of vernacular and Sanskrit terms, a repository of literary similes and conventions dealing with the various things of the world and ideas which are usually treated in poetry."[76] Its author, Jyotirīśvara Kaviśekharācārya adorned the court of Harisiṁhadeva, the last Karṇāta king of Mithilā, whose rule ended in AD 1324. The author of *VR* was a great scholar and is known for his Sanskrit prahasana *Dhūṛtta Samāgama* and a work on erotics called the *Pañcasāyaka.*[77]

The author of *Varṇa Ratnākara* exhibits considerable knowledge of the geography and people of the various regions, particularly Kāmarūpa and Oḍra.

In the very first chapter various castes and communities have been enumerated. Among the lower classes (or castes)—*mandajātīya*—is included Oḍa, which has been identified with Oriya.[78] S.K. Chatterji has surmized that "the Oḍras were clever irrigationists and expert agriculturists who took up specially this vocation of excavating tanks." He has come to this conclusion primarily on the basis of a certain passage in a twelfth century work in which reference is made to excavation of a tank by Oḍas.[79] The mention of Oḍas in *VR* along with other castes of skilled workers like weavers, oil pressers, etc., supports the above presumption and it would be interesting to explore if in the medieval times the services of excavation engineers or workmen from Orissa were utilized for digging of tanks and other civil works in Tirhut, Koch Bihar and Assam. We have already noted in Chapter 5, supra, the possibility of architects from Orissa having built the Hayagrīva Mādhava temple at Hajo in Assam. Between the fifteenth and eighteenth centuries and possibly earlier as well a large number of tanks were excavated in Assam and a large number of temples built. A thorough scrutiny of the Ahom *burañjīs* and records of Koch Bihar to search such references is likely to be a rewarding exercise.

Among the names of places and countries enumerated by *VR*, Kāmarūpa, Utkala and Śrīhaṭṭa are prominently mentioned.[80] The author does not merely mention these names; some specialities of these places are also noticed. For example, we hear of the *Silahaṭī* and *Kamaruvāla* cloth[81]—evidently, Śrīhaṭṭa, i.e., Sylhet in east Bengal and Kāmarūpa were famous for it. In all probability *Silahaṭī* is the famous Dhaka muslin and *Kamaruvāla* is the munga silk of Assam. Śrīhaṭṭa has also been noted for its *elā* (cardamom).[82] Such references clearly show that considerable trade used to take place between Mithilā and Kāmarūpa in the thirteenth century. Then, there is mention of a *sarāī* of gold.[83] *Sarāī* is a typically Assamese thing—it is a plate on a stand on which offerings are made to the deities as well as to the honoured guests. *VR* thus exhibits an intimate knowledge of the customs and etiquette of Assam. Similarly, another typical Assamese object, *Jāṭhī*, is mentioned in this book.[84] This refers to a lance-like object used only in Assam. At another place, *VR* enumerates some *mleccha* people. By this term *VR* clearly means tribal people. Many of the names are the traditional ones like *Kirāta*, *Khasa* and *Pulinda* but significantly, the list includes Koch.[85] The Koch tribe populated western Assam near the border of Mithilā and in the early sixteenth century one of their leaders became the ruler of Kamatā, subsequently called Koch Bihar. Familiarity with the things Assamese may be considered quite natural since Assam was just across the border of Mithilā, but the author of *VR* shows good knowledge of Orissa as well. It mentions *Autkali* as one of the seven dialects (*upabhāṣā*)[86] and Mahendra and Kaliṅga as hills.[87] It mentions *Vanarautu*[88] among the list of the *rājasevakas*. This word is clearly *rautā* with a prefix which was an official designation in Orissa. The word is mentioned along with *sāmanta*, *māṇḍalika*, etc. which is quite appropriate for *rautā*.

Among the women of different countries and castes we come across *Kamatāvārinī*.[89] No doubt it means a lady of Kamatāpura. It is rather disappointing that there is no mention of the women of Orissa who have been favourites of the Sanskrit writers on erotics. Our author perhaps had no experience of them!

Coming to the passage relating to gods, goddesses, scriptures and places of pilgrimage we find that the author is familiar not only with those of Mithilā but also with many of Kāmarūpa and Orissa. Kauśikī[90] and Kokāmukha[91] are the holy places in or near Mithilā;[92] along with them we also have Kāmeśvara[93] and Kāmākṣā[94] of Kāmarūpa. Significantly, even Ugratārā[95] is mentioned. Of Orissa, surely Puruṣottama[96] could not have been forgotten, but more significant is the mention of Causaṭha yoginī.[97] it is significant because in eastern India the temples of Causaṭha yoginīs are found only in Orissa and the author of *VR* is clearly referring to them.

It is highly significant to note that the *Kālikā Purāṇa* is included by the author of *VR* in the list of eighteen Purāṇas[98] and not in that of the *Upa-Purāṇas*.[99] Even *Bhāgawata* has been downgraded to the category of an *Upa-Purāṇa*. This clearly shows the *Śākta* leanings of the author on the one hand and, on the other, the great popularity of the *Kālikā Purāṇa* in Mithilā. Of the popularity of the *Kālikā Purāṇa* in Mithilā we have, of course other good evidences also. B.N. Shastri has given a long list of the *nibandhakāras* of Utkala and Mithilā who have quoted the *Kālikā Purāṇa* as an authority in their works.[100] Nearest to the time of *VR* we have the great Vidyāpati, the poet and *nibandhakāra*, in whose works we find the *Kālikā Purāṇa* to be the most-quoted scriptural authority. For example, the various *pūjāvidhis* and *balidānavidhis* in Vidyāpati's *Dūrgābhaktitaraṅgiṇī* are almost entirely based on the *Kālikā Purāṇa*.

In the *abhiṣeka* ceremony a prince is required to be bathed in the various auspicious liquids like milk, *ghṛta*, *madhu* and water from *tīrthas*. Curiously, *VR* adds *madirā* to this list.[101] This is perhaps due to the influence of tribal customs. The importance of liquor in all auspicious ceremonies among the tribals of Assam is well known.

Dīpikā Candra and Nāma-Mālikā

Dīpikā Candra and *Nāma-Mālikā* are two Sanskrit works whose authorship is attributed to Puruṣottama, the Gajapati king of Orissa (1467-1497). The relevance of these works for our study is that they were translated into Assamese, possibly very soon after their compilation.

While some information is available about the compilation and translation of *Nāma Mālikā*, the same about *Dīpikā Candra* are sadly lacking.

Nāma Mālikā, or *Harināma Mālikā*, to give its full name, in the original Sanskrit is not available but we get adequate information from its Assamese version. It is a work commenting on the attributes of Viṣṇu as given in the Purāṇas and Saṁhitās. It was compiled by Puruṣottamadeva, the Gajapati king, with the assistance of several Paṇḍitas. From an early seventeenth century hagiographical work we learn that a copy of this book was brought by Śaṅkaradeva from Orissa.[102] Later, Virūpakṣa Kājī, a minister of the king Lakṣmīnārāyaṇa of Koch Bihar, requested Mādhavadeva, the chief disciple of Śaṅkaradeva, to translate it into Assamese verse. The work was accordingly undertaken and completed in 607 verses around the year 1595.[103]

Śaṅkaradeva had probably acquired that copy of *Nāma Mālikā* during his first pilgrimage that ended in the year 1493. This means that it was acquired by him very soon after its compilation. That this book fascinated the minister of Koch Bihar and it was translated into Assamese within a century of its compilation shows the great regard in which the works of Orissa were held by the people, particularly the elite of Kāmarūpa in the sixteenth century.

Even more interesting is the case of *Dīpikā Candra*. This work is also not available in the original Sanskrit; only from its translation we know that its author is Gajapati Puruṣottama. This book is also said to have been culled out from different *Śāstras* with the aid of paṇḍitas. Who made the Assamese translation has not been stated and it is not possible to fix its date either.[104]

The book was published in the first decades of the last century and is not easily available. In fact, the present author could not succeed in procuring the book. However, it is said that the book "exposed the vices of the fallen Brahmaṇas and tyrannical kings."[105] P.C. Choudhury has recorded that it "contains legendary accounts of the rulers of ancient Assam."[106] He has further recorded that "A number of traditions centre around Ārimatta, and it appears that he was an important ruler. The genealogy given in the *Dīpika Candra* of Puruśottama Gajapati, mentions a number of rulers including one Haravinda, whose capital was at Candraprabhā on the Lohita. He was succeeded by his son Kuśaraṅga and his capital was at Ratnapura, and he is said to have ruled in Kāmarūpa, Gauḍa, Magadha and Jaintia. It also refers to a king, Śrutasena, the ruler of *Saumārapīṭha*, whose wife was Candramatī and whose capital was at Mānapura on the Brahmaputra."[107]

The students of the history of Assam very well know that the above names and facts are neither corroborated by any archaeological or epigraphic evidence nor are traceable in any of the Purāṇas. These are based entirely on legends transmitted orally from generation to generation and some of them are traceable in certain medieval texts like *Haragaurī Saṁvāda*. It is indeed interesting that these legends travelled to far off Orissa in the fifteenth century and caught the fancy of the king of Orissa to such an extent that he recorded them in a book of his. No further proof of the existence of cultural links between Kāmarūpa and Utkala, rather Oḍeṣā, as it had come to be known in the fifteenth century, is perhaps called for.

Bhakti Ratnāvalī

Bhakti Ratnāvalī is a compilation of 409 *ślokas* on the various aspects of *bhakti* culled out mainly from *Śrimadbhāgawata.*[108] Its author, Viṣṇupurī was a *saṅyāsī* from Mithilā who lived between the years 1425 and 1500.[109] He wrote a Maithili version of this book also. A copy of the Sanskrit book was presented to Śaṅkaradeva towards the fag end of his life by a Brāhmaṇa of Hajo.[110] Śaṅkaradeva was greatly impressed by the compilation and decided to translate it into Assamese. Due to his advanced age, however, he was unable to proceed with the arduous task and entrusted it to his chief disciple, Mādhavadeva, who completed it in 1,209 verses.[111] It is noteworthy that Śaṅkaradeva had himself prepared a similar compilation of 564 *ślokas* named *Bhakti Ratnākara* a few years earlier and on getting the copy of *Bhakti Ratnāvalī* he liked it so much that he said that if he had got it earlier, he would not have needed to compile *Bhakti Ratnākara.*[112]

Procurement of a copy of *Bhakti Ratnāvalī* by a Brāhmaṇa of Hajo within a few years of its compilation in Mithilā, the words of admiration for it uttered by no less a person than the great Śaṅkaradeva himself and its translation into Assamese within just a few decades of its compilation—all these facts clearly point to the great esteem of the people of Kāmarūpa for the scholarship of Mithilā in the fifteenth-sixteenth centuries.

Candrakalā Nāṭikā

This is an obscure Sanskrit drama written by Viśwanātha Kavirāja, the famous author of *Sāhitya Darpaṇa* who was also a minister of the Orissa king. A manuscript of this drama was discovered and edited by S.N. Rajguru and S.S. Das; it was published as an Appendix to *OHRJ*, Vol. VI, Part 1 in 1957. The prologue of the drama states that it was being staged in the presence of the King Niḥśaṅka Bhānudeva (1414-34). The editors have surmised that it was written by the King's Sāṅdhivigrahin, Viśwanātha, and staged in the very first year of his reign in connection with the celebrations organized to mark the king's victory over Jalāluddin, the Sultan of Gauḍa. Of interest to us, however, is the opening speech of the *Sūtradhāra*, in which he eulogizes the king and names the countries worsted by him. The list includes some of the names traditionally included in such eulogies and some well-known ones like Cola, Kośala, Vaṅga, Gauḍa, Ḍāhala, Karṇāta, etc. Then there are two unusual names: Kocha and Hāvaṅga. These undoubtedly refer to the Koch territory in western Kāmarūpa and Hābung in the north-east of Kāmarūpa. Interestingly, the first independent Koch state was founded by Viśwa Siṁha in AD 1515; the reference to the Koch country fully one hundred years earlier in a drama written in the far away Orissa by a court dignitary, therefore, assumes even greater significance. As regards Hāvaṅga, no state by this name in this region was ever formed, but as a territorial unit in the fifteenth century Hābung is mentioned in many Ahom *buranjīs* as well as in the *Vaiṣṇava* literature of Assam. However two copper plate grants found in the Lakhimpur district inform us of the existence of a line of kings with Nārāyaṇa-ending names ruiling in this region in the fourteenth century. These dated C.P. grants refer to the Kings Satyanārāyaṇa, Pratyakṣanārāyaṇa, Lakṣmīnārāyaṇa and Yaśa (or Yama?)-nārāyaṇa who are described as rulers of Sadhayāpurī that can be easily identified with the modern Sadia in the Jonai district (east of Lakhimpur)[113]. Sadia as well as the find places of the two C.P. grants fall in the old Hābung region. No further details of this dynasty are ascertainable but it can be surmised that the above named Kings were the ancestors of

Dhīranārāyaṇa and Candranārayaṇa, the Kings of the Sootea community (tribe?) vanquished by the Ahoms in AD 1522 as recorded in the Ahom *buranjīs*.[114] It is indeed significant that the author of the *Candrakalā Nāṭikā* in Orissa knew about this obscure far flung region. Viewed in conjunction with the evidence of *Dīpīkā Candra*, it is surely interesting that the history and geography of Assam were attracting the attention of the elite in Orissa in the fifteenth century. It is difficult to say why it was so, except that it appears to be a continuation of the cultural links between Kāmarūpa and Utkala that existed since the Bhauma-Kara times.

NOTES AND REFERENCES

1. *The Classical Age*, p. 296.
2. *Ibid.*
3. *Brahma Purāṇa*, Chapters 42, 45-51and 69.
4. Ibid., Chapters 41.
5. Ibid., Chapter 42.
6. Ibid., Chapter 28.
7. Ibid., Chapter 62.
8. Ibid., Chapter 28.
9. Ibid., Chapter 38.
10. Ibid., Chapter 202.
11. Ibid., Chapters 202-4.
12. Ibid., Chapter 87.
13. Ibid., Chapter 88.
14. Ibid., Chapter 219.
15. Ibid., 219.17.
16. Ibid., 219.115.
17. Ibid., 219.116.
18. Ramaranjan, Mukherji and Sachindra Kumar Maity, *Corpus of Bengal Inscriptions bearing on History and Civilisation of Bengal*, pp. 61-65.
19. *Brahma Purāṇa*, 220.23 - 27.
20. Biswa Narayan Shastri (ed.), *TīrthaKaumudī*, Introduction, pp. lxiv -lxv.
21. Ibid.
22. S.C. Banerji, *Studies in the Mahāpurāṇas*, p. 32.
23. P.V. Kane, *History of Dharmaśāstra*, vol.I, Part I, pp. 421-22.
24. Ibid., p. 6.
25. Ibid.
26. For this chronology reference may be made to the Chronological Table in P.V. Kane's *History of Dharmaśāstra*, vol. IV, pp. ix-xii.
27. Har Prasad Shastri, Preface to *Catalogue of Sanskrit Manuscripts of Asiatic Society of Bengal*, vol. III.
28. P.V. Kane, *History of Dharmaśāstra*, vol. 1, part II, p. 982.

29. Manoranjan Sastri, 'The Kāmarūpa School of Dharmaśāstra with Particular Notice of Pītāṁbara Siddhāntavāgīśa' in *Pragjyotisa Souvenir* (XXII session of the Oriental Conference, Gauhati, 1965), p. 103.
30. S.C. Banerji, op.cit., pp. 48-49.
31. Ibid.
32. Manoranjan Sastri, op.cit., p. 94.
33. Ibid., pp. 100-102 lists these works.
34. Ibid., pp. 91-92.
35. Ibid., pp. 99-101 lists these works.
36. Ibid., p. 92..
37. Ibid., pp. 96-97.
38. Ibid., p. 97.
39. S.K. Bhuyan, 'A Note on Assamese Manuscripts' in Hemchandra Goswami, *Descriptive Catalogue of Assamese Manuscripts*, pp. xix-xx.
40. List and periods as given in S.C. Banerji, *A Brief History of Dharmaśāstra*, pp. 48-57.
41. Ibid., pp. 126-134.
42. Ibid., pp. 134-146.
43. Ibid., pp. 134-135.
44. H.K. Satpathy, Preface to Atul Kumar Nanda (ed), *Vishwanath's Smṛiti Sāra Samgrahaḥ*, p. 13.
45. K.C. Panigrahi, *Hostory of Orissa*, p. 272.
46. Ibid., pp. 278-79.
47. Ibid., p. 279.
48. Ibid.
49. Ibid.
50. Ibid.
51. This list and the chronology is based on H.K. Satpathy, op.cit. He, however, mentions the date of Gadādhara as AD 1715. It is P.V.Kane who has placed Gadādhara between c. 1450 and 1500 AD.
52. S.C. Banerji, op.cit., p. 149.
53. B.K. Barua, *A Cultural History of Assam*, vol. I, p. 119.
54. Manoranjan Sastri, op.cit., p. 91.
55. B.N. Shastri (ed.), *Kālikā Purāṇa*, Introduction, convincingly establishes the date and place of origin of this *(Upa)-Purāṇa.*
56. *Kālikā Purāṇa*, Chapters 78-80.
57. Ibid., Chapters 37-40.
58. Ibid., 64.43.
59. Ibid., 64.44.
60. Ibid., 64.11.
61. Ibid., 1.1-3.
62. Ibid., 1.3.
63. Ibid., 40.87.
64. Ibid., 40.135.
65. Ibid., 80.95-100.
66. *Yoginī Tantra*, 2.9.241-243.

67. Ibid., 2.3.76.
68. Ibid., 2.4.136 and 2.4.138.
69. Ibid., 1.11.66.
70. Ibid., 1.11.61.
71. Ibid., 1.11.63.
72. For example, ibid., 1.13.8 and 1.13.10.
73. Ibid., 2.2.5 and 2.2.15-19.
74. Ibid., 2.2.26.
75. Ibid., 2.4.11.
76. Sunitikumar Chatterji and Babua Misra (ed.), *Varna Ratnākara of Jyotirīśvara Kaviśekharācarya*, Introduction, p. xxi.
77. Ibid., p. xiv.
78. Sunitikumar Chatterji, *Artavallabha Mahanti Memorial Lectures (First Series, 1964)*, p. 19.
79. Ibid.
80. *Varṇa Ratnākara*, p. 8.
81. Ibid., pp. 21 and 22.
82. Ibid., p. 13.
83. Ibid.
84. Ibid., p. 34.
85. Ibid., p. 37.
86. Ibid., p. 44.
87. Ibid., p. 57.
88. Ibid., p. 64.
89. Ibid., p. 63.
90. Ibid., pp. 12 and 56.
91. Ibid., p. 56.
92. Ibid.
93. Ibid., p. 56.
94. Ibid., p. 52.
95. Ibid.
96. Ibid., p. 56.
97. Ibid., p. 52.
98. Ibid., p. 60.
99. Ibid., p. 60.
100. B.N. Shastri (ed.), *Kālikā Purāṇa*, Introduction, pp. 23-27.
101. *Varṇa Ratnākara*, p. 22.
102. Hemchandra Goswami, *Descriptive Catalogue of Assamese Manuscripts*, No. 106, pp. 124-26.
103. Krishna Narayan Prasad, 'Māgadh', *Mādhavadeva: Vyaktitva aur Krititva* (in Hindi), pp. 51-54.
104. Hemchandra Goswami, op.cit., No. 42, pp 48-51.
105. Ibid., p. 48.
106. P.C. Choudhury, *The History of Civilization of the People of Assam to the Twelfth Century A.D.*, p. 14.

107. Ibid., pp. 118-19.
108. 'Māgadh', op.cit., p. 49.
109. Durganath Jha 'Shrīsh', *Maithilī Sāhityaka Itihāsa* (in Maithili), Part I, p. 85.
110. 'Māgadh', op.cit., pp. 47-48.
111. Ibid., p. 47-49 .
112. Ibid., p. 48.
113. Maheswar Neog, *Prācya Śāsanāvalī*, Texts, App. A, p. 93 and p. 96.
114. Ibid., Introduction (in Assamese), p. 84.

Chapter 9

The Age of Vidyāpati and Śaṅkaradeva

In the present study the period from the late fourteenth to the late sixteenth century is being designated as the age of Vidyāpati and Śaṅkaradeva for the purpose of our study.

Vidyāpati (1350-1450)[1], the great scholar, poet and *nibandhakāra* of Mithilā was the most outstanding figure of his time whose influence on the languages and literatures was felt not only in the eastern but the whole of India. His influence has been such an all-prevading one that he has been claimed even by Bengali[2] and Hindi[3] as their own. His poetry was responsible for the emergence of a new language, *Brajabolī*, in Bengal, Assam and Orissa, whose role in bringing the three regions of our study closer to each other shall be discussed in the second section of this chapter.

ŚAṄKARADEVA AND HIS DEBT TO MITHILĀ AND UTKALA

Śaṅkaradeva is a unique figure in the history of Assam. In the words of Banikanta Kakati, "Śaṅkaradeva has given Assam a new life, letters and a state. Rulers have come and gone and their kingdoms perished in the dust, but Śaṅkara's state endures and "broad in the general hearts of men his power survives."[4] Such men are rarely born in any society and Śaṅkaradeva was, therefore, truly a *Yuga Puruṣa.*

His influence on the society and culture of Assam is without parallel in the history of medieval India—it is only approximated by Nanak in Punjab and Tulasīdāsa in the Gangetic plains.

Śaṅkaradeva was born in the year 1449 at Bardowa in the Nagaon district of central Assam. A *Kāyastha* by caste, his ancestors had migrated from Kanauj only five generations earlier. A large part of Assam during this period was ruled by the semi-independent estate-holders called *Bhuiyāñs.* Śaṅkara's father, Kusumavara, was also a Bhuiyāñ chieftain called *Śiromaṇi Bhuiyāñ* because his primacy was acknowledged by the other neighbouring Bhuiyāñs. Śaṅkara's parents died when he was barely seven years old and he had to be brought up by his grandmother, Khersutī. He received good education and became well-versed in the *śāstras* and the Sanskrit lore of the time. At the age of twentyone he was married to Sūryavatī and also took over the responsibilities of the *Śiromaṇi Bhuiyāñ.* Within a few years, his wife died leaving behind a daughter, Manu. Śaṅkara became desolate and started devoting himself to religion and self-purīfication and contemplating *vairāgya.* Eventually, at the age of thirtyone, in 1481, he renounced his home and proceeded on a pilgrimage after marrying off his daughter to one Hari and entrusting his estate to two aged uncles of his father.

This pilgrimage lasted for twelve long years and took him and his seventeen companions to all corners of India, from Badarikāśrama in the north to Setubandha Rāmeśvaram in the south and from Dvārīkā in the west to Jagannāth Purī in the east. He also visited the Vrajabhūmi around Mathurā and the various places in Mithilā but his longest sojourn was at Purī. In the course of his travels he met a large number of saints, poets and holy men and absorbed the essentials of the *Bhakti* movement that was sweeping across the length and breadth of the country. Not only that, he also saw the miserable condition of the Hindu subjects of the iconoclastic foreign rulers in different parts of India, particularly in the 'Āryavarta' that he must have come to love from his study of the Purāṇas. Returning home in 1493, he found that the condition of the people under the rule of the foreigner Ahoms was perhaps no better. No doubt, they were not attacking the religion of their subjects; rather, they were themselves, slowly gravitating towards Hinduism, but the autocratic behaviour of the rulers and their cronies was often intolerable. On the other hand, the people were thoroughly disunited and following the most degenerated form of the Śaiva and Śākta religions. Even the prevailing Vaiṣṇavism was tainted with Tāntrik rituals. Remnants of Vajrayāna in the form of obnoxious rituals were also prevalent. Śaṅkaradeva at once saw the need to pull the society out of this spiritual morass and concluded that *Bhakti* was the only means for the salvation of the individual as well as the society. He started preaching this *Bhakti.* He emphasized on the one-ness of the Supreme Reality whom he called Kṛṣṇa, equality of all before Him irrespective of caste or social status and surrender before Him as one's prime duty and means of release from suffering; he also started opposing the prevailing pantheism and the atrocious bloody practices in the name of the worship of the Goddess. Based on these tenets he initiated his *Eka Śaraṇa dharma* and started giving *mantra* to his disciples including Brāhmaṇas. The entrenched orthodox Brāhmaṇa clergy complained to the Ahom monarch, Suhummung, that Śaṅkaradeva was destroying the *dharma* and the established order; the main charges against him were that he did not worship the *devī,* was a crypto-Buddhist, and being a *śūdra* i.e., a non Brāhmaṇa, he had no right to give *mantra* to anyone, much less to a Brāhmaṇa. Śaṅkaradeva could extricate himself from a very trickly situation only by the dint of his knowledge of the *śāstras* and great skill at religious disputation. Nevertheless, his persecution continued to take place every now and then and to this were added the attacks on his estate by the Kachārīs who had their kingdom to its south. For more than thirty years Śaṅkaradeva led a very trubulent life and had to flee and change his residence a number of times. Eventually, he took shelter in Koch Bihar. In the year 1534, the founder of the Koch kingdom, Viśwa Siṁha had died and his son, Malladeva alias Naranārāyaṇa had ascended the throne. The new king and his brother and commander-in-chief, Śukladhvaja, were most enlightened rulers and great patrons of learning, religion, arts and culture. Thus, Śaṅkaradeva found a very congenial atmosphere in the court and kingdom of Naranārāyaṇa. He divided his time between places in Kāmarūpa in the modern Barpeta district and Koch Bihar during the last twenty years of his life and passed away near Koch Bihar in the year 1568 at the age of 119 years. A remarkable event of this period is that in the year 1550, at the age of 101 years, Śaṅkaradeva undertook the second pilgrimage of his life. This time he was accompanied by 120 followers and went only to Jagannnāth Purī—the pilgrimage lasted for less than one year.

Narrating the life story of Śaṅkaradeva is not one of the objectives of the present study; yet, an outline of the same has been given above for a better appreciation of the discussion below. As regards the facts and events of his life, fortunately we have a lot of authentic information from the near-contemporary biographers and excellent books by modern authors.[5] Here we shall confine ourselves only to discussing the role played by Mithilā and Orissa in shaping Śaṅkaradeva's philosophy and concept of *bhakti*.

A Brāhmaṇa from Hajo named Kaṇṭhabhūṣaṇa had once gone on a pilgrimage during which he procured a copy of *Bhakti Ratnāvalī*, compiled by a *saṅyāsī*, Viṣṇupurī of Mithilā. We have already taken note of this work in Chapter 8, supra. Viṣṇupurī was named Ramāpati before taking *saṅyāsa* and was a reputed scholar of Mithilā.[6] He is known to have written many books and his period has been fixed to be AD 1425-1500.[7] He is known to have composed a few works in Maithili as well as a Sanskrit commentary, *Kāntimālā*, on his own *Bhakti Ratnāvalī*.[8] The Brāhmaṇa, Kaṇṭhabhūṣaṇa, presented his copy of BR along with a copy of *Kāntimāla* to Śaṅkaradeva who was greatly impressed by it.[9] By now Śaṅkaradeva had already composed a number of his works but henceforth he must have been influenced by *BR* and *Kāntimālā*. Another significant event in the life of Śaṅkaradeva occurred earlier when soon after his return from his first pilgrimage in 1493 he was visited by a

Brāhmaṇa from Tirhut, i.e., Mithilā, named Jagadīśa Miśra who had brought for him a copy of *Bhāvartha Dīpīkā*, a commentary on *Śrīmadbhāgawata* written by Śrīdharaswāmī of Purī.[10] He informed Śaṅkaradeva that he was instructed by a *sanyāsī* of Purī to give this book to Śaṅkaradeva.[11] Śaṅkaradeva's biographers have recorded that discussion on this book continued at Śaṅkara's residence for many years and finally, it was concluded that *Bhāgawata* was the ultimate book on *Bhakti* and, thenceforth, Śaṅkaradeva leaned heavily on the *Śrīdharī ṭīkā* for determining the tenets of his *Eka Śaraṇa dharma.*[12]

After returning from his pilgrimage in 1493, Śaṅkaradeva devoted all his time and energy to propagation of his *Eka Śaraṇa dharma* and opposing the obnoxious rites of the *Tantrikas* and superstitions as well as to spreading the message of equality of all men. He established a few *Satras*, as the centres of the new faith. In course of time every village in Assam came to build its own *nāmaghar* which became the centre for bringing about social cohesion. During the next seventyfive years of his life, Śaṅkaradeva produced an enormous amount of literature for the propagation of his ideas and recruited disciples from all castes and classes including tribals and at least one Muslim.

Even though he was an erudite scholar of Sanskrit, Śaṅkaradeva chose the language of the common man of Kāmarūpa—what we call Assamese today—for propounding his ideas because he wanted his message to reach and be understood by one and all. He composed a number of *Upākhyāna Kāvyas*, or long poems narrating episodes from the Purāṇas, the *Rāmāyaṇa* and the *Mahābhārata.* A few of these are also included in his *Kīrtana ghoṣā*, a collection of *Kīrtanas* for singing by the devotees. His *upākhayāna kāvyas* may be considered as free translations from the scriptures. He also wrote the *Uttarakāṇḍa* of *Rāmāyaṇa* which was written in order to complete the *Rāmāyaṇa* left unfinished by the poet Mādhava Kandalī of the fourteenth century. Śaṅkaradeva composed a number of devotional hymns called *Borgīta* and six dramas in Brajabulī; these will be taken up in some detail in the next section of this chapter.

Exhibition of scholarship or impressing scholars with his learning being far from his mind, Śaṅkaradeva refrained from writing in Sanskrit. In fact, the *Toṭaya*, a melodious hymn in just nine verses, is the only Sanskrit composition of Śaṅkaradeva. He also did not attempt any commentary on scriptures; rather, he compiled *Bhakti Ratnākara*, a collection of 564 verses culled out from the various scriptures, particularly the *Bhāgawata.*[13] In explaining these verses he has mostly relied on the *ṭīkā* of Śrīdharaswāmī. Scholars have also spotted the influence of Viṣṇupurī's *Kāntimālā* on the explanation of just two verses.[14]

The basic tenets of the religion propounded by Śaṅkaradeva are the oneness of the Supreme Reality whom he calls Kṛṣṇa, and his *bhakti* as the prime duty of man and the only means of *mukti* from all misery. The most potent method to achieve the goal of *bhakti* is *nāmasmaraṇa*—constantly chanting the Lord's name. He declared that all human beings regardless of their caste or social status could and should practice *bhakti.*

The system propounded by him is named *Eka Śaraṇa dharma* as well as the *Mahāpuruṣiyā dharma.* The meaning of the first term is self-explanatory; in the other name, the word Mahāpuruṣa refers to Kṛṣṇa, the Great Puruṣa, the Ultimate Cause. In later times Śaṅkaradeva and his chief disciple Mādhavadeva were also given the appellation *mahāpurṣa* because of which people often think that the *Mahāpurṣiyā dharma* refers to the *dharma* propagated by them; it is really not so, the term relates to Kṛṣṇa only. At the philosophical level Śaṅkaradeva is clearly a monist, a non-dualist. As noted above, he fashioned his teachings largely on the *Śrīdharī ṭīkā* of the *Bhāgawata.* This Śrīdharaswāmī was the head of the Govardhana piṭha at Purī, one of the four great *pīṭhas* established by Śaṅkaracarya. There is every likelihood of Śaṅkaradeva having attended the discourses of Śrīdharaswāmī on the *Bhāgawata* during his long stay at Purī; later as noted above, he obtained a copy of the *Śrīdharī ṭīkā.* He has freely acknowledged his debt to Śrīdharaswāmī. In his *Bhakti Ratnākara* he often uses phrases like *Śrīdharaswāmītaḥ śabdagataḥ, Śrīdharaswāmiṭīkaiva gṛhīta, Swāmiṭīkaivānusruta Śrīdharaswāmīvyākhyānāmeva gṛhītaṁ,* etc.[15] All this would mean that Śaṅkaradeva was a follower of Advaita as propounded by Śaṅkarācārya. It is said that the blending of Śāṅkara Advaita with *Bhakti* was achieved by Viṣṇuswāmī, Śrīdharaswāmī and Madhusūdana Saraswatī and it is this philosophy to which Śaṅkaradeva adhered. However, the great emphasis that Śaṅkaradeva places on the surrender to Him—*śaraṇa*—appears to be very close to the concept of *prapatti* expounded by Rāmānuja. The *Śrīvaiṣṇava* sect of Rāmānuja too had a strong presence at Purī in the fifteenth century and there is every reason to believe that Śaṅkaradeva was influenced by them.

Śaṅkaradeva was a teacher of *Bhakti,* first and last. It is, therefore, not of much consequence to determine the system of philosophy that he followed. For the purpose of the present study, it is sufficient to note that the source of all his religious and philosophical ideas and ideals are traceable to his experiences at Purī in Orissa. His connection with Mithilā too contributed to the crystallization of his concept as may be inferred from the Viṣṇupurī episode. In fact, it stands to reason that during his first pilgrimage while passing through Mithilā, Śaṅkaradeva may have come in direct contact with Viṣṇupurī. The latter must have been a *sanyāsī* in his sixties and Śaṅkaradeva must have been impressed not only by his command over the scriptures but also his Maithili poetry that is said to be of a high order.[16] Incidently, it may also be noted that in the *Kāntimālā,* the commentary on his own *Bhakti Ratnāvalī,*[17] Viṣṇupurī has often quoted Śrīdharaswāmī. It would thus appear that Śaṅkaradeva absorbed the same influences from Orissa as well as Mithilā.

Śaṅkaradeva was not in favour of idol-worship and in the prayer hall—*nāmaghar* or *Kīrtanaghar*—of his *satras* a copy of the *Bhāgawata* instead of an idol is installed on the *siṁhāsana,* the pedestal. Yet, he seems to have had a special reverence for Jagannātha of Purī. In fact, he had not obtained *dīkṣā* from any *guru* and it is said that he considered Jagannātha himself as his *guru.* This view gets some support from his long poem, *Oreṣā Varṇanā* (description of *Oreṣā*); he cites the *Brahma Purāṇa* as the basis of this work and extols Jagannātha in it. He is even believed to have installed a wooden image called Madana Mohana; evidently, he did so for the satisfaction of the common folk to facilitate the propagation of his new faith even though at the philosophical level he did not favour idol-worship.

Certain scholars hold that probably the idea of *nāmaghar* was borrowed by Śaṅkaradeva form the *Bhāgawataghar* of Orissa.[18] In these *Bhāgawataghars* the Oriya *Bhāgawata* of the poet Jagannātha Dāsa is installed just as the Assamese *Bhāgawata* of Śaṅkaradeva is kept in the *nāmaghars* of Assam. It is, however, difficult to agree with this view for the institution of *Bhāgawataghar* is certainly of a later origin. Jagannātha Dāsa, one of the five Oriya saint-poets called *pañca-sakha,* was almost of the same age as Caitanyā (b. 1486)[19] and, therefore, when Śaṅkaradeva stayed at Purī between 1485 and 1490 he must have been a mere child. By the time of Śaṅkaradeva's second pilgrimage to Purī in 1550, Jagannātha Dāsa had certainly written his Oriya *Bhāgawata* but it is impossible to believe that within a few years of its writing it had become so popular as to reach almost every village in Orissa and get installed in the *Bhāgawataghars.* Moreover, Śaṅkaradeva had already established more than one *satra* well before 1550 with the *nāmaghar* or *Kīrtanaghar* as its integral part.

PURĪ AS THE HOLIEST PLACE

Jagannātha Purī or the Puruṣottama Kṣetra has been one of the most popular places of pilgrimage in India ever since the concept of *tīrtha* evolved. It was undoubtedly very popular in Assam in the medieval period and that is why Śaṅkaradeva chose to spend so much time there. The devotional and intellectual ambience of the place must have prompted him to prolong his stay. Then, because of his association with the place, it became a favourite place for his followers as well.

Thus, Vanamālīdeva (1576-1683) is known to have performed a pilgrimage of Jagannātha Purī in the year 1657.[20] He was the head of the Damodarapur *satra*. This *satra* was established by the king Lakṣmīnārāyaṇa, son and successor of Naranārāyaṇa of Koch Bihar, near his capital for Dāmodaradeva, one of the chief disciples of Śaṅkaradeva.[21] Dāmodara's successor was Vaṅśīgopāladeva who was succeeded by Vanamālīdeva. Vanamālīdeva not only visited Purī, he also planned to set up a *satra* there. A plot of land was purchased and some construction work also started but the plan did not materialize.[22] By now idol worship had entered the *Eka Śaraṇa dharma*. Something that was ingrained in the psyche of the people for centuries could not be easily uprooted. It is reasonable to hold that the power and attraction of Jagannātha was perhaps responsible for adoption of idol-worship by the followers of Śaṅkaradeva within less than a century of this demise. On his way back from Purī, Vanamālīdeva not only brought the *prasāda* of Jagannātha but also a stone image of Kṛṣṇa. This image is still worshipped under the name of Yādavarāya at the Dakhinpāṭ *satra* situated on the Majuli island in the Brahmaputra in the Jorhat district. Significantly, this deity is offered cooked food every day—a reminder of Jagannātha, no doubt!

Another episode connecting Purī and Assam is worth mentioning. An indirect effect of awakening amongst the people caused by the new faith of Śaṅkaradeva was acceleration of the process of Hinduization of the Ahoms. The first seeds of Hinduism amongst the Ahom rulers were sown as early as the time of the king Sujenphā or Bāmunī Koñwar in the early fifteenth century but is started germinating only during the period of *Dihiñgiā Rājā* (1497-1539) who adopted the title of *Swarga Nārāyaṇa*. The formal entry of an Ahom monarch into a Hindu sect, however, had to wait till 1654 when the king Sutāmlā alias Jayadhwaja Siṁha took *śaraṇa* or *dīkṣā* from the head of the Auniatī satra. With the spread of Śaṅkaradeva's new faith, the Ahoms appear to be developing reverence for the Hindu *tīrthas*, particularly Jagannātha Purī. We have no record of any Ahom monarch going on a pilgrimage but the Ahom *Burañjīs* (chronicles) tell us that the King Susengphā alias Pratāp Siṁha had planned to get a tank excavated at Jagannātha Purī. It may be marked that by now the Ahom kings had started adopting Hindu names in addition to their Tāī-Ahom names; this they used to do at he time of their coronation which ceremony was now performed according to both the Ahom and the Hindu *śāstric* rituals. Pratāp Siṁha, popularly known as the *Būṛhā Rājā*, because he had ascended the throne at an advanced age, was given the epithet *Budhi Swarga Nārāyaṇa* because we was considered to be very wise, ruled for long thirtyeight years[23] from AD 1611 to 1649. The *burañjīs* record that in the year 1617, i.e., soon after his accession, he sent two envoys to Purī with a large sum of money with instruction to have a tank excavated at the holy city. The two envoys, however, failed to execute the order; instead, they spent the money on purchasing a couple of Bengali girls. The King's reaction to this offence was swift and severe. He was not called *Budhi Swarga Nārāyaṇa* for nothing; he got the two culprits beheaded and set the unfortunate girls free.[24] This episode reveals the reverence of the Ahom monarch for Jagannātha on the one hand and, on the other, hints at a possible diplomatic contact between Assam and Orissa. The Ahom King could not have contemplated any construction in a foreign Kingdom without obtaining the concurrence of its ruler. We have no way to know whose concurrence or permission was sought in this case. Orissa had already lost its independence to the Sultans of Bengal in 1568 and in 1617 it was under the rule of some governor appointed by the Sultan. Any further, exploration of the matter is, therefore, not quite relevant for the present study.

BRAJABŪLĪ, THE LINGUA-FRANCA OF EASTERN VAIṢṆAVAS

The peculiarities of the language of the poems (*padas*) of the medieval Vaiṣṇava poets of Bengal was noticed for the first time by John Beams. He noted n 1873 that the language of these poems was more akin to Maithili than to Bengali.[25] Some years later, George Grierson declared that this "was a kind of a 'hybrid' language, neither Bengali nor Maithili" used by these Vaiṣṇava poets of Bengal in their attempt to imitate the songs of Vidyāpatī, the great poet of Mithilā.[26] This language was subsequently given the name Brajabūlī—when and by whom, we do not know. The important point to note is that unlike Brajabhāṣā it is not the dialect of any particular region. Dr. Sukumar Sen says "This artificial language was given the name of Brajabūlī because it reminded one of Vraja, the land sanctified by the presence of Rādhā and Kṛṣṇa. The term Brajabūlī, however, should not be confused with the name of Brajabhākhā or Brahabhāṣā. The latter is the name of the actual spoken language, a form of western Hindi of the district round about Muttra."[27] Suniti Kumar Chatterji, writing in 1927, accepted this view about the origin of Brajabūlī and further stated that this new language of the Vaiṣṇava poetry of Bengal was a mixture of Maithili, Bengali and western Hindi (i.e., Brajabhāṣā). Regarding the background of its evolution Dr. Chatterji wrote in 1940:

> Mithila was the resort of Sanskrit students from Bengal for some three hundred years after the conquest of the latter province by the Turks. She was the teacher and inspirer of Bengal in Sanskrit learning in *Smṛti,* and specially in *nyāya.* Bengali scholars

would come back home after finishing their studies in Mithila not only with Sanskrit learning in their heads, but also with Maithili songs on their lips—songs by Vidyapati, and also probably his predecessors and his successors. These were adopted by the Bengali people, and they gave a new literary dialect, the *Brajabūlī*, to Bengal. The Maithili lyric similarly naturalized itself in Assam and in Orissa in the fifteenth century.[28]

In 1949, Suniti Babu reiterated these views and further elaborated the role of Vidyāpati when he said:

The cultural and intellectual ties between Mithila and Bengal, have always been very close. Bengalis, after the conquest of their province by the Turks and the establishment of a Musllim state, found in Mithila and in Orissa two neighbouring lands with a Hindu *regime* and a Hindu culture retained intact, and to Mithila the best scholars of Bengal were in the habit of repairing for higher Sanskrit studies for some centuries after the Turki conquest. Five hundred years ago the language of Mithila and that of Bengal were much closer to each other: a thousand years ago these were very closely agreeing dialects, if not actually the same speech. A great Maithila poet, Vidyapati, had a host of imitators in Bengal (as well as in Assam and Orissa), and these imitators followed their master to the extent of imitating his early Maithila speech in Bengal; and this resulted in the creation of an artificial mixture of Maithili and Bengali into a special dialect for *Vaishnava* religions poetry known in Bengal as the *Braja-buli*, in which Bengali poets from the second half of the 15th century down to our day have composed lyrics centring around the divine love of Radha and Krishna.[29]

There is no season to dispute these views; *Brajabūlī* was clearly evolved by the Vaiṣṇava poets of Assam, Bengal and Orissa by imitating the Maithili of Vidyāpati and mixing in it their own language—Assamese, Bengali and Oriya—with a sprinkling of *Brajabhāṣā.* The three regions, therefore, have their own distinctive brand of Brajabūlī. It is significant that this language was used only by the Vaiṣṇava poets in all the three regions. It would be interesting to explore why it did not find favour with others; the reason perhaps is that the post-Vidyāpati period for about three centuries is an almost exclusively Vaiṣṇava period not only in the eastern but the whole of northern India. Very little non-*Bhakti* literature was created during this period and *Bhakti* consisted mainly of the *Vaiṣṇava Bhakti.* No wonder, a great literary historian, Ācārya Ram Chandra Shukla has designated the period from Vikrama Saṁvat 1375 to 1700 (c. AD 1318-1643) as the *Bhakti Kāla* of the Hindi Literature.[30]

The popularity of Vidyāpati in Bengal is testified to by the contemporary records as well. Thus, it is recorded in *Śrī Caitanya Caritāmṛta* of Kriṣṇadāsa Kavirāja that the Mahāprabhu used to greatly enjoy the songs of Jayadeva, Caṇḍādāsa and Vidyāpati.[31] The disciples of Caitanya gave birth to the *Padāvalī* literature of Bengal, the sweetest part of the Bengali literature. From Grierson onwards till the 1930's the study of Brajabūlī literature centred around the *Padāvalī* literature of Bengal. With the publication of the *History of Brajabūlī Literature* by Sukumar Sen, in 1935, it was discovered that the disciples of Caitanya were not the first to write in Brajabūlī. That distinction was conferred on Yaśorāja Khān (real name Dāmodara Sen) of the early sixteenth century who is credited to have composed the long poem *Kṛṣṇa Maṅgala* and was anterior to Baḍu Caṇḍīdāsa.[32] Next poets of note were Murāri Gupta (born AD 1470) and Narahari Sarkar (born 1478), both direct disciples of Caitanya.[33]

In the Brajabūlī studies little attention was paid to Assam and Orisssa possibly because the literatures of these provinces were hardly known outside their home provinces till then. From the 1940's, however, scholars started taking notice of the Brajabūlī lliterature of Assam and Orissa and gradually they began to realize that the Brajabūlī literature did not originate in the post-Caitanya period in Bengal, but much earlier in Assam and Orissa.

It has been known all along that Rāya Rāmānanda, a disciple of Caitanya had composed songs in Brajabūlī, but it was presumed that he must have done so after coming into contact with the great master. It is now known that he had actually composed many such poems much earlier. It is recorded in the *Caitanya Caritāmṛta* that Śrī Caitanya met Rāya Rāmānanda in AD 1511 at Vidyānagara, on the banks of Godavari when the latter mesmerized him by singing a song of his own composition. Fortunately, this entire *pada* is preserved in the *Caitanya Caritāmṛta* of Kṛṣṇadāsa Kāvirāja as well as in *Caitanya Caritāmṛta Mahākāvya* of Kavi Karṇapoor. It is clearly in Brajabūlī.[34]

Then the great compositions of Śaṅkaradeva and his chief disciple Mādhavadeva that were the life support of the Vaiṣṇavas of Assam, started being noticed by the outside world. Both of them admittedly belonged to the pre-*Padāvali* period. It is now known that Śaṅkaradeva had already started composing his Borgītas in Brajabūlī when Śrī Caitanya was born in AD 1486. His near-contemporary biographers have recorded that he composed his first Borgīta '*Mana meri Rāma-caraṇehuṅ lāgu*' at Badarikāśrama[35] during his first pilgrimage, i.e., sometime in the 1480's. During this pilgrimage he had spent some time at Mithilā as well as in the Vraja region around Mathurā. This was the period when the songs of Vidyāpati were on the lips of everybody in Mithilā and Śaṅkaradeva must have been enthralled by them. He must have heard other songs in Maithili. His *Bhakti* was getting ripened during this period of his life. We have noted earlier the possibility of his having met Viṣṇupurī while in Mithilā; his Maithila poems too must have impressed him. In the sylvan surroundings of the holy Badarikāśrama the devotion of his heart spontaneously gushed forth from his lips in the form of a song in the language of Mithilā mixed with that of the Vraja—just like the first *śloka* from the mouth of the Ādikavi Vālmīki! Śaṅkaradeva assiduously cultivated this language and wrote a large number of songs—*Borgītas*—in Brajabūlī over the next eight decades. He is reputed to have written twelve scores, i.e., 240 *Borgītas* but only forty-one of these have survived. His disciples too continued to compose songs in Brajabūlī. *Borgiītas* is really a special name given only to the Brajabūlī hymns of Śankaradeva and his disciples. In all, a total of 207 *Borgītas* are extant—of these 41 are by Śaṅkaradeva, 154 by Mādhavadeva, one each by Rāmacaraṇa Thākura and Daityāri Thākurā and ten by Puruṣottama Thākura.[36] On account of their great literary merit and spiritual content the *Borgītas* have been designated as 'Noble Numbers' by Banikanta Kakati.[37]

Coming to Orissa, we have already noted the Brajabūlī compositions of Rāya Rāmānanda before AD 1511. However, the earliest Brajabūlī *padas* found in Orissa are attributed to Nṛpa Baidyanātha, popularly known as Baijaladeva.[38] Significantly, in the *bhaṇitā* of a few *padas* of Vidyāpati both these names occur.[39] In an anonymous *pada*, the names of Śiva Siṁha and Baidynātha occur together implying that these two kings were contemporaries.[40] Śiva Siṁha, the king of Mithilā, is the well-known patron of Vidyāpati in whose praise the poet has written many lines. The identity of Nṛpa Baidyanātha or Baijaladeva remained controversial for a long time. He was taken to be a king of Mithilā but no such name is found in the history of Mithilā. On the other hand, a grammar work in Sanskrit, titled *Prabodha Candrikā*, mentions Baijaladeva and his queen, Candrāvatī. He is described as the King of Paṭanā 'in the west of Utkala'. Vidyāpati also refers to Baijaladeva as 'Candālapati'; 'Candāla' is clearly the Prakritism for Candrāvatī just as 'Baijala' is that for Baidyanātha.[41] Now, Paṭanā was one of the numerous small states founded in the medieval times that continued to exist till their accession to the Indian Union in 1947-48. This state was ruled by the Cauhān rulers—in the *Prabodha Candrikā*, Baijaladeva is also described as *Cauhāna-vaṁśa-tilakaḥ Paṭanādhināthо.*[42]

About Vidyapāti's contact with Baidyanātha we have a significant reference in his short dramatic work *Maṇi Mañjarī*. The *sūtradhāra* of this drama says that it was being staged during the *yātrā* of Lord Puruṣottama.[43] This reference is just like a similar speech in *Anargha Rāghava* of Murāri Kavi noted in Chapter 7, supra, It is easy to surmise that the poet Vidyāpati met Baidyanātha Nṛpa during some such ratha yātrā festival at Purī and inspired him to compose poems in Oriya mixed with Maithili, i.e., the Brajabūlī of Orissa.

The earliest Brajabūlī poem in Orissa has, however, been traced to an even earlier period. King Kapilendradeva (1434-1466), the great warrior-king or Orissa, is credited to have written a Sanskrit drama, *Paraśurāma Vijaya* in which there is a song, the language of which is identified as *Brajabūlī*.[44] It clearly pre-dates Nṛpa Baidyanātha.

Before concluding this section, we may take note of a unique feature of the Brajabūlī literature of Assam, viz., its dramas. The Brajabūlī poets of neither Orissa nor Bengal, wrote anything but *padas* but Śaṅkaradeva attempted dramas too. In this respect, Śaṅkaradeva was a great innovator. The type of drama evolved by Śaṅkaradeva is called the *Ankiyā Nāṭa.* Birinchi Kumar Barna has written "Śaṅkaradeva was possibly influenced by his witnessing some of the plays of the Maithili poets, for instance the *Pārijāta Haraṇa* of Umapati when he was in Bihar in the heyday of Vidyapati's fame."[45] The influence of Maithali poets is no doubt a distinct possibility, rather a certainly, but Dr. Barua was perhaps not aware that the tradition of drama in Mithila at that period was weak and very different from the technique adopted in the *Ankiyā Nāṭa.* Only one drama, *Dhūrtta Samagāma*, a *prahasana*, is known to have been written in Maithili in the pre-Vidyāpati period. Even *Dhūrtta Samāgama* was written only a generation before Vidyāpati by Jyotirīśvara Kaviśekharācāra, the author of *Varṇa Ratnākara* that has been noted in Chapter 8, supra. Regarding Umāpati, Grierson and, following him, other scholars believed that he belonged to the thirteenth-fourteenth century.[46] But later researches have established that he actually belonged to the eighteenth century. He was active during the period of Maharaja Raghava Siṁha of Mithilā (1707-1740) and appears to have adorned the court of Hindūpati, a Bundela chief and descendant of the famous Chatrasāla.[47] So, the technique of the *Ankiyā Nāṭa* was entirely a creation of Śaṅkaradeva who wrote as many as six dramas in this idiom. Mādhavadeva and other disciples of Śaṅkaradeva too wrote a number of dramas in Brajabūlī. The dramas written in Assam comprise the entire dramatic literature of Brajabūlī.

We may, incidentally, make an interesting observation about the absence of the tradition of drama in Maithli. Dr. Jayakanta Mishra has frankly admitted: "In Mithila proper there is no evidence of any great dramatic activity in the vernacular till the installation of the Khaṇḍavālakula to power in 1557."[48] So much for Dr. B.K. Barua's observation about Śaṅkaradeva being influenced by the Maithili drama, Dr. Mishra goes on to describing the works of Śaṅkaradeva and other dramatists of Assam as the 'Maithili drama in Assam'.[49] It is clearly unfair to the Assamese literature because these dramas being written in the *Brajabūlī* of the Assam variety are the property of the Assamese literature. Even more interesting is the view of the Hindi Scholars claiming these dramas to be a part of the Hindi literature. Dr. Dasharath ojha finds the use of 'Old Hindi' in these dramas of Assam.[50] Regarding the language of Śaṅkaradeva's dramas he says, "Not only the songs but the entire play is in Maithili with a touch of Assamese."[51] Such claims are evidently based on the view held by many scholars that Maithili is but a dialect of Hindi like the Brajabhāṣā or Avadhī. And claiming Brajabūlī for Hindi is even easier because of the presence of the Brajabhāṣā elements in it.

In the previous section we had noted the great role played by Orissa and Mithilā in the evolution of Śaṅkaradeva's new faith. In the present section we have seen Mithilā's role in his literary development. It would be relevant to say that, in all probability, in this aspect too he owes a debt to Orissa as well.

In discussing the possible contact between Vidyāpati and Nṛpa Baidyanātha, we have seen that Vidyāpati's drama was being staged at Purī. Thus, Śaṅkaradeva's exposure to Maithili may not have taken place exclusively in Mithilā. He is likely to have heard the Maithili songs of Vidyāpati and Brajabūlī songs of Nṛpa Baidyanātha, and possibily, even Rāya Rāmānanda (who might have written some songs before 1490) during his sojourn at Purī as well. The language, literature and religion of Orissa and Mithilā all combined to create the persona of Śaṅkaradeva. This was the finest hour of the cultural alignment between Kāmaraūpa, Kaliṅga and Mithilā.

NOTES AND REFERENCES

1. Jayakanta Mishra, *A History of Maithili Literature,* vol. I, pp. 134-165 give details of the life and works of Vidyāpati including his date. Also see Durganath Jha 'Shrīsh', *Maithili Sāhityaka Itihāsa* (in Maithili), Part One, Chapter III, pp. 27-66.
2. Ācārya Ram Chandra Shukla, *Hindi Sahitya Kā itihāsa,* (revised and enlarged edition, reprint, 1984), Chapter 4, p. 41.
3. Ibid.
4. Banikanta Kakati, *The Mother Goddess Kāmakhyā,* p. 82.
5. The old biographies have been edited by Maheswar Neog under the title *Guru-charita-kathā* and by Upendra Chandra Lekharu as *Kathā-Guruchartitra* (both in Assamese). Both these compilations also contain accounts of some of the chief disciples and successors of Śaṅkaradeva. Modern works on the life, times and works of Śaṅkaradeva include *Śankaradeva and His Time* by Maheswar Neog, *Śankaradeva, Vaishnava Saint of Assam* by B.K. Barua, *The Neo-Vaishnavite Movement and the Satra Institution of Assam* by S.N. Sharma, *Yuganāyaka Mahāpuruṣa Śānkāradeva* by Dimbeswar Neog (in Assamese) and *Śankaradeva: Sahityakāra aur Vicāraka* by Krishna Narayan Prasad 'Māgadh' (in Hindi).
6. Durganath Jha 'Shrish', op. cit. Part One, Chapter IV, p. 85.
7. Ibid.
8. Krishna Narayan Prasad 'Māgadh', *Mādhavadeva: Vyaktitva aur Krititva* (in Hindi) pp. 47-48 and Appendix I.

9. Ibid.
10. Krishna Narayan Prasad 'Māgadh', *Śaṅkaradeva: Sāhityakāra aur Vicāraka* (in Hindi), pp. 9-11.
11. Ibid., p. 28.
12. Ibid.
13. Ibid.
14. Ibid.
15. Ibid., p. 108.
16. Durganath Jha 'Shrish', op. cit.
17. Krishna Narayan Prasad 'Māgadh', *Mādhavadeva: Vyaktitva aur Kritiva*, Appendix I.
18. Mayadhar Mansinha, *History of Oriya Literature*, p. 98.
19. Ibid.
20. Benudhar Sarma, *Dakṣinapāt Satra* (in Assamese), p. 51.
21. Ibid., p. 37.
22. Ibid., p. 38.
23. Hiteswar Barbarua, *Ahomar Din* (in Assamese), p. 714.
24. Ibid., p. 127.
25. *Indian Antiquary*, January 1873, p. 7.
26. George Abraham Grierson, *Maithili Chrestomathy*, p. 34.
27. Sukumar Sen, *A History of Brajabūlī Literature*, p. 3.
28. Suniti Kumar Chatterji, *Varṇa Ratnākara of Jyotirīśvara-Kaviśekharacārya*, Introduction, p. xxi.
29. Suniti Kumar Chatterji, in *Introduction* to Jayakanta Mishra, *A History of Maithili Literature*, vol. I, p. viii-ix.
30. Ram Chandra Shukla, op. cit., p. 43.
31. Shailendra Mohan Jha, *Brajabolī Sāhitya* (in Hindi), p. 5.
32. Ibid., p. 75-76.
33. Ibid., p. 77-81.
34. Ibid., pp. 254-55.
35. Krishna Narayan Prasad 'Māgadh', *Śaṅkaradeva: Sāhityakāra aur Vicāraka*, p. 9.
36. Jayakanta Mishra, op. cit., pp. 177-78.
37. Banikanta Kakati, *Puranī Asamiyā Sāhitya* (in Assamese), pp. 57-58.
38. Shailendra Mohan Jha, op. cit., pp. 247-48.
39. Ibid.
40. Ibid.
41. Ibid.
42. Ibid., p. 248.
43. Ibid., p. 251.
44. Ibid., p. 253.
45. Birinchi Kumar Barua (ed), *Aṅkīyā Nāṭa*, Introduction, pp. x-xi.
46. Jayakanta Mishra, op. cit., pp. 301-308.
47. Ibid.
48. Ibid., p. 287.
49. Ibid., Chapter IX.

50. Dasharath Ojha, *Hindi Nāṭaka: Udbhava aur Vikāsa,* makes such a claim. In fact, he makes the same claim in respect of *Paraśurāma Vijaya,* the drama written by the King Kapilendradeva in which a *Brajabūlī* song is found.
51. Ibid., p. 46.

Chapter 10

Śākta and Vajrayāna Traditions

All the three regions of our study have been the known centres of *devī* worship. The *Devī Purāṇa*, a work composed about the end of the seventh or the beginning of the eighth century states that the *Devī* was worshipped in her different forms in different places, for instance in Kāmarūpa, Kāmākhyā, Bhoṭṭadeśa, etc. H.H. Wilson is of the view that "Assam, or at least the north east of Bengal, seems to have been in a great degree the source from which the Tāntrik and Śākta corruption of the religion of the Vedas and Purāṇas proceeded."[1] Charles Eliot also says, "Śāktism, in the sense of a definite sect with scriptures of its own, if not confined to the north-east corner, at least has its headquarters there."[2] Traditionally, the Śākta cult is considered to have its centre in Kāmarūpa with its chief temple at Kāmākhyā.[3]

It will be interesting to study how far the roots of the Śākta cult may be traced into the traditions of the tribal autochthons of Assam. We have already noted, in Chapter 4, supra, that Kāmākhyā was probably a minor tribal deity of some matriarchal tribe such as the Khāsī or the Gāro and it was Naraka, an 'Aryan' adventurer from the western country of Mithilā, who raised her to the status of the Supreme Goddess. This probably happened in the early centuries of the Christian era. We have also surmised that Naraka was probably brought up in some kind of a Śākta tradition which presumption is reasonable because the worship of the goddess had already started in the Madhyadeśa around the first century BC.[4] well before which time the culture of Mithilā had become an extension of that of the Madhyadeśa. It is, however, difficult to determine the antiquity of the Śakti worship either in Mithilā or in Kāmarūpa with any degree of certainty, though it may be said with confidence that the Śakti worship is closely related to the development of the Tantras.

The theory that the Hindu Tantras had their origin in the Mahāyāna doctrine of the Tārā-centred Tantras is no more favoured by most scholars. There is, no doubt, a similarity between the practices of the two systems but there is really no ground to presume that the one was born out of the other. The existence of the *Śakti Pīṭhas* in almost all parts of India, the prevalence of animal sacrifice at all these places and the archaeological and literary evidence of the existence of some of them even in the Gupta period surely point to their pre-Vajrayāna origin. Nonetheless, it is a fact that the Śakti worship as obtained in the early medieval period in eastern India was inextricably mixed up with the Tāntrik tradition of Vajrayāna that originated around the eighth century. Emphasizing the 'non-Aryan' origin of Tāntrikism, P.C. Choudhary says, 'All its elements—the use of magic and charms, the revolting rites, the use of wine, the belief in efficacy of mantras and sex worship—are found in other primitive cultures all the world over and the high antiquity of the cult is pointed out by all. *The Aryans only systematized it* (emphasis added).'[5] The role of Naraka vis-á-vis Kāmākhyā appears to be that of such systematization.

The Tantras are broadly divided into orthodox and heterodox, the former including the *Āgamas* and the *Yāmalas* with their supplements and the latter, both Hindu and Buddhistic, are represented by different schools of Kulācāra, Vāmācāra, Sahajayāna, Vajrayāna, etc.[6] Citing the opinion of P.C. Bagchi, Choudhury says further, "While mid-India was the centre of the orthodox system, outer India was that of the heterodox one, of which the famous centres were Kāmarūpa, Pūrṇagiri, Oḍḍiyāna and Jālandhara."[7] It is tempting to trace the origins of this system into the cult of the Vrātyas, which is said to be fully represented in the *Atharvaveda*.[8] The Vrātyas, representing a definite cultural milieu of eastern India with Magadha as the centre appear to have developed an independent cult of their own; the Ṛgvedic reference to *Śiśna-deva, Pumān, Strī* and *Muradeva* perhaps refers to the deities of the Vrātyas.[9] The heterodox Tantras of *devī* worship may have evolved from the concept of this *Strī*.

The attempts to trace the antiquity and origin of the Tantras—both Hindu and Buddhist—have not yielded any definitive conclusions.[10] Nevertheless it is known that the Tantras were widely prevalent in eastern India from the early medieval times. Benoytosh Bhattacharya, who was the author of the theory that the Hindu Tantras were born out of the Buddhist Tantras, has stated "the Buddhists generally believe that the Tantras were introduced into Buddhism by Asaṅga, the elder brother of Vasubandhu, who flourished between AD 280-360."[11] He has, however, further noted that not much is known about the role of Asaṅga and a sober chronology of the Tantras can be constructed from the seventh century. He determines the date of Indrabhūti as AD 717 and on this basis assigns Padmavajra, the first *guru* to AD 693.[12]

Following another tradition, he fixes the date of Saraha, as AD 633 and that of his disciple, Nāgārjuna as AD 645.[13] He says, "When we fix the time of Saraha, we practically go to the root of the Buddhist Tantra or Tantrayāna, because Saraha is reputed to be one of the chief promulgators of the *Tāntrik* religion".[14] K.L. Barua believes that Saraha was a contemporary of the Kāmarūpa king

Ratnapāla of the late tenth century.[15] We shall come to the association of Saraha with Kāmarūpa a little later.

According to *Pag Sam Jon Zan*, the Tāntrik Buddhism first developed in Uḍḍiyāna, which is identified with Oḍra or Oḍaviṣa (i.e., Orissa), notwithstanding the earlier controversies about its location.[16] Some of the earliest names in the Tāntrik tradition are associated with Uḍḍiyāna and Kāmarūpa. Indrabhūti, the third in the *śiṣya-paraṁparā* from Padmavajra, was a king of Uḍḍiyāna and father of Padmasaṁbhava who conjointly with the famous logicians Śāntarakṣita erected the monastery of Sām-ye in Tibet in the year AD 749.[17] The period of Indrabhūti fixed as AD 687-717, therefore, appears to be reasonable and the beginning of the Buddhist Tantra may also be reasonably fixed in the late seventh century. In the *śiṣya-paramṁparā* of Saraha, the fourth name is that of Luipā whose date has been fixed as AD 669 by Bhattacharya.[18] He was a fisherman from Uḍḍiyāna and was also known as Matsyendranātha or Machindranātha.

It appears that the Buddhist Tantra got enmeshed with the Śākta religion of the Hindus quite early in its evolution. We have noted earlier that one of the earliest Śākta works, *Devī Purāṇa* was perhaps composed around the end of the seventh or early eighth century. It probably originated in Bengal. Then, by the end of the ninth century, the *Kālikā Purāṇa* was written in Kāmarūpa. It would, therefore, appear that the Hindu Śāktism in Kāmarūpa and Vaṅga and the Buddhist Tantra in Uḍḍiyāna or Oḍra-Kaliṅga were developing simultaneously and influencing each other. Such exchange is attested to by the mention of the sacred places of one system in the scriptures of the other. By the time of the *Kālikā Purāṇa*, the story of the Dakṣa-Yajña and dismembering of the dead body of Satī by Viṣṇu had well-developed and so had the story of the burning of Kāma by Mahādeva Śiva. This gave rise to the concept of the *pīṭhas* of Śakti and the prime importance to the *Yonimaṇḍala* at Kāmākhyā in Kāmarūpa.[19] Kāmākhyā and Kāmarūpa were adopted as places where the *sādhanā* of different deities could be practiced most efficaciously. In *Sādhanāmālā*, which is a collection of 312 *sādhanās* of the various Buddhist deities, Oḍḍiyāna, Kāmākhyā, Kāmarūpa, Pūrṇagiri and Śrihaṭṭa are mentioned as the Vajrayāna *pīṭhas*. In this text the most prominent and most frequent mention is that of Oḍḍiyāna and a number of *sādhanās* are said to have originated there—*Uḍḍiyāna-vajrapīṭha-vinirgata*. In the *sādhanā* no 232, Uḍḍiyāna, Pūrṇagiri, Kāmākhyā and Śrihaṭṭa are mentioned together.[20] Similarly, in the *sādhanā* no. 234, Uḍḍiyāna, Pūrṇagiri, Kāmarūpa and Śrihaṭṭa are mentioned while invoking the goddess Vajrayoginī.[21] While the identification of Pūrṇagiri has not been satisfactorily done so far, that of the other three is not in doubt. The important point to note here is that Kāmarūpa, Kāmākhyā, Pūrṇagiri and Uḍḍiyāna were sacred *pīṭhas* of the Śāktas as well. The *Kālikā Purāṇa* records that the *yoni* of the goddess fell at the Kāmagiri in Kāmarūpa, i.e., Kāmākhyā, a portion of the neck fell at Pūrṇagiri, two thighs fell in Uḍḍiyāna and her breasts fell at Jālandhara. It is interesting that all these places except Jālandhara have been adopted by the Vajrayāna, evidently, because Jālandhara was not in eastern India. It may be mentioned that the early Śākta works speak of only four *pīṭhas* as in the *Kālikā Purāṇa*; in course of time their number rose to fiftyone and in certain traditions to as many as 108.[22] The list of the four *pīṭhas* in the various early works do not tally but all of them include Kāmarūpa-Kāmākhyā. Similarly, the list of fifty-one *pīṭhas* differs from text to text—clearly, the writers of these texts gave importance to their local deities who had no importance for the other text writers.

Reverting to the early development of the Śākta and Vajrayāna traditions, we find that they were not only adopting the sacred places of each other but also the deities. Thus, the *Kālikā Purāṇa*, declares Tārā and Cāmuṇḍā to be the one and the same.[23] At one place this Śākta text even enjoins the use of a Vajrayāna formula while invoking certain goddesses. It says that Narāntakā, Tripurāntakā, Devāntakā, Yamāntakā, Vetālāntakā, Durdharāntakā, Ghanāntakā and Śramāntakā—the eight *dvārapalikās* of the goddess Tīkṣṇakāṇtā—are to be duly worshipped in the eight directions of the *maṇḍala* and each of them is to be addressed first by her name followed by *vajrapuṣpaṁ svāhā.*[24] We should remember that *vajra puṣpe svahā* is a formula used in the Vajrayāna *sādhanās*, as, for instance, in the two *sādhanās* mentioned above.

Mention may also be made of the goddess named Ugratārā, whose temple is still extant in Guwahati. The present temple was built only in the Ahom period but the ruins at the place prove that on this spot there existed a temple in the tenth-eleventh century. Ugratārā is also called Ekajaṭā and both these names occur together in the *Kālikā Purāṇa* at more than one place.[25] There is an Ugratārā temple in Mithila too. This goddess is also worshipped in the Buddhist Tantra, in which she also gets the name of Mahācīnatārā. Thus, in the *Sādhanamala* in *sādhanā* no. 91, Mahattarī Tārā is called Ekajaṭā[26] and in the *sādhanā* no. 101, Mahācīnatārā is named as Ugratārā.[27]

It appears that the interaction between the Śākta and Vajrayāna systems was really a part of the wider phenomenon of the cultural exchanges between Kāmarūpa and Oḍra-Utkala-Kaliṅga from the seventh century onwards.

The Buddhist Tāntrikism traditionally recognizes eightyfour teachers known as the *Siddhas*; most of them belonged to eastern India, including a number of them to Oḍra and Kāmarūpa. Saraha, one of the earliest, if not the first, among them, also known as Rāhulabhadra, was, according to Tārānātha as well as *Pag-Sam-Jon-Zam*, born of a Brāhmaṇa and *Ḍākinī* in the city of Rājñī in 'Eastern country'. K.L. Barua locates this place in ancient Kāmarūpa and identifies it with the modern village of Rani, a few km to the west of Guwahati.[28] Regarding his date, however, Barua is disinclined to assign him to such an early date as the seventh century and considers him to be a contemporary of the Kāmarūpa king Ratnapāla (late tenth century).[29] On Saraha, Barua further notes, "It appears that, though born in Rani, he learnt the *Mantrayāna* in Orissa and became a *Siddha* in Maharashtra after having performed there the *mahāmudrā* ritual with a female ascetic. It is further stated that he was an adept both in the Brahmaṇical and Buddhist lores and flourished during the reign of King Candanapāla of Prācyā. He worked some miracles in the presence of King Ratnapala and his Brahmaṇa minister, and thereby converted both of them to the Buddhist faith. He must have spent a part of his life in Oḍḍiyāna, for in the *Sādhanāmālā* there are two *sādhanās*, the author of which is Saraha and wherein it is stated that these *sādhanās* were introduced by him from Oḍḍiyāna (*Iti Sarahapādāvatārita-Uḍḍiyāna-vinirgata-Trailokya-vaśaskara-lokeśvara-sādhanaṁ-samāptaṁ*). This does not, however, show that he belonged to Oḍḍiyāna, though he may have, as stated in the colophon, adopted certain rituals practiced in Oḍḍiyāna."[30] Barua has further pointed out that according to the Tibetan work *Grub-to'b*, Rāhulabhadra or Saraha was a śūdra from Kāmarūpa.[31] This substantially tallies with the other account. The direct disciple of Saraha was Nāgārjuna who was also a famous physician. He appears to have introduced the worship of Ugratārā, imported from Tibet. In the *Sādhanāmālā*, the *sādhanā* no. 127 for invoking Ekajaṭā ends with the colophon: *Ekajaṭā sādhanaṁ samāptaṁ. Āryanāgārjunapādaiḥ bhoṭeṣu uddhṛtamiti.*[32] Barua has tried to establish that Nāgārjuna had close association with Kāmarūpa and may have actually hailed from there; his name as a great physician is still current in the popular tradition.[33] Some other *Siddhas* also belonged to Kāmarūpa. Luipā, the great-grand disciple of Saraha, assigned to AD 669 by Bhattacharya[34] and to the early eleventh century by Barua,[35] is said to have been a fisherman of Oḍḍiyāna[36] but if he is identical with Mīnanātha or Matsyendranātha or Machendrarnātha named in the Tibetan works *Grub-to'b* and *Bka-ababs-bdanldan*, then he too hailed from Kāmarūpa.[37] Barua would also have us believe that Jālandharapā alias Haḍīpā too belonged to Kāmarūpa and was a contemporary of the king Dharmapāla (late eleventh century).[38] Bhattacharya places Jālandharapā in AD 705.[39] The chronology of the *Siddhas* as given by

Barua though supported by weighty arguments, is difficult to be accepted in view of the definite date of AD 749 when the Sam-ye monastery in Tibet was founded by Padmasaṁbhava, son of Indrabūti.

As noted above, not only did Vajrayāna originate in Oḍḍiyāna, a number of the earliest *Siddhas* belonged to that country. We have already noted the names of Indrabhūti and Luipā. Another notable name is that of Śavarīpā, *guru* of Luipā and disciple of Nāgārjuna. He was undoubtedly from Oḍḍiyāna and a member of the Śavara tribe. Bhattacharya assigns him to AD 657.[40] Another significant name is that of Lakṣmīkarā, sister of the king Indrabhūti, who was married to a prince of Saṁbhala, again in Oḍḍiyāna, and attained *Siddhi.* Being a disciple of Indrabhūti, she has been assigned to AD 729 by Bhattacharya. Could there be a connection between her and Lakṣmīkara, mentioned in the later charters of the Bhauma-Karas as the originator of the dynasty? If so, Indrabhūti and Lakṣmīkara might be the other names of Kṣemaṅkaradeva, known to be the originator of the Bhauma-Kara dynasty. Chronologically the possibility is very much there since, as we have noted in Chapter 3, supra, Kṣemaṅkaradeva was appointed as viceroy at Tośalī by the conqueror Harṣadeva around AD 725.

That the Buddhism in the form of Vajrayāna became a dominant religion in Orissa during the Bhauma-Kara age has been well-established.[41] The archaeological remains of Ratnagiri, Udayagiri, Lalitagiri, and those around Jajpur as well as the Vetāl temple at Bhubaneswar bear ample testimony to the flourishing state of this religion. That the region was attracting scholars and *sādhakas* from far and near is exemplified by the episode of the Bhikṣu Prajñā. An inhabitant of Kapiśā in the Gandhāra region of the north-west frontier of India, he is said to have practiced *Yoga* in a monastery in Orissa and was sent as an emissary to the Chinese emperor by the ruler of Orissa who, according to the Chinese sources, "had a deep faith in the Sovereign Law."[42] Bhikṣu Prajñā had presented a copy of *Gaṇḍavyūha* authographed by the Orissan king to the emperor Te-tsong in AD 795. This Orissan king has been identified with Paramatathāgata Śivakaradeva Unmaṭṭasiṁha,[43] who ascended the Bhauma-Kara throne in AD 748 (see Chapter 3, supra) and who was the grandson of Kṣemaṅkaradeva, the founder of the dynasty, sought to be identified with Indrabhūti as well as Lakṣmīkara, brother of Lakṣmīkarā above.

The above discussion by no means implies that the Śāktism was developed exclusively in Kāmarūpa nor that the Vajrayāna exclusively in Orissa. The entire eastern region including Mithilā, Vaṅga, Gauḍa and Magadha was contributing to these developments. The proponents of the two systems moved about all over the region and beyond and went on assimilating different influences from the various regions. In the process, not only Śāktism and Vajrayāna influenced each other but they also incorporated the elements of Śaivism and even Vaiṣṇavism. Discussing the growth of Śāktism in Orissa, Panigrahi says, "In the early part of Orissan history Sāktism established itself as a separate cult, but it later merged into Saivism so much so that its separate entity is hardly discernible. The Śākta shrine of Virajā at Jajpur existed in the pre-Christian era. . . . In the later stages of Orissan history before the Gupta period, the Śākta shrine of Virajā seems to have been dominated by Buddhism. . . . The Buddhist influence seems to have been eliminated in the Gupta period and it seems to have been re-converted into a pure Brahmaṇical shrine. It was again influenced by Tāntrik Buddhism in the Bhauma period . . . . the Buddhism of this period was a mixed form of religion in which Buddhism, Śaivism, Śāktism and Tantrism had become strangely amalgamated . . . . There are several Śākta images, particularly of Cāmuṇḍa, at Jajpur which were the objects of worship by the Saktas, Saivas and Buddhist Tāntrikas."[44]

One of the important sects born out of this amalgamation of systems is the *Nāthapantha* which has a pan-Indian presence even today. This sect considers Śiva as the Supreme Being and the *Ādiguru* and lays great emphasis on Yoga; so much so that its followers came to be known as *Yogīs* or *Jugīs* all over India. Its close link with Vajrayāna is seen from the fact that the eightyfour *Siddhas* are fully recognized in this system. In fact, the first precepter of this sect is none other than Matsyandranātha, who is identical with Luipā. Matsyendra's chief disciple was Gorakṣanātha or Gorakhanātha who attained *nirvāṇa* at Gorakhpur in eastern Uttar Pradesh and is a legendary figure in the whole of India. According to a popular legend, Matsyendranātha once went to a *Pramīlā rājya* where he was enticed by its female ruler and gave up the path of *sādhanā*. Then his disciple, Gorakhanātha went there and rescued his *guru* from the clutches of his enchantress. This *Pramīlā rājya*, according to the local tradition, was located at Kandali in the Nagoan district in Assam. The story of Machendranātha's fall and his rescue by Gorakhanātha had already become popular by the fourteenth century in eastern India as, very interestingly, the great Maithila poet and scholar, Vidyāpati made it the theme of his drama *Gorakṣavijayaṁ*, considered to be the second earliest dramatic work in Maithili.

Most of the *Siddhas* belonged to the lowest castes or tribes; for instance, Hāḍīpā was of the Haḍī or scavenger caste, Dhobīpā was a Dhobī or washerman, Luipā was of the fisherman caste and Śavarīpā belonged to the Śavara tribe. A noteworthy feature of these *Siddhas* is that while they composed their basic Tantra works in Sanskrit, they also composed songs in the language of the common folk. These songs, known as *Caryāpadas,* have been composed in a language that was the common language of the whole of eastern India—from the region of Kāśī and Kośala in eastern Uttar Pradesh through Mithilā and Magadha in Bihar to Bengal and Kāmarūpa in Assam and Oḍra and Utkala in Orissa. This language usually called the Apabhraṁśa, evolved from the Māgadhan or eastern Prākṛta, was the predecessor of the modern Assamese, Bengali, Maithili, Oriya and eastern Hindi and that is why it is claimed by the scholars of all these languages as their own. Elements of this language are traceable even in Punjabi, Gujarati and Marathi which is explained by the peripatetic nature of the Siddhas and their followers. The policy of preaching the religion in the language of the common folk was continued by the saint-poets of the *Bhakti* movement from the fourteenth century in all these regions. The composers of these *Caryāpadas* and *Tantras* were preaching a kind of mysticism on the one hand and, on the other, also the equality of all men and women regardless of their caste, sex or station in life. This philosophy was also inherited by the saint-poets of the *Bhakti* movement. The first among them was the Saint Kabir, who was born in the weaver community that followed the *Nātha* or *Jugī* sect.

It is now necessary to have a quick look at the development of the Śākta and Tāntrik religion in Mithilā. As in Assam and Bengal, Śāktism is a living faith in Mithilā too. We do not know whether any of the early Tantras was actually composed in Mithilā. However, the origin of the *Mārkaṇḍeya Purāṇa,* that contains the *Dūrgā Saptaśatī* is ascribed to Mithilā by some scholars. Then, we know that the *Kālikā Purāṇa* had great influence in Mithilā. We have noted earlier (Chapter 8, supra) the great influence *KP* exercised on the *nibandhakāras* of Mithilā; in particular, the *vidhis* in *Dūrgā-bhakti-taraṅgiṇī* are almost exclusively based on *KP.* Upendra Thakur has said, "The worship of Śakti was predominant in Mithilā and Bengal. There are still many *pīṭhas* and centres of Tāntricism where *Sādhakas* from different parts of the country come to practice *Sādhanā.* Every household has a *Gosāunī* (Śakti goddess). Moreover, the first verse taught to a child is in praise of Śakti.... Not only there are a large number of Tāntrik works written and compiled in Sanskrit,... but the very script of Mithilā, called Mithilākṣara or Tirhutā has developed in accordance with *Tāntric Yantras.* The history of this peculiar development of the *Varṇas* has been elaborately dealt with in the *Kāmadhenu Tantra* and the *Varṇoddhāra Tantra.* The *añji* sign in the beginning of Maithili alphabet is again due to the Tāntric influence, for it represents the Kuṇḍalinī (*Mūlādhāra*).... Another very important result of this Tāntric predominance over the Maithilias has been the composition of the popular *Gosāunī-ka-Gīta*

(The song of the Goddess Durgā) in Maithili literature, without which no auspicious religious ceremony can ever begin in Mithilā."[45] He states further, "In ancient Mithilā, *Dakṣiṇācāra* was more popular and widely pracised. . . . But in course of time (probably about a century ago) the Maithilas came to be intensely influenced by the *Vāmācāra* practices. . . . Vasiṣṭha and other *sādhakas* followed *Dakṣiṇacāra* and were great devotees of the goddess Tārā... Tāntrik Buddhism, as we know, also greatly influenced it with the result that Mithilā came into contact with, Mahācīna (Great China). *Dakṣiṇacāra* was therefore, (and is still) looked upon with high regard.... Side by side with *Dakṣiṇacāra, Vāmācāra* and *Kaula* also gained much popularity and soon gave rise to *Abhicāra Karma* among the low classes and women... it was this *Karma* that largely contributed to the unpopularity of the Tantras in general and growing hatred for the *Sadhakas* in particular in Mithilā, Bengal and Assam."[46]

We have noted in connection with the Naraka episode that it is possible that the early Śāktism, developed in Madhyadeśa, had reached Mithilā in the early centuries of the Christian era and from there it was taken to Kāmarūpa by Naraka. We have also said that the Vasiṣṭha legend perhaps hints at a conflict between the followers of the *Dakṣiṇācāra* introduced by Naraka and those of the *Vāmācāra* that existed there among the local tribes; in this conflict not only did the former lose but Naraka also lost his life.

In the historical times, we know that the Tāntrik Buddhism travelled from Oḍḍiyāna to Tibet and China. En route, it made a stronghold in Nepal too. As regards Nepal, the *Nātha Pantha* also registered a strong presence there; Machendranātha is a principal divinity in Nepal and Kāmākhyā too is greatly revered there. The route to Tibet and China passed through either Mithilā and Nepal or Kāmarūpa and Bhutan. The Vajrayāna masters, therefore, must have left their footprints in Mithilā. As regards the Hindu Śākta sect, it is somewhat strange that the early texts, including the *Kālikā Purāṇa*, do not locate any important *pīṭha* in Mithilā. However, there is a *dhyāna* of the goddess Kauśikī in Chapter 61 (KP, 61.71) who may have some connection with Mithilā because Kauśikī is the ancient name of the river Kosi. However, there are shrines of Jvalāmukhī, Caṇḍī, Tārā, Kālī, Dūrga, etc., at different places in Mithilā—all being the goddesses in the early texts.[47]

In the later times, when the concept of fifty-one Śākta *pīṭhas* developed in the late medieval period, some texts assigned some *pīṭhas* to Mithilā. For example, the *Rudra Yāmala* names Mithilā in its list of eighteen *pīṭhas*. Another *pīṭha* is listed as Aṅga which is also a part of Mithilā in the present study.[48] I do not know to which particular shrine of the present day these *pīṭhas* refer.

Before concluding this chapter, it would be appropriate to take a brief look at some of the important Devī shrines in Assam and Orissa and correlate them with the observations made above. Kāmākhyā, the holiest of the holy shrines, eulogized both in the Śākta and Buddhist texts, has figured repeatedly in this chapter. The *Kālikā Purāṇa* names a number of places in Kāmarūpa that are sacred to the various goddesses; some of these sites have been identified. Of these, Ugratārā has already been mentioned. K.L. Barua opines that her temple was perhaps erected by Ratnapāla in the late tenth century after he was converted to Buddhism by Saraha or Nāgārjuna.[49] While the present author has not been able to agree with Barua's view about the contemporaniety of Saraha and Ratnapāla, there is every possibility of Ratnapāla having adopted Buddhism and then built the Ugratārā temple. One of the most famous goddesses in the medieval Assam was Tāmreśvarī whose temple was located at Sadiya in the eastern Arunachal Pradesh. She was the titular deity of the Sootea tribe and was popularly known as *Kesāī Khātī* meaning'eater of raw flesh.' She has been identified with Dikkaravāsinī of the *Kālikā Purāṇa.* It is the name of a river as well as the deity and has two forms Tīkṣṇakāntā and Lalitakāntā. In the first form she is identical with Ugratārā and Ekajaṭā[50] while the other form is one with the goddess Maṅgalacaṇḍikā.[51] Up to three centuries ago, Tāmreśvarī used to receive human sacrifices, the merits accruing from which have been greatly extolled in the *Kālikā Purāṇa* which says that the goddess remains satisfied for full one thousand years if a human being is sacrificed before her and for one hundred thousand years when three men are sacrificed.[52] We have noted that the Śākta influence in Kāmarūpa assumed prominence from the ninth century and for the next six hundred years it was the principal faith of the people of Assam till it was supplanted by the neo-Vaiṣṇavism of Śaṅkaradeva in the early sixteenth century. Nevertheless, it was never completely uprooted and continues to be adhered to by a section of the people. Many Ahom and other rulers patronized it in the medieval period and Devī shrines continued to be erected. These shrines were built at a number of places that are mentioned in *KP* and where ruins of the early medieval temples can still be seen. Dīrgheśvarī temple on the Brahmaputra opposite Guwahati is one such place—it is built perhaps at the site of the city of Durjayā, the capital city of the dynasty of Brahmapāla and Ratnapāla. At many places temples of Kāmākhyā were built, the most prominent among them is the one at Silghat in the Nagaon district.

We may take note of a building at Chhaygaon, a few km west of Guwahati, whose importance has not been realized so far. It is a circular structure called the *merghar*, the present brick structure is built on old stone foundations. Fragments of sculptures and architectural members of the ruins of ancient temple or temples are lying scattered in the vicinity. The door-frame of a temple, belonging to the eleventh-twelfth century is also preserved under a shed. The *merghar* is associated with the folk tale of Behulā-Lakhindar and Cāñd Saudāgar. This folk tale is popular throughout eastern India and in Bengal many sites are associated with it.

My guess is that the circular plan of the structure and its association with the Behulā legend indicates that it was a Śākta shrine, possibly a temple of the Cauñsaṭha Yoginī. The temples of Cauñsaṭha Yoginī have been found at Bheraghat near Jabalpur, at Khajuraho, at Mitawali and at two places in Orissa, viz., Hirapur and Ranipur Jharial. All of them have a circular plan and belong to the eleventh to thirteenth centuries. A thorough scrutiny of the ruins of Chhaygaon, and an excavation, if possible, is likely to yield interesting results. It may be mentioned that in the Behulā story, the greatness of the Devī has been narrated; again, it is connected with serpants—an association with Manasā, the Snake-goddess!

Interestingly, in the ruins of Mahasthan, the extensive site of the ancient Puṇḍranagar, on the western bank of the Karatoya in the Bogra district of Bangladesh, one of the mounds is known as Lakhindarer 'Meḍh' (no doubt the same as 'mer', the meaning of which is not clear). It was excavated in 1960 by the Department of Archaeology, Government of Bangladesh. An extract from its report follows.

> ...originally this stupendous ruin at the Medh constituted an imposing terraced sub-structure of a roughly cruciform plan surmounted with a central shrine of complex outline, dedicated probably to the Buddhist Faith. Over the sub-structure is an octagonal plinth which, as mentioned, may originally have carried a stupa, but now completely gone. This stupa was replaced by a square shrine (26'10" square outside) and porch during the Sena period (11th-12th century AD). A grand staircase on west gave access to the shrine but the doorway of the shrine and porch was later blocked and the floor level raised to an unknown height. The excavation inside the shrine revealed a small intrusive cell containing human skeleton—probably of an anchorite—and underlying that was found a circular brick-paved pit of 12'8" in diameter. A stone slab of 1'8" x 1'6" was discovered at the centre of the shrine which bore 12 shallow holes with a larger hole in the centre containing a tiny gold leaf, about an inch square. This square leaf bore, in *repouse* relief, the figure of a recumbent bull which strongly indicates that the later or overlying shrine was a Śiva Temple. However, nothing noteworthy was discovered underneath the stone-slab.[53]

Not having had an opportunity to see the site of Mahasthangarh nor to examine the antiquities discovered there. I am not in position to comment on the above report. Yet, to hazard a guess, the shrine might have been a Śākta one, possibly, that of the Cauñsaṭha Yoginī, and the human skeleton found in the excavation could be that of the victim of a sacrifice and not of an anchorite.

A regards Orissa, we have already noted about the goddess Virajā at Jajpur whose antiquity goes back to the pre-Christian era. We have also noted the views of Panigrahi how the character of Virajā changed from time to time. The image of Virajā now under worship, which is that of a two-armed Mahiṣāsuramardinī, belongs to the fifth century AD at the latest.[54] The temple, next in antiquity to the original Virajā, is the Vetāla deul at Bhubaneswar which is really the oldest temple of the Buddhist Tāntrikism. It belongs to the early Bhauma period (eighth century) and has Cāmuṇḍā as its presiding dcity. In the Bhauma period three other Śākta temples were erected at Bhubaneswar, only two of which are extant and these are now known as Mohinī and Uttareśvara.[55] About Vetāla, Panigrahi has remarked, "a study of its sculpture and architecture indicates that the strange esoteric rites including human sacrifice, were being performed there."[56] Another notable temple of the late Bhauma period, is the Vārāhī temple at Chaurasi. Sapta Matṛkā worship seems to have been widely prevalent in Orissa and Vārāhi is also one of them. An ancient Śākta temple was that of Rāmacaṇḍī at Konark whose image was shifted to its present site by Coḍagaṅga, according to a fifteenth century tradition.[57] A number of temples of the late medieval period contain older images; the most notable among such shrines is the Maṅgalā at Kakatpur. The stone image of Maṅgalā is identified to be Tārā in the *lalitāsana* posture assignable to the eighth-ninth century.[58] It is significant to note that the Maṅgalā of Kakatpur is intimately connected with the Jagannātha of Puri. Before the *nava kalevara* of Jagannātha, the priests appointed to search for the *neem* tree for the carving of the new images, first visit the Maṅgalā to seek her guidance and proceed in accordance with her direction![59] Viewed in the light of the Buddhist association of Jagannātha and the Maṅgalā actually being Tārā, this tradition assumes greater significance.

Among the other Śākta temples of Orissa, having an early origin, the noteworthy are the Khambeśvarī Thākuranī at Aska, the Tārā-Tāriṇī *pīṭha*, the goddess Hiṅgulā at Gopalaprasad and the Samaleśvarī temple at Sambalpur. The last-named is of particular importance as the deity there is aniconic. It is just a large block of stone in the middle of which there is a projection with a narrow groove regarded as the mouth. This is reminiscent of the rock worshipped as Kāmākhyā in Assam in which the groove in the centre is considered to be the *yoni* of the goddess. Then there are more than one temples dedicated to Maṅgalacaṇḍī that remind us of the Lalitakāntā form pf the goddess Dikkaravāsinī of Assam noted earlier.

As in the other regions under study, the Devī temples continued to be erected in Orissa and her worship continues to be popular. Among he most notable shrines at present is the Caṇḍī at Cuttack. The most significant aspect of the development of the Śākta traditions in Orissa is, first, the convergence of the Hindu and Buddhist traditions as exemplified by the Tārā being worshipped as Maṅgalā at Kakatpur and, secondly, her adoption in the cult of Jagannātha. The shrine of Vimalā attached to the Jagannātha temple at Puri is a reminder of the Tāntrik association of the Lord of the Universe and to confirm it, certain Tāntrik rituals are still performed there. For instance, once a year the goddess Vimalā is offered rice smeared with the blood of a goat that is sacrificed outside the temple precincts. That the orthodox priests of the purely Vaiṣṇava Jagannātha still allow such a practice is not of minor significance. Association of Śakti with Jagannātha is also proved by the presence of a female form in the Triad who came to be identified as Subhadrā with the Vaiṣṇavization of Jagannātha. At this stage, another goddess was also annexed to Jagannātha when in the early twelfth century, under the influence of Rāmānuja, a temple of Lakṣmī was built by the side of that of Jagannātha. Tāntrik association of Jagannātha is also attested to by the Tāntrik text *Jñānasiddhi* attributed to Indrabhūti and assigned to the eight century. It opens with a salutation to Jagannātha 'worshipped by all sages who have conquered all their desires.'[60]

NOTES AND REFERENCES

1. H.H. Wilson, *Preface to Viṣṇu Purāṇa.*
2. Charles Eliot, 'Hinduism in Assam' in *JRAS*, 1920, p. 1153.
3. B.K. Barua, *A Cultural History of Assam*, p. 166.
4. An image of Mahiṣāsuramadinī belonging to the Kuṣāna period found at Mathurā clearly points to such a conclusion.
5. P.C. Choudhury, *The History of Civilisation of the People of Assam to the Twelfth Century* AD., p. 414.
6. Ibid.
7. Ibid.
8. Radhakrishna Choudhury, 'The Cult of the Vrātyas' in *IHQ*, vol. XXXIV, No. 3&4, Sept. and Dec. 1958, pp. 258-69.
9. Ibid.
10. Benoytosh Bhattacharya, *Sādhanamālā*, vol. II, Introduction, p. xl.
11. Ibid., p. xl.
12. Ibid., p. xlii.
13. Ibid., p. xliii.
14. Ibid.
15. K.L. Barua, 'Kamarupa and Vajrayana' in *JARS*, vol II, No. 2, July 1934, pp. 44-49.
16. Bhattacharya, op. cit., p. xxxviii.
17. Ibid., p. li.
18. Ibid., p. xliii.
19. D.C. Sircar, *The Śākta Pīṭhas*, pp. 5-7.

20. Bhattacharya, op. cit., pp. 452-53.
21. Ibid., pp. 455.
22. D.C. Sircar, op. cit., pp. 11-42.
23. *Kālilkā Purāṇa*, 61. 92-95. The last *śloka* ends with the words '*eṣa Tārāhvayā devī Cāmuṇḍeti ca gīyate*'.
24. Ibid., 80. 42-43.
25. *Kālikā Purāṇa*, 61. 59-60 and 79.80.
26. Benoytosh Bhattacharya, *Sādhanamālā*, vol. I, p. 177.
27. Ibid., p. 209.
28. K.L. Barua, op. cit.
29. Ibid.
30. Ibid.
31. Ibid.
32. Bhattacharya, *Sādhanamālā*, vol. 1, p. 265-67.
33. K.L. Barua, op. cit.
34. Bhattacharya, *Sādhanamālā*, vol. II, Introduction, p. xliii.
35. K.L. Barua, op. cit.
36. Ibid.
37. Ibid.
38. Ibid.
39. Bhattacharya, op. cit, p. xliii.
40. Ibid.
41. K.C. Panigrahi, *History of Orissa*, pp. 307-13.
42. Ibid., p. 70.
43. Ibid., p. 71.
44. Ibid., pp. 330-31.
45. Upendra Thakur, 'Development of the Tantric Religion in Mithilā' in *IHQ*, vol XXXIV, no. 3&4, Sept. and Dec.1958, pp. 200-202.
46. Ibid., pp. 202-03.
47. Ibid., fn 9 at p. 195.
48. D.C. Sircar, op. cit., pp. 17-18.
49. K.L. Barua, op.cit.
50. *Kālikā Purāṇa*, 80.37.
51. Ibid., 80.52; Also see Banikanta Kakati, *The Mother Goddess Kamakhya*, pp. 55-63.
52. Ibid., 67.18; The verse reads as follows:
    "*Nareṇa balinā devī sahasraṁ parivatsarān.*
    Vidhidattena cāpnoti tṛptiṁ lakṣaṁ tribhirnaraiḥ."
53. Nazimuddin Ahmed, *Mahasthan—A Preliminary Report of the Recent Archaeological Excavations at Mahasthangarh*, pp. 50-51.
54. K.C. Panigrahi, op. cit., p. 331.
55. Ibid.
56. Ibid.
57. Ibid., p. 334.
58. H.C. Das, *Sakta Pithas—A Study*, p. 132.
59. Ibid., p. 131.
60. K.C. Panigrahi, op. cit., p. 339.

Chapter 11

Epilogue

A perusal of the contents of the present work would show that while it contains separate chapters entitled 'Kāmarūpa and Kaliṅga' (Chap. 3) and 'Kāmarūpa and Mithilā' (Chap. 4), there is no separate chapter on the third arm of the triangle, viz., 'Mithilā and Kaliṅga.' The primary reason for this omission is the paucity of material for writing such a chapter and, as a matter of fact, most of the material relevant for it relates to the topics excluded from the present study as mentioned in Chapter 1. However, the six chapters from Chapter 5 to 10, dealing with the specific aspects of the study contain all that is relevant to the connection between Mithilā and Kaliṅga. The following paragraphs of this chapter may be read in the light of this clarification.

CONCLUSIONS OF THE STUDY

Kāmarūpa, Kaliṅga and Mithilā appear to have shared a common political destiny from the time of the epics to the medieval period. In the Mahābhārata war the rulers of all the three kingdoms had fought on the side of the Kauravas. In the historical times Kāmarūpa and Kaliṅga managed to remain outside the Gupta empire while Mithilā became a part of it. In the post-Gupta period the history of all the three regions shared a common feature inasmuch as they had to constantly resist the imperial designs of the Later Guptas, the Pālas and the Senas. In the period after AD 1200 the history of all the three regions is characterized by their successful resistance to the invasions of the Turko-Afghan rulers of Delhi, Bengal, Jaunpur and the southern states. This was a feat in which Bengal had failed whose last Sena ruler, Lakṣmaṇasena was defeated in AD 1199. The Muslim rule could be established in Mithilā in the fourteenth century, in Orissa in the sixteenth century and in Assam (only in the Koch Bihar portion) as late as the seventeenth century. It is a curious fact of history that in spite of having a common political interest for well nigh six centuries, the rulers of the three regions never seem to have made a common cause of fighting their common enemies. Or, the historians of India have really not tried to explore this 'fact'? Only one attempt at forming a federation of Hindu states against the Mughals seems to be the one made by the King Rūdra Siṁha of Assam which, however, did not come to much due to his untimely death in 1714. This episode, however, has not been examined in the present study, as the author considered it to be beyond its scope.

In the sphere of political history, the most important event covered in the present study is the founding of the Bhauma-Kara dynasty in Orissa in AD 736. There is an old hypothesis that this dynasty was related to the Bhaumas of Assam. New and convincing evidence has been found in the present study that confirms this hypothesis. On the basis of certain epigraphic evidence, it appears beyond doubt that the king Harṣadeva of the Śālastaṁbha dynasty of Kāmarūpa conquerred the regions of Oḍra, Kaliṅga, Kośala, etc., that comprise the modern Orissa, in c. AD 725 and appointed a relation of his, Śivakaradeva, as his viceroy with headquarters at Guhadevapāṭaka in Tośalī. Śivakara's son, Kṣemaṅkaradeva declared independence in 736 and became the founder of the new dynasty, known as the Bhauma-Karas, that ruled till c. AD 940. The capital city of Guhadevapāṭaka appears to have grown out of the campaign headquarters of Harṣadeva.

Establishment of the Bhauma rule in Orissa heralded an era of intense cultural exchanges between Kāmarūpa and Kaliṅga-Utkala in the fields of arts, religion, Dharmaśāstra and other literature. Particularly in the field of art and architecture, the two regions exhibit very close similarities for about seven centuries from the eighth century. Such closeness is also reflected in the religious traditions and legends of the two regions. For instance, the traditions related to the Jagannātha and Mādhava cults of Orissa and those relating to the Virajā Kṣetra have close parallels in Assam. The art traditions in the post-Gupta period appear to have travelled from the region of Sarnath to Assam and Orissa as well as Bengal through the Māgadhan region and given rise to the development of a unique east Indian school of art. Various sub-schools of this school developed in the regions of Magadha, Kāmarūpa, Vaṅga and Utkala, all joined by some common strands and inter-acting with each other.

Eastern India witnessed the last and most intense phase of 'Aryanization' or the spread of Vedic culture from the closing days of the Guptas and this was achieved, in a large measure, by migration of the learned Brāhmaṇa scholars from the Madhyadeśa to the various regions of eastern India. These scholars were invited by the rulers of the eastern kingdoms and settled on large tracts of land, most of which was deforested and cultivated by them for the first time. These Brāhmaṇas settled in Mithilā and north Bengal, that was a part of Kāmarūpa, in the first instance, in the fifth and sixth centuries, and from these colonies they dispersed to the various places in Bengal and Orissa between the seventh and the thirteenth century. Encouragement to the Brāhmaṇas of Madhyadeśa to settle in their territories appears to have been the deliberate policy of the rulers in this age in order to raise the level of education and intellectual environment among their subjects. The policy appears to have borne ample fruits as is evidenced by the production of a vast body of *Smṛtinibandhas* as well as other works in Sanskrit in the three regions covered by the present study and in Bengal.

The same period also witnessed the development of Śāktism and Buddhist Tantra. In all these developments, the religious leaders and other scholars of the three regions had close inter-action and exchange of ideas. The Tāntrik tradition travelled to Tibet from Orissa, Bengal and Assam during this period.

Towards the end of this period, i.e., around the thirteenth century the Assamese, Bengali, Maithili and Oriya languages started their course as separate distinct languages evolving out of a common speech of the east, Māgadhan or Eastern Prākrit. Of this speech the earliest examples are found in the *Caryāpadas* of the Buddhist *Siddhas* composed between the seventh and the thirteenth century which the protagonists of Assamese, Bengali, Maithili, Oriya and Hindi all claim to be their exclusive property.

In the fourteenth century was born Vidyāpati, the nightingale of Mithilā, one of the most outstanding figures of the medieval literature of India. The influence of his language and poetry was so powerful in Assam, Bengal and Orissa that it gave birth to a new dialect, Brajabūlī, which became the *lingua-franca* of the eastern Vaiṣṇavas and a great force in fostering unity of these regions with the Indian heartland through the Vrajabhūmi, the land of Kṛṣṇa. The earliest poems in Brajabūlī were written in Orissa by the end of the fifteenth century, i.e., within decades of the demise of Vidyāpati (in AD 1460). About the same time Brajabūlī was employed by Śaṅkaradeva in Assam. Śaṅkaradeva (1449-1568) was a part of the contemporary neo-Vaiṣṇava Bhakti movement of India and initiated a unique form of Vaiṣṇavism in Assam that proved to be a great unifying factor for the people of Assam and, in fact, gave birth to the Assamese identity. He also proved to be the most powerful poet of Brajabūlī. Mithilā and Orissa played the most significant role in the creation of the persona of Śaṅkaradeva. The author calls the age of Śaṅkaradeva as the 'finest hour' of the alignment of Kāmarūpa, Kaliṅga and Mithilā, that commenced almost a thousand years earlier.

SCOPE OF FURTHER WORK

Ever since the study of Indology began about two centuries ago, considerable research has been done to show the differences between the various regions, linguistic groups, followers of different religious persuations, etc. Such endeavours of the scholars fitted very well in the general programme of 'divide and rule' of our British masters. The fact that the earliest Indologists were mostly the members of the Indian Civil Service or other employees of the British Government is perhaps not a matter of coincidence. It is unfortunate that the said trend in the Indological studies does not appear to have been reversed even after we attained independence. Even today, we find what I term as, the 'divisive studies' far outnumbering, to again coin a term, the integrative studies'.

The present study is a humble contribution to such 'integrative studies'. Even though the author feels that he has been able to throw light on some dark corners of the early medieval history of eastern India, the subject deserves to be studied in much greater detail and depth by competent scholars.

In the second section of Chapter 1, while describing the scope of the present study, and how it had to be restricted due to the limitations of time and resources, the author had indicated some of the topics that were being left out. In addition, the treatment of some of the topics covered by the author has been rather sketchy on account of the same limitations. In the following paragraphs, an attempt is being made to indicate some of the areas that could be profitably studied.

Linguistic Aspects

On the language of the *Caryāpadas*, Suniti Kumar Chatterji has observed, "As a matter of fact, the language represents a stage of common speech which is very much akin to what we would conceive to be Old Oriya or Old Assamese as much as Old Bengali."[1] I may add that Rahul Sankrityayana and many other historians of Hindi literature consider this language as Old Hindi.[2] As a matter of fact, the four major languages of eastern India, viz., Assamese, Bengali, Maithili and Oriya and the dialects such as Magahī and to a large extent, Bhojpurī, have all developed from the Māgadhi dialect of Prākṛt and Apabhraṁśa, each with its own special features. Inter-relations between these languages is a subject of rather technical study and may be taken up by scholars of philology and linguistics. Since these languages are joined by the same umbilical cord, their speakers are bound to have had strong cultural links during their formative period. A study to identify these links and to situate them in the pan-Indian context would he a fascinating exercise.

Anthropological and Pre-Historic Aspects

Commenting on the megalithic culture obtaining in Assam, P.C. Choudhury states, "A far closer link between the Assam tribes and those of Orissa may be gathered from their common megalithic practices."[3] Assam here surely denotes the province as it existed at the time of independence, i.e., before the states of Nagaland, Meghalaya, Mizoram and Arunachal Pradesh were carved out of it. In fact, a comparative study of the tribes of the north-east with those of Orissa, Jharkhand and Chhattisgarh, not only in terms of their megalithic practices but in a comprehensive manner, may yield results interesting for the anthropologists as well as the historian. A study of the spatial distribution of the various linguistic and ethnic groups to which these tribal communities belong may provide valuable clues for the solution of many problems of Indian history and sociology. Studying the spread of the various pre-historic cultures, particularly the neolithic, may be of special interest.

Under this head, we may also consider the study of folk tales, folk songs and customs prevalent in the tribal and other communities.

One aspect of daily life usually left out in the scholarly works is that of food and culinary methods and habits of the people. Inter-regional and inter-community comparison of these aspects is likely to reveal cultural contacts not otherwise suspected.

Historical or Semi-Historical Legends and Songs

Such legends and songs are popular in all the three regions of our study; some of them use symbolism and allegories of value for the historian while some others contain a core element of history itself. Some of these legends are current in more than one region; it should be fascinating to trace their source and course of their travel. For instance, the legend of Behulā-Lakhindar and Cāñd Saudāgar is quite popular in the eastern districts of Uttar Pradesh, Mithilā, Bihar, Bengal and Orissa. A reference to it has been made in Chapter 10 since the core of the legend is Śākta in nature. Similar is the case of legends about Gorakhanātha and Yogī Bharthарī.

Dharmaśāstra Traditions

Some notice of the Dharmaśāstra traditions in Mithilā, Assam, Bengal and Orissa has been taken in Chapter 8 but the subject is very vast and deserves greater attention. During the discussions with scholars the author learnt of similarities or differences between the different schools that have significant historical and cultural implications. For instance, the renowned Sanskritist of Assam, Mm. Dr. Biswa Narayan Shastri, who passed away in the year 2002, had once told me about certain problems on which the *nibandhakāras* of Kāmarūpa agreed with their Maithila counterparts and both vehemently opposed the views of the Bengal school. Could such agreements and disagreements be based on political rather than intellectual considerations? Barring a few very early and very late ones, the *nibandhakāras* of eastern India flourished between the eleventh and the fourteenth century. This was the period when the history of India was taking an absolutely new turn and modern Hinduism was taking shape; in fact, these *nibandhakāras* were a product of this phenomenon as well as contributors to it. A really comprehensive study of the growth of the *Smṛti* literature during the early medieval period is likely to yield multi-dimensional results and help us in understanding the Indian society.

In this connection, I would like to stress on one point that is equally relevant to the other topics mentioned here and it is that in the course of the present study, the author often felt the need to include Bengal within its ambit. The history, culture and society of the three regions of the present study are intimately connected with those aspects of Bengal which has a common border with all the three regions. A more meaningful study should, therefore, cover all the four regions. With the inclusion of Magadha too, the study will truly become a study of eastern India.

Religious Traditions

Śākta and Vajrayāna traditions have been briefly studied in Chapter 10. It would be useful to study them in greater detail and to relate them to the development of arts and literature.

Development of Music and Dance

Mithilā has a strong musical tradition of a thousand years. Nānyadeva, the first Karṇāta king (1097-1133), was an accomplished musicologist and wrote a commentary on Bharata's *Nāṭyaśāstra.* He was perhaps the first person to accord classical status to the popular music. Jayakanta Mishra says, "The earliest reference to local (called "Popular" as distinguished from Classical) *rāgas* and *rāginīs* is found in the *Caryāpadas.* Mahārāja Nānyadeva (1097-1133), however, seems to have first patronised and developed the popular *rāgas* on regular lines. After him, Jayadeva (c. 1120), the author of the *Gītagovinda* exercised the greatest influence on the evolution of the Mithilā School."[4] It is significant to note that all poets of eastern India, begining from Vidyāpati in Mithilā, from the fourteenth century onwards indicate the *rāga* in which each *pada* was to be sung. A comparative study of the *rāgas* used by the various Brajabūlī poets of Assam, Bengal, Mithilā and Orissa and relating it to the *rāgas* found in the *Caryāpadas* and indicated by Nānyadeva and used by Jayadeva will surely be really fascinating. In the *Satras* of Assam, a special kind of music developed from the sixteenth century which is known as the *Satriyā* music. There is need to study its structure vis-a-vis the forms prevailing in Mithilā and Orissa. In the fourteenth-fifteenth century some musical treatises were also written in the regions of our study. *Saṅgīta-Dāmodara* is one such work that was written either in Mithilā or in Kāmarūpa. A comparative study of such eastern treatises with the other contemporary works, e.g., those of Rāṇā Kuṁbhā (fourteenth century) by some knowledgeable scholar will be a good contribution to the cultural history of India. Even more interesting could be a study of the development of dance. While Orissa developed the famous Odissi dance form, in Assam the *Satriyā* dance was evolved, that is still not so well known outside the state. A comparative study of these dance forms and exploring their textual context, particularly with reference to the *Sarasvatīhṛdayālaṅkārahāra* of Nānyadeva is likely to be a significant contribution to the history of classical Indian music and dance. Incidentally, just like *Saṅgīta Dāmodara*, there is a treatise on dance, *Śrīhastamuktāvalī* written by Śubhaṅkara Thākura. He is claimed both by Assam and Mithilā.

NOTES AND REFERENCES

1. S.K. Chatterji, *Artavallabha Mahanti Memorial Lectures* (First Series, 1964), p. 30.
2. Rahul Sāṅkrityāyana, *Hindī Kāvyadhārā* (in Hindi), pp. 1-13.
3. P.C. Choudhury, *The History of Civilisation of the People of Assam to the Twelfth Century A.D.*, p. 62.
4. Jayakanta Mishra, *A History of Maithili Literature*, vol. I, p. 32.

Select Bibliography

[This list includes only the books. The list of articles, being too lengthy, has been excluded; the references of the journals in which they appear have invariably been indicated in the text.]

A. ORIGINAL SOURCES IN SANSKRIT

(i) The *Rāmāyaṇa* of Vālmīki

(ii) The *Mahābhārata*

(iii) The Purāṇas, particularly
the *Viṣṇu* (tr. and intro. by H.H. Wilson, 5 vols., London, 1864-70),
the *Mārkaṇḍeya* (with Hindi tr. by Kanhaiya Lal Misra, Allahabad: Hindi Sahitya Sammelan, 1996)
the *Garuḍa*
the *Brahma* (Anandasrama Sanskrit Series, 1895)
the *Kālikā* (tr. and intro. by Biswa Narayan Shastri, 3 vols., Delhi: Nag Publishers, 1993)
the *Ekāmra* (ed. by U.N. Dhal, Delhi: Nag Publishers, 1986)

(iv) *Ācāra Nirṇaya of Śri Gopāla Nyāyapañcānana Bhaṭṭācārya* (ed. and intro. by Atul Kumar Nanda; Bhubaneswar: Urmila Nanda, 2001)

(v) *Dūrgābhaktitaraṅgiṇī of Mahākavi Vidyāpati Thakkura* (ed., Hindi tr. and Sanskrit intro. by Kashi Nath Misra, Darbhanga: K.S.D. Sanskrit University, 2001)

(vi) *Kṛtya Kalpataru of Bhaṭṭa Lakṣmīdhara, Tīrthakāṇḍa* (ed. and intro. by K.V.R. Ayangar; GOS no. 98, Baroda: Oriental Institute, 1942)

(vii) *Kāmākhyā Tantraṁ* (ed. and intro. by Biswa Narayan Shastri, Delhi: Bharatiya Vidya Prakashan, 1990)

(viii) *Nīlādri Mahodaya* (pub. details not known)

(ix) *Rāmacaritaṁ of Sandhyākaranandin* (ed. by H.P. Sastri; revised, tr. and ann. by R.G. Basak, Calcutta: The Asiatic Society, 1969)

(x) *Smṛti Sāra Saṅgraha of Viśwanātha Miśra* (ed. and intro. by Atul Kumar Nanda, Bhubaneswar: Urmila Nanda, 2001)

(xi) *Śrihastamuktāvalī* (ed. and intro. by Maheswar Neog, New Delhi: IGNCA & MLBD, 1991)

(xii) *Sādhanamālā* (ed. and intro. by Benoytosh Bhattacharya, 2 vols., GOS nos. 26 and 41, Baroda: Oriental Institute, reprints, 1968)

(xiii) *Śuddhi Cintāmaṇiḥ* (ed. and Sanskrit intro. by Jayamant Misra, Sriramachandra Jha, Prabhu Narayan Sharma and Dharmanath Jha, Darbhanga: K.S.D. Sanskrit University, 1985)

(xiv) *Tīrtha Kaumudī of Pītāṁbara Siddhāntavāgīśa* (tr. and ed. by Biswa Narayan Shastri; Guwahati: Anundoram Borooah Institute of Language, Art & Culture (ABILAC), 1998)

(xv) *Virajākṣetramāhātmya* (ed. and intro. by Upendra Nath Dhal, Delhi: Nag Publishers, 1984)

(xvi) *Yoginī Tantra* (tr., ed. and intro. by Biswa Narayan Shastri, Delhi: MLBD, 1984)

(xvii) *Yoginī Tantra* (with Hindi tr. by Pt. Kanhaiya Lal Misra, Mumbai: Lakshmi Venkatesvara Press, 1984)

B. ORIGINAL SOURCES IN ASSAMESE

(i) Works of Śaṅkaradeva:
Mahāpuruṣa Śrīmanta Śarikaradeva Vākyāmṛta (ed. by a Board of Editors, Srimanta Sankaradeva Sangha, Nagaon (Assam), 1998)

(ii) Works of Mādhavadeva:
Mahapuruṣa Mādhavadeva Vākyāmṛta (ed. by a Board of Editors, Srimanta Sankaradeva Sangha, Nagaon (Assam), 1994)

(iii) Biographies of the Vaiṣṇava Saints of Assam by the medieval writers:

(a) *Guru Carita Kathā* (ed. and intro. by Maheswar Neog, Guwahati: Lawyers Book Stall, 1986)

(b) *Kathā Guru Caritra* (ed. and intro. by Upendra Chandra Lekharu, Nalbari: Dattabarua Publishing Co., 1952)

(iv) *Darrāṅga Rāja Vaṁśāvalī of Sūryakhaḍī Daivajña* (ed by H.C. Goswami, Guwahati: DHAS, 1930)

C. ORIGINAL SOURCES IN MAITHILI

(i) *Mithilā-Paraṁparāgata Nāṭaka-Saṅgrahaḥ* (Vol. I) containing *Dhūrtasamāgamaṁ* of Jyotirīśvara and *Gorakṣavijayaṁ* of Vidyāpati (ed. and Maithili intro. by Shashi Nath Jha, Darbhanga: K.S.D. Sanskrit University, 1985)

(ii) *Pārijātā Haraṇa Nāṭaka of Umāpati* (ed. and intro in Maithili by Jayadeva Misra, Madaneshwar Misra and Yoganand Jha, Patna: Maithili Akademi, 1984)

(iii) *Varṇa Ratnākara* of *Jyotirīśvara Kaviśekharācārya* (ed. and intro. by Suniti Kumar Chatterji and Babua Misra; Bibliotheca Indica Series, Calcutta: Royal Asiatic Society of Bengal, 1940)

D. ORIGINAL SOURCES IN BENGALI

(i) *Śrīcaitanya Caritāmṛta* of Kṛṣṇadāsa Kavirāja (ed. by Pt. Nityanand Goswami, Calcutta: Sulabh Library, Third edition)

(ii) *Śrīcaitanya Caritāmṛta Mahākāvya* of Kavi Karṇapoora (Pub. details not Known)

MODERN WORKS IN ENGLISH

Ahmed, Nazimuddin — *Mahasthan* — A Preliminary Report of the Recent Archaeological Excavations at Mahasthangarh (Deptt. of Archaeology & Museums, Govt. of Bangladesh, Dhaka, Third edition, 1981).

Alam, A.K.M. Shamsnl — *Sculptural Art of Bangladesh* (Deptt.of Archaeology and Museums, Dhaka, 1985).

Akhtar, Naseem — *Patna Museum Catalogue—Stone Sculptures and Other Antiquities* (Patna, 2001).

——— *Patna Museum Catalogue—Terracottas, and Metal Images* (Patna, 2001).

Alumni Association — *J.N. Banerjea Volume* (Calcutta University, 1962).

Bagchi, P.C. — *India and China* (Bombay: Hind Kitabs Ltd., Second Edition, 1950).

Bandyopadhyay, Bimal — *Metal Sculptures of Eastern India* (Delhi: Sandeep Prakashan, 1981).

Banerjea, J.N., — *Development of Hindu Iconography* (Calcutta, 1956).

Banerji, R.D. — *History of Orissa,* 2 vols. (R. Chatterji, Calcutta, 1931)

——— *The Medieval School of Eastern India Sculpture* (Delhi, 1933).

Banerji, S.C. — *A Brief History of Dharmasatra* (New Delhi: Abhinav Publications, 1999).

——— *Studies in the Mahapurāṇas*

Barpujari, H.K. (ed.) — *The Comprehensive History of Assam,* 5 Vols. (Guwahati: Publication Board, 1990-94).

Barua, B.K. — *A Cultural History of Assam* (Early Period) (Guwahati: Bina Library, Guwahati, Third edition, 1986).

——— *Ankiya Nat* (DHAS Guwahati, Third edition, 1983).

——— *Sankaradeva Vaishnava Saint of Assam* (Calcutta, 1960).

——— *Studies in Early Assamese Literature* (Guwahati, 1953).

——— *History of Assamese Literature* (New Delhi: Sahitya Akademi, 1964),

——— *Assamese Literature* (PEN, Bombay, 1962).

Barua, K.L. *Early History of Kamarupa* (Shillong, 1933).

——— *Studies in the Early History of Assam* (M. Neog (ed.), Jorhat and Guwahati: Asam Sahitya Sabha, 1973).

Basak, R.G. *History of Noth-Eastern India* (Calcutta, 1967)

Behera, K.S. and Donaldson, Thomas, *Sculpture Masterpieces From Orissa* (New Delhi: Aryan Books International, 1998).

Bhandarkar, R.G. *Vaishnavism, Saivism and Minor Religious Systems* (Reprint, Varanasi, 1965).

Bhattacharya, Benoytosh *Buddhist Esoterism* (Oxford University Press, 1932).

——— *The Indian Buddhist Iconography* (London, 1924).

Bhattasali, Nalini Kanta *Iconography of Buddhist and Brahmanical Sculptures in the Dacca Museum* (Dacca, 1929)

Bleck, E.F., Claus, Peter J., Goswami, P.D. and Handoo, J.L., *Folktales of India* (Delhi: MLBD, 1989).

BORI *List of Tirthas* (*being offprint from* Kane's *History of Dharmasastra, pp. 733-828)* (Poona: BORI, 1953).

Chakladar, H.C. *Aryanisation of Eastern India* (Calcutta, 1962).

Chatterji, S.K. *The Place of Assam in the History and Civilisation of India* (Guwahati: Gauhati University, 1955).

——— *Artavallabha Mahanti Lectures* (First Series, 1964) *The People, Language and Culture of Orissa*

(Bhubaneswar: Orissa Sahitya Akademi, 1966).

——— *Origin and Development of Bengali Language*, Vol. 1 & 2 (London: George Allen & Unwin, 1927).

——— *Kirāta-Jana-Kṛti* (Calcutta: Royal Asiatic Society of Bengal, 1951, Reprint, 1998)

Chaudhury, P.D. *Archaeology in Assam* (Guwahati: Deptt. of Archaeology, Govt. of Assam, 1964).

Choudhury, N.D. *Historical Archaeology of Central Assam (from earliest time to 12th century A.D.)* (Delhi: B.R. Publishing Corporation, 1985).

Choudhury, P.C. *The History of Civilisation of the People of Assam to the Twelfth Century A.D.* (Revised, Third edition, Delhi: Spectrum Publications, 1987).

Choudhury, R.D. *Archaeology of the Brahmaputra Valley of Assam* (Delhi: Agam Kala Prakashan, 1985).

——— *Catalogue of the Inscriptions in the Assam State Museum* (Guwahati, 1987).

——— *The Sculptures of Assam* (Guwahati: Assam State Museum, 1987).

——— *Catalogue of Metal Sculpture in the Assam State Museum* (Guwahati, 1988).

——— Catalogue of Stone Sculptures—*Assam State Museum* (Guwahati, 1998).

Choudhury, R.D.& Kalita, Naren *Manuscript Paintings from Kamarupa Anusandhan Samiti* (Guwahati: K.A.Samiti, 2001).

Danaldson, T.E. *The Iconography of Vaiṣṇava Images in Orissa* (New Delhi: D.K. Printworld (P) Ltd., 2001).

Das, Biswarup — *The Bhauma-Karas —Buddhist Kings of Orissa — and Their Times* (New Delhi: Oriental Publishers & Distributors, 1978).

——— *Orissa—Social Cultural and Religious Aspects* (Delhi: Sundeep Prakashan, 1985).

Das, H.C. — *Sakta Pithas - A Study* (Bhubaneswar: Bharati Prakashan: 1999).

Dasgupta, Rajatanand — *Manuscript Painting of Eastern India* (Varanasi, 1972).

Eliot, Charles — *Hinduism and Buddhism*, 1-3 (London, 1922, 1933).

Gait, E.A. — *A History of Assam,* Third edn. Calcutta, 1926.

——— *List of Archaeological Remains in the Province of Assam* (Shillong, 1897).

Ganguly, D.K. — *Historical Geography and Dynastic History of Orissa.*

Gauhati University — *Aspects of Early Assamese Literature* (Guwahati, 1959).

Gnoli, Reniero — *Nepalase Inscriptions in Gupta Characters, Part I-Texts* (Istituto Italiano Per Il Medio Ed Estremo Oriente Serie Orientale Roma Vol. X, Roma, 1956).

Gopal, Lallanji and Verma, T.P. — *Studies in the History and Culture of Nepal* (Varanasi: Bharati Prakashan, 1977).

Goswami, Hemchandra — *Descriptive Catalogue of Assamese Manuscripts* (Calcutta: University of Calcutta, 1930).

Goyal, Shankar — *History and Historiography of the Age of Harsha* (Jodhpur: Kusumanjali Prakashan, 1992).

Grierson, G.A. *Linguistic Survey of India* 1-5 (Calcutta, 1903-9).

——— *Maithili Chrestomathy* (Extra No. JRASB, 1880-82).

Hazra, R.C. *Studies in Upa-puranas,* 2 vols. (Calcutta, 1958).

Jayaswal, K.P. *The Imperial History of India* (Patna, 1931).

Jha, Makhan *Civilizational Regions of Mithila and Mahakoshal* (Delhi: Capital Publishing House, 1982).

——— *Folklore, Magic and Legends of Mithila* (Patna: Jyoti Publications, Year n.s.).

Kamarupa Anusandhan Samiti Guwahati, *Readings in the History & Culture of Assam* (Guwahati, 1984).

——— *A Source Book of the Archaeology of Assam and Other States of North-Eastern India* (Guwahati, 1984).

——— *Abhinandana-Bhāratī* (Guwahati, 1982).

Kakati, Banikanta *The Mother Goddess Kamakhya* (New edition, Guwahati: Publication Board, Assam, 1989).

——— *Visnuite Myths and Legends* (Gauhati, 1952).

——— *Assamese: Its Formation and Development* (Third Edition, Guwahati: Lawyer's Book Stall, 1972).

Kane, P.V. *History of Dharmasastra,* vol. 1 and vol. 4 (GOS Class B, No. 6, Second editions, 1968 & 1975 and 1973).

Kulke, H., Eschmann, A. and Tripathy, G.C. *The Cult of Jagannath and the Regional Tradition of Orissa* (New Delhi, 1978).

Law, B.C. *Indological Studies* Part III (Allahabad: Ganganath Jha Research Institute, 1954).

——— *Geography of Early Buddhism* (London, 1932).

——— *Some Kṣatriya Tribes of Ancient India* (Calcutta, 1924).

——— *Studies in Indology*, vol. I (Mm Dr. Umesh Mishra Memorial Volume) (Allahabad, 1967).

Mahtab, H.K. *The History of Orissa*, 2 vols. (Cuttack, 1959-60).

Majumdar, N.G. *Inscriptions of Bengal, III*, (Rajshahi, 1929).

Majumdar, R.C. *History of Bengal*, Vol. I (Dacca, 1943).

Majumdar, R.C. and Pusalkar, A.D. (ed.) *The History and Culture of the Indian People* [Vol. 1-5, Vol. 3, *The Classical Age* (1970); Vol. 4, *The Age of Imperial Kanauj* (1964)], (Bombay: Bharatiya Vidya Bhawan).

Mansinha, Mayadhar *History of Oriya Literature* (New Delhi: Sahitya Akademi, 1962).

Mishra, Jayakanta *A History of Maithili Literature*, vol. I (Allahabad: Tirabhukti Publications, 1949).

Misra, Binayak *Orissa Under The Bhauma Kings* (Calcutta, 1934).

——— *Dynasties of Medieval Orissa* (Calcutta, 1933).

Misra, K.C. *The Cult of Jagannatha* (Calcutta, 1971).

Mitra, Debala *Bronzes from Achutarajapur, Orissa* (Delhi, 1978).

Mittal, Amar Chand *An Early History of Orissa* (Varanasi: Jain Cultural Research Society, 1962).

Mohapatra, Ramesh Prasad *Temple Legends of Orissa* (Bhubaneswar: Orissa Sahitya Akademi, 1989).

Mookerjee, Radha Kumud — *Ancient Indian Education* (Reprint, Delhi: MLBD, 1989).

Mukherjee, P. — *The Gajapati Kings of Orissa* (Cuttack, 1981).

Mukherji, R.R. and Marty, S.K. — *Corpus of Bengal Inscriptons bearing on History and Civilisation of Bengal* (Calcutta: Firma K.L. Mukhopadhyay, 1967).

Mukherji, B.N. — *Eastern Indian Art Styles* (Calcutta: K.P. Bagchi & Co., 1980).

Nath, R.M. — *The Background of Assamese Culture* (Shillong, 1948).

Nath, Vijay — *Puranas and Acculturation* (New Delhi: Munshiram Manoharlal Publishers Pvt. Ltd., 2001).

Neog, Maheswar (ed. & intro.) — *Prācya Śāsanāvalī* (Guwahati: Publication Board, Assam, 1974).

——— *Sankardeo and His Times* (Guwahati, 1965).

——— (ed.) *Pragjyotish Souvenir* (All India Oriental Conference, XXII Session, Guwahati, Jan, 1965).

——— (ed.) *Studies in the History and Culture of Assam* (Guwahati, 1973).

Neog, Dimbeswar — *New Light on History of Asamiya Literature* (Guwahati: Xuwani Prakas, 1962).

——— *Yuganayak Mahapurush Sankardew* (Jorhat, 1952).

Neog, M. & Sarma, S.N. (ed) — *Prof. Birinchi Kumar Barua Memorial Volume* (Guwahati, 1966).

Orissa Tourism — *Places of Interest in the District of Puri* (Brochure; Bhubaneswar).

——— *Cuttack* (Brochure; Bhubaneswar).

Panigrahi, K.C. — *History of Orissa* (Cuttack: Kitab Mahal, 1981).

——— *Archaeological Remains at Bhubaneswar* (Orient Longman, 1961).

——— *Chronology of the Bhauma-Karas and Somavamisis of Orissa* (Madras, 1961).

Pargiter, F.E. — *Ancient Indian Historical Tradition* (Reprint, MLBD, 1962).

Pradhan, S. (ed.) — *Orissa - History, Culture and Archaeology* (New Delhi: D.K. Printworld (P) Ltd., 1999).

Ray, H.C. — *Dynastic History of Northern India*, 2 vols. (Calcutta, 1931).

Raychaudhuri, H.C. — *Political History of Ancient India* (5th and 6th edn., Calcutta, 1953).

——— *Studies in Indian Antiquities* (Second edition, Calcutta: University of Calcutta, 1958).

Rajguru, S.N. — *Inscriptions of Orissa*, 4 vols. (Bhubaneswar, 1958-66).

Rath, B.K. — *Cultural History of Orissa* (Delhi: Sundeep Prakashan, 1983).

Sahu, N.K. — *Buddhism in Orissa* (Cuttack, 1958).

——— *History of Orissa* (Cuttack: Utkal University Publication, 1956).

Sarasvati, S.K. — *A Survey of India Sculpture* (Calcutta, 1957).

Sarma, Dimbeswar — *Kāmarūpaśāsanāvalī* (Guwahati: Publication Board, Assam, 1981).

Sarma, S.N. — *Epics and Puranas in Early Assamese Literature* (Guwahati: Bani Prakash, 1972).

——— *The Neo-Vaishnavite Movement and the Satra Institution of Assam* (Guwahati, 1966).

Sastri, Manoranjan and Choudhury, P.C. (ed. & intro.) — *Smriti-Jyotiṣa-sārasaṅgraha* (Guwahati, 1964).

Sen, Sukumar — *History of Bengali Literature* (New Delhi: Sahitya Akademi).

——— *History of Brajabuli Literature* (Calcutta, 1935).

Shaha, Rishikesh — *Ancient and Medieval Nepal* (New Delhi: Manohar Publications, 1992).

Shastri, Ajay Mitra — *Inscriptions of the Sarabhapuriyas, Panduvamsins and Somavamsins*, 2 Parts (Delhi: ICHR & MLBD, 1995).

Shastri, Biswa Narayan — *Kālikāpurāṇe Mūrtivinirdeśah* (Delhi: IGNCA & MLBD, 1994).

Singh, G.P. — *The Kiratas in Ancient India* (New Dehli: Gian Publishing House, 1990).

Sircar, D.C. — *Select Inscriptions bearing on Indian History and Civilisation* (vol. I, Calcutta University, 1942; vol. II, MLBD, Delhi, 1983).

——— *The Sakta Pithas* [Extracted from JRASB, Letters, vol. XIV, 1948, pp. 1-108] (MLBD, year n.s.).

——— *Studies in the Society and Administration of Ancient and Medieval India* (Calcutta, Firma K.L. Mukhopadhyay, 1967).

——— *Indian Epigraphy* (Delhi: MLBD, 1965).

——— *Indian Epigraphical Glossory* (Delhi: MLBD, 1978).

Subudhi, U.K. *The Bhauma-Karas of Orissa* (Calcutta, 1978).

Thakur, Upendra *History of Mithila* (circa 3000 BC-AD 1556) (Darbhanga: Mithila Institute, 1956).

——— *Some Aspects of Ancient Indian History and Culture* (New Delhi: Abhinav Publications, 1974).

——— *Studies in Indian History* (Varanasi & Delhi: Chaukhambha, 1989).

Thaplayal, K.K. *Inscriptions of the Maukharis, puṣpabhūtis and Yaśovarman of Kanauj* (Delhi: ICHR & Agam Prakashan, 1985).

Tripathi, C.D. *Aspects of the Medieval History of Assam* (Shimla: IIAS, 2002).

Tripathi, R.S. *History of Ancient India* (Varanasi, 1942).

——— *History of Kanauj* (Varanasi, 1937).

Tripathi, Snigdha *Inscriptions of Orissa*, vol. 1 (Delhi: ICHR & MLBD, 1997); vol. 2 (Delhi: ICHR & Pratibha Prakashan, 2000) and vol. 6 (Bhubaneswar: State Museum 1974).

Utgikar, N.B. and Paranjpe, V.G. (ed.) *Collected Works of Sir R.G. Bhandarkar*, vol. 1 (GOS class B No. 1, Poona: BORI, 1933).

Vasu, N.N. *Social History of Kamarupa*, I-3 (Calcutta, 1922, 1926, 1933).

——— *The Archaeological Survey of Mayurabhanja* (Reprint, Delhi: RareReprints, 1981).

Vishva Bandhu (ed.) *Siddha Bhāratī (Siddheswar Varma Fel. Volume,* Hoshiarpur: VVRI, 1950).

F. MODERN WORKS IN ASSAMESE (A), BENGALI (B), HINDI (H) AND MAITHILI (M)

Barbarua, Hiteswar *Ahomar Din (A)* (Guwahati: Publication Board, 1981).

Barua, Gunabhiram *Assam Burañjī(A)* (Reprint, Guwahati: Assam Publication Board, 1972).

Bharati, Dharmavir *Siddha Sāhitya(H)* (Delhi: Vidya Prakashan Mandir, 1988).

Gohainbarua, Padmanath *Asamar Burañjī (A)* (Reprint, Guwahati: Assam Publication Board, 1976).

Jha, Parameswar *Mithilā Tattva Vimarśa (M)* (Tarauni, Darbhanga: Parameshwar Pustakalaya, Year n.s.).

Jha, Shailendra Mohan *Brajaboli Sāhitya (H)* (Patna: Bihar Grantha Akademi, 1974).

Kakati, Banikanta *Purani Asomiyā Sāhitya (A)* (1950).

——— *Purani Kāmarūpar Dharmadhārā (A)* (1955).

'Māgadh', Krishna Narayan Prasad *Saṅkaradeva: Sāhityakāra aur Vicāraka (H)* (Patiala: Punjabi University, 1976).

——— *Mādhavadeva: Vyaktitva aur Krititva (H)* (Guwahati: Purvottar Pradeshiya Marwari Sammelan, 1979).

Mahanta, Bap Chandra *Mahapuruṣa Saṅkaradeva (A)* (Jorhat, 1968).

——— *Asamiyā Jāti, Bhāṣā āru Sāhityar janmakathā (A)* (Jorhat, 1996).

Majumdar, Mamat Chandra — *Hājo aru Dhopgurī Satrar Camū Itivritta (A)* (Brochure, Smti Dipan Majumdar, Hajo; V edn., 2000).

Motichandra — *Sārthavāha (H)* (Patna: Bihar Raṣtrabhāṣā Parishad, 1966).

Neog, Dimbeswar — *Yuganayak Mahāpuruśa Śaṅkaradeva (A)* (Jorhat, 1949).

Neog, Maheswar — *Pavitra Asam (A)* (Jorhat: Asam Sahitya Sabha, 1960).

——— *Śrī Śrī Śaṅkaradeva (A)* (Guwahati, 1963).

——— Guru Carit (Rāmānanda Dwija racita) (A) (Guwahati, 1957).

Ojha, Dasharath — *Hindi Nāṭāka: Udbhava aur Vikāsa (H)* (Delhi: Rajpal & Sons, New edition, 2000).

Pandit, Gunendra Nath — *Śaiva Darśana Āru Sāhityara Paṭabhūmi* (A) (Barnibari, Kamrup: Ratikant Prakashan, 1964; second edition, 1984).

Pandey, Rajendra — *Dharmadruma- Dharmaśāstra Kā Itihāsa (H)* (Second edition, Ranchi, 1989).

Sankrityayana, Rahula — *Hindī Kāvyadhārā (H)* (Allahabad: Kitab-Mahal, 1945).

Sen, Deeneschandra — *Baṅgabhāṣā ār Sāhitya (B)* (1942).

Sen, Kshiti Mohan — *Bhāratīya Madhyayugina Sādhanā (B)* (1935).

Sharma, Benudhar — *Dakṣinapāṭa Satra (A)* (Guwahati, 1967).

Shukla, Ram Chandra — *Hindī Sāhitya Kā Itihāsa (H)* (Revised and Enlarged edition., Reprint, Varanasi: Nagari Pracharini Sabha, 1984).

Sukul, Kuber Nath — *Vārāṇasī Vaibhava (H)* (Patna: Bihar Rāṣṭrabhāṣā Pariṣad, 1971).

Tiwari, Ram Pujan — *Brajabūlī Sāhitya (H)* (Patna: Granth Vitan, 1960).

Tomar, Kanika — *Brajabhāṣā evaṁ Brajabūlī— Tulanātmaka Adhyayana (H)* (Varanasi: BHU, 1959).

Tripathi, Chandra Bali — *Dharmarāja Yudhiṣṭhira (H)* (Revised edition, Chandra Mauli Mani, Lucknow, 1991).

Upadhyaya, Baladeva — *Sanskrit Śāstroñ Kā Itihāsa (H)* (Varanasi: Sharada Mandir, 1969).

Utkala Raṣtrabhāṣā, Pracār Sabhā — *Rāṣtrabhāṣā Rajata Jayantī Grantha (H)* (Cuttack-1).

Index